WAITING FOR GOD

'For since the beginning of the world men have not heard, nor perceived by the ear, neither hath the eye seen, O God, beside thee, what he hath prepared for him that waiteth for him.

Isaiah 64 : 4

WAITING FOR GOD

DAILY HELP FOR THOSE WHO CAN'T SEE THE WOOD FOR THE TREES

DERICK BINGHAM

Ambassador

WAITING FOR GOD
Copyright © 1988 by Derick Bingham
All rights reserved

AMBASSADOR PRODUCTIONS LTD
Providence House
Belfast BT5 6JR

ISBN 0 907927 24 6

HIGHWAY BOOKS
Marsh Barton
Exeter EX2 8RD

ISBN 1 871563 30 5

Printed in the United Kingdom by
  Ambassador Productions Ltd.

Dedication

This book is dedicated to:
Ivor and Hilary Jones who have, with great
faithfulness and kindness, constantly shown me the
wood despite the trees.

Acknowledgements

Cover photograph — Edmund Nägle FRPS

Our thanks to Mrs. Deidre Cousins for preparing the manuscript of this book for publication with patience and accuracy

Thanks is also due to Mr. Simon Biggarstaff for his evocative and excellent drawings which illustrate this book. We deeply appreciate the painstaking work he put into his illustrations.

Introduction

You know how it is; the pressure of life gets to you and all you can see is the endless detail of duty and responsibility. So great is the detail you cannot see where it is all leading, you lose your sense of direction. Trees are pleasant, they are sturdy and tall and useful. Trees are great fun to climb as a child and refreshing to sit down under as an adult, but, they are not everything. You need to stand back and see the woods they make up and then have a look over the common and the fields and mountains and sky that lie beyond the woods.

It reminds me of the cartoon I once saw of a U.S. President sitting in a blown apart White House and virtually all that is left is his desk and phone. There he is in the cartoon, holding the phone close and saying. "Show me the big picture!" That's exactly what I aim to do in this book. I aim to show you that if you wait for God you will see your life from a totally different perspective. I aim to show you the trees, then the woods and then to reach for the stars.

Derick Bingham

JANUARY

The archers used to cut straight staves from its large trunk and made their longbows because the yew tree provides timber with greater elasticity and strength than any other timber known to man.

Yet, the dark, mysterious evergreen yew tree is particularly associated with churchyards because it provides year-round shelter under its large spread for the christian preacher and his congregation. Some churchyard yews are estimated to be 1,500 years old, even older than the nearby church buildings themselves.

May you find, as the wind blows across your life in the coming months, a year-round shelter which even far surpasses that of the yew tree. The Lord is your refuge and strength and not only for a few thousand years but for eternity. He will not fail you. Wait for Him.

January

1

A New Year stretches out in front of you. It will be a year of both breathtaking joys and inevitable sorrows. There will be tangles of circumstances weaving around the coming months which will leave you confused and wondering. Whispers in your heart might suggest 'There is no way out of this'.

Tell me, as you stand on the height of the common and see that wood down there through which you must walk in these coming days, what do you think is meant by those words in Genisis 2 : 2 which say that the earth was "Without form and void"? Interesting words? Whatever they may ultimately mean there can be no doubt that God spoke to the formless, empty earth and it became sea and dry land, seed and grass: he spoke and the stars, the moon, the sun, the fish and birds, insects and trees came into being at his word.

If God could do all that with something which was without form, and void, what could he not do with your precious life if you were to yield it to his guidance and care day by day? The answer is, lots! Only, remember, as you pass through the woods of this year, those famous words of William Longstaff.

January

They were spoken a long time ago but they are as fresh and relevant as ever. Think long upon them and obey them. They will save you endless heartache. What are they?

'Take time to be holy, let him be your guide;
And run not before Him whatever betide
In joy or in sorrow, still follow your Lord,
And looking to Jesus, still trust in His word'.

2

JUDGING ANGELS

'Out of the ground the Lord God formed every beast of the field and every bird of the air and brought them to Adam to see what he would call them. And whatever Adam called each living creature, that was its name', says the Bible.

It must have been an utterly amazing experience for Adam to co-operate with God in administering Eden. It will be equally amazing when you, christian, help God to administer the new heaven and the new earth. All the training you are getting in the decisions you will make to-day is training for reigning. If you don't believe me read 1 Corinthians 6 : 1-3. If we shall judge angels surely we need some experience in judging and deciding things now. So, don't shirk the responsibilities you have to face to-day: you 'aint seen nothin' yet!

January

3 _____

She couldn't wait, could she? 'God knows that the day you eat it your eyes will be opened and you will be like God, knowing good and evil,' said Satan (Genesis 3 : 5).

Her eyes were ravished by the pleasantness of the fruit, her appetite yearned to be satisfied, and her mind longed to be widened by a new experience.

Eve took of the fruit and also gave to her husband — we have all seen the results. Africa is tortured by famine; places like Mexico City are devastated by earthquakes; the Mediterranean is plagued by the menace of terrorism; and Ireland North and South, has groaned daily for over 400 years.

Eve started something that day in the Garden of Eden which cost God the cross of Calvary. Impatience like Eve's will drag you into hell itself if you are not careful.

We all love new experiences and 20th century people want them sooner, immediately if possible. Even Eve would have been surprised at our fast-lane living. Surely the Christian must learn to be different to the rest of contemporary society.

People of the modern generation must often think of the Christian as a frightened rabbit in a minefield — hopeless and frightened, unable to cope with the realities of present-day life. But they are wrong — the Christian is like an eagle in a storm. 'But they that wait upon the Lord shall renew their strength; they shall mount up with wings as eagles; they shall run, and not be weary; and they shall walk, and not faint'. (Isaiah 40 : 31).

The Christian sometimes tends to walk when the crowd is running, but never let it be said that believers are dead-beats and cannot move fast when it is necessary.

Christians are called to wait upon the Lord — to wait and wait and wait again. Then they are called to wait some more. Because of their impatience a temptation may look attractive to Christians, and it might seem to widen their experience — but they have been warned that if this desire has not been directed by God's Word and Spirit, they had better leave it well alone.

Are our activities born out of communion with God? No matter how impressive they may be, if God has not initiated them they will not bring true happiness.

Are you about to rush into an exciting new experience? Are you about to give up a commitment that seems unspectacular, mundane and troublesome? Remember what Uncle Remus said: 'You can't run away from trouble, because there ain't no place that far'. Wait upon the Lord, impatient one.

How do you know whether or not something you want to do is pleasing to the Lord? Remember the man who asked his wife whether his shirt was dirty or clean — 'If it's doubtful, it's dirty,' she replied.

Wait, then, upon the Lord. And if you doubt the wisdom of this, ask Eve.

January

4

'Why are you angry and why is your countenance fallen?' said God. Cain gave no answer and huffed. But huffing with impatience is a very dangerous emotional condition, especially when it involves huffing with impatience at God's ways.

Abel's offering of a lamb for his sins was accepted by the Lord but Cain's offering of what he had grown in the ground was refused. 'Without the shedding of blood there is no remission' — that is God's Word regarding forgiveness but Cain wouldn't have it. Isn't it strange that the man who would not have the shedding of a lamb's blood then ruthlessly turned and shed his own brother's?

'Behold the Lamb of God', said John on the banks of the Jordan. Millions won't have his cross but have shed more blood in this 20th century than perhaps any other.

I remember a young Chinese man in Hong Kong handing me a piece of paper with the blood of heathen priests upon it. 'Put this upon your door in Ireland', he said, 'Then you will have peace'.

'But I don't need it', I replied. 'Two thousand years ago the Lamb of God shed his blood for me at Calvary and the Scriptures teach that he made peace through the blood of his cross'.

'You're lucky', he sighed. 'Your religion is so simple. All you have to do is believe'.

I wouldn't define it as luck but let me define it in a true story. One day a General came to one of Ulster's most beautiful parks, Tollymore Park. He had been wounded in the Battle of Waterloo and came to stay with his friend, Lord Roden, who was a deeply commited Christian.

The General longed to have peace with God but didn't know how to get it. One day, standing in Lord Roden's library at Tollymore the General's eyes fell on a little poem above the mantlepiece. It read:

'In peace let me resign my breath,
And thy salvation see,
My sins deserved eternal death,
But Jesus died for me.'

The General believed the truth of the poem and was converted to Christ on the spot.

Over and over again all across the world I find people ignorant of one of the greatest doctrines of the Bible, the finished work of Christ. From South Korea to South Down I have found people who simply think God's salvation is to be earned. By church attendance, by Bible reading and prayer they seek to have their good deeds outweigh their bad deeds.

The doctrine of Cain, presenting God with the work of their hands is still a common belief for many. 'Nothing in my hand I bring, simply to the Cross I cling' is a fast receding attitude in the Western world.

If Cain despised the blood of the lamb of Abel 'how much more severely do you think a man deserves to be punished', wrote the writer of Hebrews, 'who has trampled the Son of God underfoot, who has insulted the Spirit of grace?'

It is significant that Cain was a fugitive for the rest of his life. He never found rest because he couldn't wait and rest in God's way of salvation. Can you?

January

5

FACING BOTH WAYS

Poor Cain: he was never satisfied? He didn't want God's way of redemption yet when he became a fugitive from God he didn't want that either: 'I shall be hidden from your face', he complained to God.

Don't be like Cain, a person 'facing both ways'.

'As a rule man's a fool
When its hot he want's it cool
When it's cool he want's it hot
Always wanting what it's not'

6

ON WALKING WITH GOD

My wife's grandmother once said to me that she had enjoyed over sixty years of unbroken fellowship with God. No one else has ever said that to me before or since. Do you know of anyone who ever said such a thing to you?

'After he begot Methuselah Enoch walked with God three hundred years' says Genesis 5 : 22. I like to think that the little lad who was to become the world's oldest person influenced his dad to walk closer to God. Has a little one entered your house or family circle recently? May its coming do to you what I like to think it did to Enoch.

Methuselah means 'When he's gone it shall come' and by calculation we learn that the flood came the very year Methuselah died. As Enoch walked closely with God he obviously knew that judgement was coming.

I heard my godly friend Dr. James Montgomery Boice of Philidelphia teach this truth one evening. After the service a lady approached him angrily. 'I only believe in a God of love, not in a God of judgement', she said. 'Then you must not be walking closely with God', said Dr. Boice, quietly.

7

HE WAITED FOR 120 YEARS!

Imagine yourself witnessing for the Lord to a generation of people absolutely given over to the pursuit of physical pleasure. If it tasted good they drank it, if it felt good they did it. Nor would these people be deterred by the slightest flicker of conscience when it came to using violence. Does this sound familiar?

Imagine trying to warn these people that the judgement of God was coming. Imagine pleading with them to repent toward God before his wrath fell on their defenceless heads, for the wages of sin is death. Imagine a reaction of total indifference as the generation around you continue pursuing their own goals relentlessly, ignoring your warning with an incredulous look.

Now carry on down this road of your imagination. Imagine keeping up this witnessing for ten years with no sign of anyone believing your message. In 20 years you are still witnessing, and continue for 30, 40, 50, 60, 70, 80, 90 years! In 100 years you are

January

still telling people the judgement is coming but by this time the signs of it seem further away than when you started. God has promised that he is going to send his judgement in the form of a flood, that you must build a vessel to withstand that flood. To the guffaws of the surrounding generation you build away and continually witness to the truth of God's Word for yet another 20 years.

The end result of your witness is that only your immediate family are saved when 'all the fountains of the great deep are broken up' and 'the windows of heaven' are opened. Think about it: seven people besides yourself believe God's Word and survive the deluge. Incredible!

Noah didn't have to imagine all this — it actually happened to him. If anybody ever experienced the pressure of waiting for God, Noah is the grandfather of them. Why, if for a fortnight I preach God's Word of coming judgement on all those that do not obey the Gospel and nobody repents and believes, I wonder sometimes if it is worth going on!

Do some weary eyes fall on these lines who in 30 years of faithful Sunday school teaching have never witnessed a pupil believing the Word to the saving of that pupil's soul?

Perhaps some youth leader is weary of his work of trying to reach a generation that finds Spielberg's film, ET more exciting than the story of a baby found in a backyard who had come from the alien world of Heaven and was in fact God incarnate, come to save us from our sins. Maybe not one of your teenagers have shown the slightest interest in receiving him as Saviour but gratefully queue up to drink your coffee, eat your crisps and play on your snooker table any time you care to open the door.

There may be a missionary scanning these lines who has long served the Lord in some overseas nation, and when it comes to writing a news letter home has 'not one soul with which to greet them' — not only this year, but for the last 25. You are hardly counted a success by the Christian world around you. True?

The time has come to quit the fanatical love of statistics of 'how many were there' and 'how many responded' and start leaving spiritual results to 'Heaven's Morning News' (the Judgement Seat of Christ).

Faithfulness is a rare virtue. Waiting on God when the signs seem to be that he is not going to deliver is just about the most unsensational, difficult experience you could have. It certainly crucifies the flesh and its desires, that's for sure. It will certainly bring you ridicule. But it is eternally worth it. Ask Noah.

8

WHERE DO YOU PUT A MILLION INSECTS?

Taking a cubit to be 17.5 inches, the ark was 438 feet long, 72.9 feet wide, 43.8 feet high. It can be shown that such a ship could be titled to just short of 90 degrees and immediately right itself again. The total volumetric capacity was 1,400,000 cubic feet.

Biological taxonomy experts say that there are less than 18,000 species of mammals, birds,

January

reptiles, and amphibeans living in the world today. This number might be doubled to allow for extinct land animals and allowing for two of each species there might have had to have been room for over 72,000 animals on the ark. Since that ark by modern measuring standards could have carried 120,000 sheep and the average size of an animal is less than that of a sheep only 60% of its capacity would have had to have been used for animals. There was room for 1,000,00 species of insects as well as food for all the animals and ample room for Noah and his family to have comfortable living quarters.

Lesson? Quit thinking that the story of the ark was a fairy story and remember that if God could care for up on 1,000,000 insects, 72,000 animals and a family of 8 when the whole world was perishing around them that same God can handle your day. Cheer up!

9

DON'T RUSH THE DOOR

When the ark rested on Mt. Ararat it is important to remember that there was no mad rush for the door. Noah and his family had to wait for 7 months before they got out. It must have taken some patience to wait for God's timing especially with thousands of animals to look after.

For 2½ months Noah could see the tops of the nearby mountains but it then took a further 47 days of waiting finalised by the return of the dove with 'a fresh olive leaf'. This showed that the seedlings from the hardy olive tree were already beginning to grow again on the mountain sides. Noah could at last see the wood for the trees! It may be some time before you can distinguish the difference but your God is Noah's God. He will not fail you. One of these days he will let you go from that 'mountain' where you rest at the moment to do greater things for Him. You wait and see.

10

WHEN SOMEONE YOU LOVE WHISPERS

I lay on a soft sofa at Dubai's airport, exhausted by the heat of the Middle East, as the airliner refuelled. Men dressed in long flowing white robes sauntered around me, and I fell to thinking about Abraham, as the site of Ur of the Chaldees could not have been too far away from me. Great as the city must have been, the most significant thing anybody remembers about it was that Abraham left it!

It was no easy move for Abraham. None of us know all that is involved when we tear ourselves from the familiar scenes of our Ur of the Chaldees to follow God into a life of separation to his will. Abraham had the promises of God that he would become a great nation. 'Dust' and 'stars' were the similies God used to describe Abraham's coming descendants, He believed the Lord and pulled out of Ur heading for a city whose builder and maker was God.

But where were the promised children? Abraham and Sarah waited. And waited. And waited some more. There were no signs of any children. Ten

January

slow-moving years passed, but surely this godly couple knew God would act in his own way and in his own time.

Abraham was so sure God would give him the land, as promised, that he would not even take so much as a shoe latchet from the King of Sodom. Surely he and Sarah would wait for God for children. Hadn't God promised?

Unfortunately they didn't wait for God.

'See now', said Sarah, 'the Lord has restrained me from bearing children. Please go in to my maid: perhaps I shall obtain children by her'. And Abraham heeded the voice of Sarah ... and ... Hagar conceived ... (and) bore Abraham a son ... Ishmael'.

Temptation to leave off waiting for God is all the more deadly when it is whispered to you by someone you love. It is very interesting to note that all of Abraham's sorest trials were related to those he loved best.

Sarah, in jealousy, turned against Hagar and in her met all the agonies of all unwanted mothers since time began. It is fascinating that all Arabs, following Mohammed's example, claim descent from Ishmael, Hagar's son. 'He shall be a wild man', said God. 'His hand shall be against every man and every man's hand against him and he shall dwell in the presence of his brethren'. As Ishmael and Isaac were later to struggle, so Arabs and Jews struggle to this very day.

The next time we hear a news bulletin about the Arab-Israeli conflict let's meditate on the sobering fact that it is directly related to a couple who were not prepared to wait for God and chose surrogate motherhood instead.

But there was more waiting involved. Hagar, smarting under the hatred of Sarah, fled into the wilderness, where the Angel of the Lord met her. 'Return to your mistress and submit yourself under her hand'. It was a difficult thing to do, but to Hagar's credit she went back and waited for God to set her free to return to her native Egypt. For 13 years she waited and endured, and then God let her go free. It is easy to act like Abraham and Sarah and try to take a detour from God's will. It is also very easy in a fit of impatience and wounded pride to run for the wilderness like Hagar, and try to make our way out of our difficulties. Let us all come to learn this lesson quickly — that we will only conquer by yielding to the lot which God has ordained for us. In acceptance lies peace.

11

WHEN GOD SAYS 'GET OUT'

There are times when we can wait too long to fully obey the Lord's call. Let us always remember that Abraham certainly did leave Ur of the Chaldees at Gods command but he did not immediately strike out for Canaan. He went about 600 miles north west to Haran whereas Canaan was about the same distance due west. Soon it became apparent to Abraham that his father no longer intended to go on to Canaan. In fact Abraham's father Terah got involved in idolatry and stayed at Haran until his death (Joshua 24 : 2, 14, 15).

January

Is there a member of your family or circle of friends who are holding you up from Gods will? I know what it is to hear views expressed from people you respect that would thwart Gods plan in ones life. Beware of all views which would dull that still small voice within you that says 'This is the way walk you in it'. Shut your heart to their dulcet tones for if you listen you will waste years of your life out of the will of God for you. When God says 'Get out' then get out completely.

12 ————————

A Beacon

Abraham was severly tested by God when he eventually arrived at Canaan. When he arrived in the place of Gods will for him he discovered that there 'was a famine in the land'. The very Canaan that he had been led to seemed to be no longer able to support him! If only he had waited on God but he stepped out of Gods will again and went down into prosperous Egypt. Eventually he was restored by God and exercised great faith but his mistake stands as a beacon.

Are you tempted to side step the testing of God? A compromise between the methods of the world and Gods will and promises often works well at first. Ultimately it is a disaster. Just because there is a famine of one kind or another around you at the moment is no reason for moving. Wait, I say, on the Lord.

13

THE MAN WHO ITCHED

Lot itched. He itched for a lifestyle that had some sophistication. The heat of the Middle Eastern countryside might be the habitat of his uncle Abraham, but the city of Sodom lay in the plain of Jordan which was well irrigated everywhere. Lot itched for Sodom and Satan scratched him where it itched. He was to live to be very sorry.

What's wrong with a well irrigated plain? Nothing, God creates them in virtually every country on earth. The problem is created when you head down into one out of the will of God.

What's wrong with living in a sophisticated city? Nothing. Babylon was a city which had great sophistication and fabulous irrigation — on its rooftops grew the famous 'hanging gardens'. There were, no doubt, as many sinners living in Babylon as in Sodom, yet Daniel lived there and had one of the greatest ministries for God in history.

The lesson of Lot echoes down to the 20th century Christian. Living in Sodom in the will of God is fine, but living there out of the will of God is a disaster. Angels had to eventually snatch Lot out of Sodom because the Scriptures plainly state that despite their warnings 'he lingered'.

Think of it: he who couldn't wait for God and hurried into Sodom, now waits to see if he can somehow accommodate the will of God to suit his own ends. He now wants to wait against God. It won't work — surely he knows this. He knows God

January

always keeps his word. Life with his uncle proved it. 'Get out of this place', he warns his son-in-law, yet hangs back himself. Incredible.

All this time Abraham was unscathed. The man of faith waited for God and was rewarded incalculably. Lot chose by sight and not by faith. He mixed with the ungodly when there was no occasion for doing so and settled down into a stupid state of soul. Did he gain anything? Certainly not. Sodom was no better the day the angels dragged him out than the day he entered in. None of his family were even nudged Heavenwards. He lost his wife, he lost his testimony and the Scriptures leave him in a state one just hasn't the stomach to meditate upon.

And mark well that the New Testament teaches that Lot was a believer: a believer who unfortunately failed to wait for God. Wouldn't he have been a wiser man to wait for an indication from God as to where he should go rather than to rush on and have those chilling words of Moses written over his biography 'And Lot chose for himself all the plain of Jordan and pitched his tent even as far as Sodom'?

Let those four little words burn in your heart before you make that telephone call, sign that document, get on that aircraft, leave that church: 'Lot chose for himself'.

A few moments' meditation on Lot's motivation and you may well put that phone down, or have that flight cancelled. It may even make you go back to that local church you threatened to leave this week.

14

To Incalculable Fortune with Company

Does God leave a visiting card and say 'Come and visit me some time?' Does he leave us to find our own way through life until we meet up with him at the end? Does he leave you to find your own way out of the wood?

Let me put it this way: did Abraham leave Rebecca to find her own way across the desert to find his son Isaac? Did he not send his servant Eliezer to guide her? So it is that the Lord does not leave us to find our own way to the marriage supper of the Lamb. God sends his Holy Spirit to be our comforter and guide.

If you can't see the wood for the trees remember the question put to Rebecca by her family who wanted her to stay at home at least another ten days. 'Will you go with this man?', they said. They knew Eliezer was the key to her future. Let me ask you, bewildered one, 'Will you go with the Holy Spirit today?' As he speaks to you through the Bible, obey his promptings. He knows where the oasis are, when it is time to strike camp and when it is time to rest, he is your intercessor with the Father (Rom. 8: 26). If you follow his leading, like Rebecca, he will lead you to incalculable fortune.

January

15

Epitaphs can be amusing. This one, in England, certainly brought a smile to my face:

> 'Beneath this sod a lump of clay
> Lies Arabella Young,
> Who on the 21st May
> Began to hold her tongue.'

Epitaphs can be haunting, too. In the Protestant cemetery in Rome is a stone erected at John Keats' grave. Keats, one of England's greatest poets, requested this epitaph to be etched on the stone: 'Here lies one whose name was writ on water'. Sad, haunting words, those. Few epitaphs, though, could ever be as far-reaching as Abraham's, the man who learned to wait for God.

What is the simple secret of Abraham's international renown? Was it that Abraham had great intelligence? Was it that he possessed fabulous wealth? No. The basis of his character was a mighty faith. His epitaph can be summed up in three simple words: 'Abraham believed God'.

A minister said to me recently, 'I think we have in the Church a lot of spiritual atheists' — meaning Christians who live as if God did not exist. But Abraham is not like them. He believes God and leaves Ur of the Chaldees. He believes God and lets Lot choose. He believes God and is prepared to do anything he asks, even to the offering of Isaac for sacrifice.

January

Did his mighty faith make him impractical? Was he a recluse, cut off from daily living with its pressures? Certainly not. Heavenly-minded men are of great earthly use. Let's list what Abraham adds to his faith.

He adds goodness: he rescues the selfish Lot and he feeds angels. He adds knowledge: he knows God better at the end of his life than when he started. He adds self control: he curbed his spirit when Lot's herdsmen quarrelled with his.

He adds patience: he has a constant sense of the presence of God in his life, until he becomes known as 'the friend of God'. He adds brotherly kindness and was not lacking in tenderness toward his family.

To all of these fruits of the Spirit, as listed in 2 Peter 1 : 5, he adds the most important of all — he adds love, and as a result is open-hearted, courteous, and able to break out into hearty laughter.

How do we measure up? What will our epitaph be? When we have read Abraham's life the impression placed on our hearts is that he leaves us not admiring himself but longing after God. What a way to live! What an epitaph to leave behind! Go to it, friend.

16

A CASE OF LENTIL STEW

The Red Fox is a haunt of mine. I often escape with my wife to this little coffee shop, tucked away in the beautiful village of Hillsborough in County Down.

January

We sit by its fire, talk to its pleasant staff and exult in the delicious soups they prepare. Their soups frequently make my day.

I do have one problem, though: I don't like lentil soup. I am embrassed when The Red Fox soup of the day is lentil because I do not wish to offend 'mine hostess'! She got to know this and, bless her, lets me have an alternative soup on 'lentil days'. The truth is, I'm spoilt!

In the Bible, though, Esau is a 'lentil man'. Coming in weary from hunting, he sold his birthright to Jacob for lentil stew. It was no fair swop. Esau's birthright included twice as much of his father's inheritance as any other member of his family, but he chose the immediate: he couldn't wait.

No regret on Esau's part could undo the loss he brought upon himself. The bitter tears he shed could not bring back what could have been his. The stupidity of his action earned him the nickname Edom, which literally means 'Red', after the lentil stew.

Esau's family and its generations were all dubbed with the same nickname. They were called Edomites, and were constantly tainted with their forefather's trait: they grabbed the immediate and ignored a promise of future blessing.

Herod was an Edomite, and look at him — he chose Roman political power, for he was Caesar's puppet — rather than the kingship of the little Lord Jesus. Warned by scholars of Jewish law that the Messiah would indeed be born in Bethlehem, he tried to kill the child.

January

Troubled by the news of the eastern sages who had seen the star, Herod reckoned he would rather have the adulation of the crowds and build his castles than give his heart and life to the Christ of God and have an incalculable spiritual inheritance. He was a true Edomite — he couldn't, just couldn't, wait for God.

Are we any better? We all quote Jim Elliott of Ecuador and say, 'He is no fool who gives what he cannot keep to gain what he cannot lose,' but do we really believe it? Some do. Many a Christian deeply involved in his or her local church has to set aside promotion in their career in order to put the Lord's work first. Many a Sunday school, Bible class or youth fellowship leader has had to frequently give up an afternoon or evening for the young folks' sake while other friends gaily trip out to some social event somewhere.

Thousands of 'career girls' in the history of the Christian Church have laid aside their careers to spend their lives in Christian service in some seemingly remote corners of God's earth. Many a young Christian lad has refused a relationship with a very attractive unconverted girl because it would be what the Bible graphically describes as an 'unequal yoke'.

Immediate blessing for faithfulness has not always been experienced. Joseph found that faithfulness cost him a long prison sentence. John the Baptist found faithfulness to the Lord cost him a gruesome death. Paul found faithfulness meant loneliness, severe beatings, shipwreck, misunderstanding and eventual execution.

Was it worth it? I have no doubt that these men would reply that had they 50,000 lives to give they would let the Saviour have every one of them.

Esau and Herod have now lived their lives; what pleasure they had is gone forever. The lentil stew is long since finished and Herod's castles and amphitheatres are now mere Mediterranean rubble, but the Word of the Lord endures forever. It pays to wait for God, whether or not you like lentils. And there I rest my case.

17

THE SCHEMER WHO BECAME A PRINCE

Anyone can count the seeds in one apple but only God can count the apples in one seed. The seed that was Jacob didn't look like producing many apples: it looked a rotten seed.

Jacob is a man in a hurry: waiting is not his guideline. Scheming and conniving he bargains for Esau's birthright and cons his father into blessing him first. Rushing, pushing, shoving, Jacob's early life is one headlong rush away from waiting for the will of God to unfold: that is, until God stops him and transforms him.

Jacob's moment comes one night when he is alone. His wives, his eleven sons, and his possessions are all on the other side of 'the ford Jabbock'. Isolated, God moves in to challenge the schemer.

Suddenly a man appears and wrestles with Jacob until the dawn. When it was all over Jacob has no doubt that the man was God.

January

Has God been wrestling with you? Has God's pressure been on your life to obey him, to serve him, to have no will but his will? Don't, for any sakes, resist him. Jacob, at first, resisted and had a dislocated hip as a result.

How many a person has 'taken God on' and proved that the chastening of the Lord can be severe? The Scriptures do not teach that God punishes a believer; that punishment fell on the sacred head of the Lord Jesus at Calvary and the moment Christ is accepted as Saviour, the penalty and punishment for sin is lifted.

But God does chasten his children and the chastening is sometimes grievous. In fact the Scriptures teach that if a person is not chastened of the Lord at some time then that person is not his child.

The Lord's chastening always has a purpose: it is to draw us closer to himself, to slow us down, to make us holier, to loosen our grip on things that are transitory.

'What is your name?' asks the man. 'Jacob,' comes the answer. It was a confession. His name means 'Deceiver' and Jacob was owning up at last.

What was the result of his confession? Transformation! 'Your name shall no longer be Jacob but Israel, Prince with God.' The chastening had its effect and is it any wonder that the Scripture comments, 'the sun rose on Jacob'?

Do some weary eyes scan this page? Maybe you have long tried to run from God's will and have known the chastening of the Lord. Like Peter the Lord's look upon you has brought a flood of tears and heartbreak.

January

Like Jacob you look back and know how much better it would have been to obey God than to resist him, to have waited for God than to scheme and plan on your own, to have let your brother have his promotion than to try to take it for yourself and bring down sorrow on your head.

Yet, when the will is won, all is won. In every sphere of life the will settles alternatives and Jacob's will relented to God's.

Anyhow, Jacob's life did not lead to disaster, after all. In God's hands from the seed of Jacob came Joseph. And that can't be bad. Can it?

18 ——————————

CAN GOOD COME OUT OF A BAD HOME?

How would you like it if your father was a con man? How would you like it if your father were then conned in turn by his father-in-law into marrying the wrong woman? What if your brothers were into rape, incest, heartless cruelty and were, to put a fine point on it, plain downright hoodlums?

Into such a home was born what was arguably the godliest of all men in Scripture. There were few to equal him in character, perception and consistency. He was to prove God like few have ever done. His name was Joseph.

If God could use Joseph in such a tremendous way despite the fact that he came from an incredibly difficult background then let no-one ever say that their home or environment are a hindrance to leading a godly life and leaving a mark on their generation for God. Nothing can stop us from being

January

or having a blessing if we let God have his way in our lives. It is certain that we cannot choose our relatives but we can choose whether or not we will live for God. Let's choose carefully today.

———————————— **19**

FAVOURITISM STINKS

'Father's Day', the small boy pointed out, 'is just like Mother's Day only you don't spend so much!' 'Parents', said Peter Ustinov, 'are the bones on which children sharpen their teeth!'

'Wouldn't it be wonderful to be as brilliant as our children thought we were when they were young and only half as stupid as they think we are when they are teenagers?', someone asked. Yes, it certainly would.

Despite all the arguments about parenthood one thing is very clear in Joseph's life in the Bible, his father Jacob showed favouritism and favouritism in any home is wrong. It caused Jacob to naively send Joseph to Shechem to see his sons. If Josephs' brothers 'Couldn't even speak peaceably' to Joseph at home what would they not do to him if they got him alone? Jacob couldn't see it because favouritism puts parents out of touch with their childrens feelings. Have you several children and one is your blue-eyed boy or blue-eyed girl? With all my heart I warn you to stop showing favouritism to that child. Don't wait to stop. Stop, now! If you don't you will live to see it whiplash back at you one day from your then grown-up, insecure and angry children. Selah.

January

20

BE WARNED

Three things ruin most men; greed, glory and girls. None of them ruined Joseph and, by Gods grace, none of them need ruin you; but be warned.

21

A TWO YEAR WAIT

Of all the things God has taught me from the life of Joseph I think that his long wait in the prison is the most thrilling. Joseph asked the butler to speak a word for him but he forgot all about Joseph for two years. In those two years Pharaoh interviewed all the wise and intelligent men of Egypt in order to try to get them to interpret his dreams. When Joseph eventually stood before him with the interpretation he could immediately compare him with all the rest and there was no comparison! That two year wait was worth it all. So, stop drumming those finger tips on your desk, stop pacing the floor, refuse to toss and turn in your bed tonight with anxious care. If God makes you wait two years for something it will be all the better when it comes.

22

GOD NEVER OVERLOADS

'I do not pray for a lighter load but for a stronger back' said Philip Brooks. When Joseph became Governor of Egypt Pharaoh said to all the Egyptians, 'Go to Joseph; whatever he says to you, do'.

God gave Joseph two little boys, one he called Manasseh meaning 'God has made me forget' and the other, Ephraim, meaning, 'God has made me fruitful.' In the naming of his boys Joseph witnesses to us even in our day of the great secret of the success of his life. The load of responsibility got no lighter for Joseph as he grew older but God had helped him forget the bitterness of his past life and made him fruitful. God will do the same for us. He will strengthen our backs for the load he lays on them. Go on with your ministry for God today, my friend. Don't get discouraged. God will not break your back with the load.

23

OF ALL THE PEOPLE . . .

Don't write people off. Why? If God could change Judah, Joseph's brother, he could change anybody. Have you given up on someone? Do you think they are lost in the wood and will never be recovered. Just pause a moment today and think.

Judah was one of the most unsavoury, immoral characters in all Scripture and yet he changed and became the man who brought his father to his senses and even said he would take the blame forever if he did not bring his young brother, Benjamin, back home. When at a later date Joseph said he would keep Benjamin it opened up the flood tide of Judah's heart. He pled that such a thing would kill his father and offered to take Benjamin's place as a slave 'for how shall I go up to my father if the boy is not with me?' It was Judah's irresistible speech that brought Joseph to tears and brought him to the tremendous point of revealing who he really was to his brother. It was truly Judah's finest hour and it broke all Joseph's restraint in two until he could hold back his glory no more. It is fascinating to remember that from Judah's tribe sprang the Saviour of the world.

24

CONSCIENCE

'Oh Yes' said the Indian, 'I know what conscience is. It is a little three cornered thing in here' — he laid his hand upon his heart — 'that stands still when I am good: but when I am bad it turns around and the corners hurt very much. But if I keep on doing wrong, by and by the corners wear off and it doesn't hurt any more.' Does your conscience still hurt you? Be glad.

25

IT WAS A QUESTION OF WAGGONS

If you think you know the will of God for your future life, my friend, you are in for a shock; nobody knows the will of God for their entire life. Jacob, I reckon, thought that Canaan was the place in which he was to live for the rest of his days but when Joseph's waggons arrived he soon saw that it was to be Egypt. In youth, middle age, or, even in old age, God may greatly change your circumstances around. You never know what a day may bring so don't panic if the wood in which you are living at the moment appears to be very dark. The waggons of Gods provision may soon arrive to take you to a place where the sun shines much more brightly. Remember he is silently planning for you in love.

26

ALL IS NOT NECESSARILY GOOD BUT . . .

'But as for you, you meant evil against me,' said Joseph to his brothers 'but God meant it for good, in order to bring it about as it is today'. Joseph clearly believed that although everything that happened to him was not necessarily good it clearly would work together for good. Joseph acknowledged that his brothers had done wrong and that was good for them to hear but Joseph also showed that he believed that God was using all the experiences of his life to accomplish divine purposes.

January

Show me a man, woman or child who lives with such a belief and I will show you such a belief adds great contentment to their lives. Every difficulty will be an opportunity to them instead of every opportunity being a difficulty. They will learn that nothing happens by chance. What we think is all wrong in the circumstances of our lives God is actually turning around for our good. If Joseph left a legacy of theology during those special years as leader of Egypt, his theology of the sovreignity of God in life and limb must stand at the forefront. Imbibe his doctrine in your life.

27

A QUESTION OF BONES

I do not wish to seem morbid, but a friend of mine has asked me to preach at his funeral service! 'I want you to preach on Joseph's bones,' he asked.

Now, my friend is no fool. For over 50 years he has known Christ as his Lord and Saviour. Also my friend does not suffer fools gladly, and when he says he wants a message at his funeral service on the subject of Joseph's bones he really wants a message at his funeral service on Joseph's bones! What is he on about? Let's investigate.

'"I am dying," said Joseph, as recorded in Genesis 50 : 24-25, "but God will surely visit you and bring you out of this land to the land of which he swore to Abraham, to Isaac and to Jacob." Then Joseph took on oath from the children of Israel, saying, "God will surely visit you and you shall carry up my bones from here".'

January

Joseph's instruction regarding his bones showed clearly that he believed blessing for God's people was on the way. 'We are not here to stay,' he was saying, 'so please take my bones out of here when the Lord takes you all out!'

For 200 years those bones lay in Egypt, for 'they embalmed him,' the Bible says. As slave masters thrashed them and Pharaoh tried to exterminate them the Hebrews must have often wondered about Joseph's last words. Where was this promise of God's coming?

Decades passed and things got worse instead of better and still there was no sign of the exodus Joseph had predicted. Then it came one day as a result of a baby's tears. Pharaoh's daughter was moved by the child in the ark of bullrushes and had him brought up as her own son.

It was that same Moses who led the great exodus of the Hebrews out of Egypt and, as they pulled out, he ordered that Joseph's bones be brought with them.

For 40 years those people wandered in the wilderness and everywhere they went, Joseph's bones went with them! So hundreds of years after Joseph's promise of God's intervention, they buried his bones in Canaan. It was a long wait but God fulfilled Joseph's dying promise to the very last detail.

And what of us? Many of our loved ones have died in Christ and we who are alive wait for our Lord's return. Waiting for him is not easy, and I reckon our friends in prison for their faith or the many who are persecuted for their witness in other lands must find it even harder. But come he will.

January

'For the Lord himself shall descend from heaven with a shout, with the voice of the archangel, and with the trump of God: and the dead in Christ shall rise first:

Then we which are alive and remain shall be caught up together with them in the clouds, to meet the Lord in the air: and so shall we ever be with the Lord'. 1 Thessalonians 4 :16-17.

When I read that thrilling promise it makes me think that I might not have to preach that funeral service on Joseph's bones after all! Maranatha!

28 _____

A DOG IS AT HOME IN THIS WORLD

As Joseph often thought about Canaan and had made preparation even for his bones to go there, so the christian often thinks about Heaven. As these cold January days draw to a close I want to warm your heart with some thoughts about Heaven.

I often think about Heaven. I am not the only one, either, as I discovered recently when doing some research into what a few well known people had to say about it. I leave you with some of their thoughts today.

'If you are not allowed to laugh in Heaven I don't want to go there,' said Martin Luther. 'A dog is at home in this world because this is the only one a dog will ever live in', wrote Vance Havner. 'One breath of Paradise will extinguish all the adverse winds of earth', wrote A. W. Pink. 'There aren't just enough songs about Heaven', sings Joni Earechson Tada.

January

Speaking in Lancashire, Lady Catherwood, daughter of Martyn Lloyd Jones, the God gifted expositor, told of praying with her sister one day at her father's bedside. She prayed out loud that God would spare her father for a little longer. She recounted how her father leaned over and wrote on a piece of paper, 'Don't hinder me from the glory!' What a way to die! What a place to go to!

29

IS HEAVEN A REAL PLACE?

Questions often flood our minds about Heaven. Is Heaven a real place? Where is it? If I'm a christian will I go there immediately? How long will it take me to get there? Would I know my friends? Would they know me? What would I look like in Heaven? Could I eat? The plain fact is that Heaven is for us a great mystery.

Is Heaven a real place? It certainly is for the Lord Jesus said 'I go to prepare a place for you'. Heaven is not merely a state of mind. It is in fact a place of indescribable beauty. 'Eye has not seen, nor ear heard, nor has it entered into the heart of man the things that God has prepared for them that love him'. Heaven is also a place of perfect rest. It is called in Scripture, 'A sabbath rest for the people of God'. On the sabbath God rested from his creatorial work and explored it and said 'Behold, it was very good'. So Heaven will be place of endless exploration of all that God is and has done in Christ. You will know then in a way you cannot know now what the love of

God really is. 'If you were to swim,' said Tozer, 'in the ocean of God's love forever you would never come to the shore'. Why? Because there is no shore to the love of God! It is limitless.

> 'Oh! The deep, deep love of Jesus,
> Twould take ages to explore,
> Just one drop from that vast ocean,
> Just one grain from off its shore.'

30

THE STORY OF THE TOY SOLDIERS

Heaven is a place of open vision. This will make a great difference because the things that happen here on earth are so hard to understand. We know that not all things that happen to us are good but it is very difficult to understand that all things work together for good to them that love God. One thing is sure, you may not be able to trace God in everything in your life but you can always trust him. He sometimes appears to draw straight lines with a crooked stick. I cannot fully explain the things that are happening to me now. I cannot see as God sees. But in heaven I'll know. Heaven is a place of open vision with no glass between. 'Now we see through a glass darkly: but then face to face', said Paul, 'Now I know in part: but then shall I know even as I am known'.

A little boy gazed in at the toy soldiers in a toy shop window every day as he went on his paper round. One day the shop owner missed him. He enquired as to where the child was and discovered that he had had an accident and was in hospital, unconscious. The shop owner took the toy soldiers and got the mothers permission to place them at the foot of the injured boy's bed. One morning, when he regained consciousness, the first thing he saw was the soldiers. When the soldiers were in his hand, with a smile he exclaimed, 'Oh! Look, mother, look! Here are the soldiers and there is no glass between . . .'

31

WILL WE KNOW ONE ANOTHER IN HEAVEN?

I am often asked the question as to whether or not we will know one another in Heaven. The answer is that we will certainly know one another there. The Lord Jesus said, 'You shall see Abraham, Isaac and Jacob and all the Prophets in the Kingdom of God'. After all Moses and Elijah knew each other on the Mount of Transfiguration though they had never met on earth and they still had the same names. 'Then,' said Paul 'shall I know even as also I am known'. The one great difference is, we shall be changed praise God!

Does the prospect of Heaven merely take us into an impractical area of thinking? Certainly not! 'You are citizens of Heaven', wrote Paul to the christians at Philippi. We are to model our lives on the culture of Heaven. The worlds value system is not to be ours. Like Abraham we are to confess that we do not belong down here and are looking for a city whose builder and maker is God. Heaven's prospect should

January

not only effect how we live but how we feel. It should be a constant source of comfort and joy. If it isn't then the reason must be that we have become too comfortable on earth. We have succumbed to the subtle love of softening things. If our life style is subtly causing the pull of earth to cancel out the pull of Heaven let us check the imbalance. If we do this we shall truly be able to say 'I have a desire to depart to be with Christ which is far better'. It will be goodbye to January forever!

FEBRUARY

Think of it: bean rods, pea sticks, corn ricks, baskets, buildings and the chocolate and confectionery industry have all owed a great deal to it. It is always a bush rather than a single-stemmed tree. It is called the Hazel. In the woods its nuts get eaten by pheasants, pigeons, jays, sharp-toothed squirrels and dormice and in chocolate by me for I am, as they say, a fruit and nut case! Maybe you are the same!

In February the Hazels catkins, well ahead of its leaves, expand to become the famous drooping "lambs tails", packed with golden pollen. The Hazels branches have amazing powers of regeneration when they are cut back and the process called "Coppicing" is practiced to ensure repeated supplies of rods and poles.

So too does the Heavenly woodsman cut back and prune things in our lives. God's "coppicing" is not necessarily pleasant but it produces tremendous results. When it happens, be patient, wait for Him, it ensures great future usefulness in life. Go through February days, patiently.

February

1

WHAT IF GOD IS NOT THERE?

I was in a restaurant the other day with a friend. Near to me were some young men who were constantly annoying a girl who was serving tables. On and on they went until I could stand it no longer. 'Leave her alone, fellows,' I asked.

'So he's got higher standards than us?' one mocked. I repeated the request. 'I'll come and stuff that chicken down your throat,' one threatened as he cast a glance at the meal I was eating. When I pointed out that I was involved in Christian work they calmed down and departed later. 'We nearly got stuffed chicken for lunch there, brother!' quipped my friend as we set out for home.

When Moses saw an Egyptian annoying one of the Hebrews he didn't request him to stop — he murdered him. It was not God's time to free the Hebrews from Egyptian tyranny nor was it God's way to have them murdered by Moses.

Moses had not waited for God's time and now had to flee the country. It is as well to make sure our activity in life is born out of communion with God, or we too will end up out of God's will. What is often forgotten though, is what Moses did next. As Moses fled to Midian he stopped to rest by a well. Seven young women came by to draw water but were prevented from doing so by some male chauvanistic shepherds. And what happened to the famous temper brooding by the well? Was there a showdown? Did he murder the shepherds? No, the Bible says Moses stood up and helped the young women and his gentleness won him the heart of Zipporah who became his wife.

Moses was to learn unusual meekness, for the children of Israel would have tried even the patience of Terry Waite! No sooner had Moses gone up Mount Sinai to talk with God than the Hebrew people made a golden calf and worshipped it!

'How long will these people reject me?' said God, 'I will disinherit them . . . and I will make of you a nation greater and mightier than they' (Numbers 12 : 11-12).

How would you have reacted to such an offer? Moses refused it: 'The Egyptians will hear it . . . and say . . . the Lord was not able to bring his people to the land which he swore to give them.' Moses cared for the greatness of God's name more than fame for himself.

For me, though, Moses' finest hour came when God suggested to him that he take the people to the promised land without their Lord. 'If you don't go with us, carry us not up at all' was Moses' reply.

Moses knew that if he did not have God's presence that land flowing with milk and honey would mean nothing. Redemption from Egyptian slavery and a safe passage to economic security

February

wasn't enough for Moses. He must have God with him or all else was pointless. Even Heaven without God is nothing.

I once heard Ethel Waters sing to 50,000 people at an open-air service. The title of her song was, 'Where Jesus is 'tis Heaven there'. It moved me to tears then, and I'm sure Ethel, in Heaven, can sing it with even greater assurance now.

I'm quite sure Moses, had he known the song, could have sung it with all his heart for he esteemed 'the reproach of Christ greater riches than the treasures of Egypt . . . for he endured as seeing him who is invisible'.

Above all pride of race, face, or place the presence of the God who is there satisfied his heart. How about you?

> 'What matter where on earth we dwell?
> On mountain top or in the dell?
> In cottage or in mansion fair?
> Where Jesus is 'tis Heaven there!'

2

SOMEBODY LIKE THAT?

He was a top flight soldier: a West Point Academy graduate. In battle he led his new recruits through a Viet Cong ambush and got all but one of his men to safety.

That one left behind was severely wounded and the young lieutenant could hear him crying for help. To run into muderous crossfire to save him was asking for certain death but he braved it, saved him and received certain death. He caught a bullet in the back and was killed instantly.

February

Months later the one who was rescued returned to the United States and the parents of the dead hero invited him to dinner. He arrived at the house drunk, told obscene jokes and showed no concern for his hosts.

The mother collapsed in tears when he had gone and cried: 'To think our precious son had to die for somebody like that'. Do you ever think of what it means to be a Christian? It means to be bought with a price and it carries with it very serious responsibilities.

You may say, 'I am saved and therefore I am free'. True, but free for what? To do as you like?

You remember when the first-born males were redeemed by the blood of the Lamb in Exodus chapter 12? Were they free?

They were free of the avenger but they were not free from the responsibility they had to the one who redeemed them.

Exodus 13 : 1 says: 'Sanctify unto me all the first born . . . it is mine' On Arrival in Canaan those first-born could be bought back (Exodus 13 : 11-13).

The first-born were automatically in what we would call 'full-time service' if not bought back. You will remember Hannah did not redeem her first-born, Samuel, so he remained in 'full-time service' all his days.

Crossing the wilderness God did an amazing thing. God substituted all the first-born out of Egypt for Levites. We are told 22,273 Levites were available but they were not enough: 273 were left over!

February

Were they relieved of their responsibilities for nothing? Certainly not: 1,365 shekels of silver (8 oz to a shekel) had to be paid to redeem them.

Those Levites now represented the first-born and were offered as living sacrifices (Numbers 8 : 5-11) in the service of the great Tabernacle.

All went well until a Levite called Korah rebelled. He didn't accept that the redeemed by the Passover Lamb were God's particular possession.

Moses challenged him and his cohorts to come to the door of the Tabernacle the next day to see what God thought. God opened the ground and it swallowed them alive (Numbers 16 : 1-50).

When the Israelites complained that Moses had 'killed the people of the Lord' God sent a plague among the people and 14,700 of them died.

Lesson? When God says something is his, he means its. No wonder Paul says: 'I beseech you therefore, brethren, by the mercies of God, that you present your bodies a living sacrifice, holy, acceptable to God which is your reasonable service. And do not be conformed to this world but be transformed by the renewing of your mind that you may prove what is that good and acceptable and perfect will of God'.

If it is bad enough for an unconverted soldier not to seem to care less about the one who saved his life, is there a worse sin under heaven than for redeemed souls to rebel against their responsibilities to the one who redeemed them at Calvary? Selah.

3

The second appearance

It was a fabulous structure, nothing has ever been seen like it, before or since: £7 million wouldn't build it today. Several million people lived around it in tents but God lived in a special part of the actual structure itself. It was called the Tabernacle.

The dimensions were 15 ft by 45 ft and it was constructed of three tons of gold, five tons of silver, four tons of brass and an assortment of jewels, fine wood and fancy tapestries.

It was, in fact, a portable house of worship and financed by the farewell gifts to the children of Israel by their Egyptian captors. It was the epitome of simplicity to dismantle and reassemble.

It could be quickly moved by 8,500 carriers when the cloud of the Lord's presence moved forward.

Two chapters in the Bible are given to the creation of the world but over 40 chapters to the Tabernacle. It was the first dwelling place that God had on earth as far as the Bible records it.

It was the expression of God's over-whelming desire to live with people. That's why it was so important.

The Tabernacle was a parable for the present (Hebrews 9 : 9), it was a shadow of things to come (Hebrews 8 : 5), it was a prophecy (Hebrews 9 : 24).

These facts are illustrated so clearly in the instructions carried out in the Tabernacle by the High Priest on the great day of atonement.

February

First of all he appeared before the people and then entered into God's presence in the Tabernacle in a place called the Holy of Holies.

He dare not enter without the blood of a slain animal which he then sprinkled on the fabulous gold lid of the Ark of the Covenant called the Mercy Seat. Two cherubim stood over this seat and there God met with him.

Outside, the huge crowd waited to see if their representative was accepted by God. Jewish legend even has it that the people would tie a rope around the High Priest when he entered God's presence in order to drag him out again if he got into trouble!

Imagine the anxious wait of those crowds as they waited for God to indicate his acceptance of the sacrificial blood shed for their sin.

Suddenly they would hear the sound of the bells on the High Priest's garments as he moved towards them. What a relief! Their rejoicing at his second appearance can only be imagined.

Remember, the Tabernacle was a parable, a shadow of things to come, a prophecy. 'Of what?', you may ask. 'Of Christ', I would quickly answer.

Did not he appear in this world, once, to put away sin? On the third day he rose again and entered into the Holiest of All, even Heaven itself. The question we are all asking is very straight-forward: has he been accepted?

Praise God he has been truly accepted! The blood he shed is powerful to the cleansing of all sin. It never needs to be shed again; 'So Christ was offered once to bear the sin of many. To those who eagerly wait for him he will appear a second time, apart from sin, for salvation' (Hebrews 9 : 28).

February

If there was jubilation at the second appearance of the Old Testament High Priest what will our reaction be at our High Priest's second appearance? Does the prospect thrill you or has the love of softening things dulled your enthusiasm for Christ's second appearing?

Is our lifestyle subtely upstaging our view of Heaven? If it has, then let's repent of our lethargy and may we soon be saying with the great Samuel Rutherford as we wait for the Lord's return:

'O Time, why dost thou move so slowly?
O Sin, be removed out of the way,
O Day, oh fairest days, dawn.'

4

DOES GOD EVER GET HUNGRY?

The Old Testament tabernacle contained almost every New Testament truth in type and picture, and, each picture is worth a thousand words. Take the table of shewbread.

This table stood on the right hand side of the holy place as you entered and approached the presence of God. On it were twelve loaves for God which were taken after a week and eaten by the priest.

What is the lesson? As we often invite our friends for a meal to our table to enjoy food together so God wants to be friends with us. The religious leaders of Christs day hated him because he received sinners and ate with them. God's salvation is likened to a man who made a banquet for his son. Bread tells us that God is the means of life and Christ is the bread

February

come down from Heaven. He is saying we are hungry for the bread of life and he can feed us. That is why we are never satisfied with this world for we were not made for it. This world is but the childs toys meant to prepare us for the next. To go out into eternity without Christ is to go out into meaningless loneliness.

If you have trusted Christ you will 'sup' with and from him but he says in Revelation 3 : 20 that he will also 'Sup with you'. You have something to give and as the shewbread was for God, as we worship, we feed the very heart of God.

I started to write today's entry in an airport lounge filled with very frustrated people. They were held up because Airlines couldn't see the wood for the fog! Yet, as I wait in an airport lounge I can lift my heart to my lovely Lord and feed his very heart despite the frustrations around me. I don't know where you are sitting today but remember that just as the shewbread fed both ways: so does worship! Think about it and you will find it's true.

5

SOFT, WARM AND COMFORTING

I love lamplight: it is soft and warm and comforting. In the tabernacle there was a beautiful golden lampstand. In that sacred dwelling there was no other source of light because all natural light was excluded. The soft light would cast its rays upon the beautiful gold covered boards that formed the walls and upon the hangings and curtains of fine twined linen embroidered with cherubim of blue and scarlet. Everything in that sacred room foreshadowed the glory and beauty of him who was to come. Nothing, no nothing in that holy place marred its beauty.

There were different varieties of gold in the tabernacle but the lampstand, all of it, was beaten out of a solid piece of gold. There was no wood in it at all. It speaks so beautifully of Christ. Christ was not merely the expression of God, he was God. To say that Christ wouldn't have been a true man if he didn't make mistakes is a blasphemy. Christ was God of very God. He was 'solid, pure gold' 'In the beginning was the Word and the Word was with God and the Word was God', says John. He is God absolute. There is no knowledge of God without him. To differ from him is to depart from the living God, it is to go out into unalleviated darkness for ever. The priest serving in the tabernacle walked in the light, so do we. It is soft, warm and eternally comforting. Lead kindly light, indeed.

6

WHAT'S IN AN ALMOND?

Many bachelors tend to go in for naked light bulbs but married men find that soon the lady of their home brings in a pleasant lampstand or two. Most people like a little style with the light in their homes.

It is fascinating to discover that the shaft of the golden lampstand in the tabernacle was a stylized tree. It had a bud, flower petals and a cup shaped like

February

an almond to represent fruit. It was made to look as if it were alive.

Is it any wonder that John wrote of Christ 'In him was life and the life was the light of men'? As we look at all creation around us we are only thinking God's thoughts after him. To find the meaning of life we have to trace it to its source. Ask people what is the purpose of life and you will get some amazing answers. The doctor might say 'To heal folk'. I say 'To heal what for?' Others might say 'The purpose of life is to work'. I say 'To work what for?'. 'To make money to eat', they reply. I say 'What for? To live? What is the end of it?' People say 'I'm not worried about the end. I'm just here to enjoy it.' Tell that to someone crippled or paralysed. Tell that to someone who will have to spend the next 30 years in bed. If life is mainly for enjoyment they would be better dead, would they not? There must be more to life than mere enjoyment or life is meaningless for many people.

Life only makes ultimate sense if it is in harmony with the personal God who gave it. When we get to know the Lord, then comes the bud of promise, and the flower of beauty. The almond of the lampstand shaft preaches us a very powerful lesson. The almond tree was known as 'the waker tree' to the Hebrews for the almond tree is the first tree in the Middle East to wake up out of the deadness of winter. Almonds are a symbol of resurrection life. So it is that life in Christ who is the light of the world is Life. Enjoy it today.

7

No power failures

When I lived at my grandmothers in the country for six months as a child, while my father had a new house built, I used to go to bed by light that came from a little oil lit lamp. What long shadows that little hand carried lamp cast!

The light in the tabernacle was oil light. Zerubabel once saw a visionary lampstand at a time of great national crisis in Israel and it was supported by pipes from an olive tree. The message to him was 'not by might nor by power but by my Spirit saith the Lord'. Israel's light of spiritual witness was not to be maintained by human power but was to be maintained by the Spirit of God.

So it is that the Spirit of God will enable us to witness to our lovely Lord in these dark days. Are you in hospital today? Are you in an awkard business situation? Do you face frightening problems in your local church? Are you in a home where the Lord is not loved? Fear not: the oil of the Spirit will not be cut off. Shine on.

8

Not just gilt-edged

Now for one of the finer points of Bible teaching. Think deeply with me. The Bible does not say that when the priest lit the tabernacle lampstand light that it was to show up what was in that sacred place.

February

It did show up what it contained but that was not its primary purpose. It was to primarily 'Give light over against the lampstand'. Isn't that fascinating? The light of the lampstand was actually to cast light back upon the beauty of the lampstand itself. The light was in fact to show up the vehicle of light.

It is true that the Holy Spirit speaks to the world, (John 16 : 8-11). It is true that the Holy Spirit speaks to the believer (John 16 : 13). Yet when all this is done the Holy Spirit's prime witness is to turn the believer's eye on Christ. As the light of the tabernacle gave light to show up the fabulous gold of the lampstand so the Holy Spirit draws our eye to Christ the great vehicle of light. Please read John 16 : 15 carefully before you face the day. As your day unfolds may you see the fabulous gold that is your possession. The possession is not just gilt-edged: it is pure gold all the way through. Thank God for Jesus!

9

TAKE HOLD OF HOPE

On the four corners of the altar of sacrifice in the outer court of the tabernacle there were horns, made of one piece of wood and overlaid with copper. In the ancient world when a man accidently killed someone and was in danger of being killed himself by the murdered mans kith and kin he would run to the sanctuary and take hold of the horns of the altar. As long as he held the horn he was safe until the elders came and investigated the case. The horns were a place of refuge.

Calvary, christian, is your place of refuge. The New Testament says that christians are people who have 'Fled for refuge to take hold of the hope set before them'. You cannot be struck down if you lean on Calvary's work alone. Oh! safe and happy shelter! Oh! refuge tried and sweet.

'The soul that on Jesus
Has leaned for repose
He'll never, he said it,
Desert to its foes,
That soul though all Hell
Should endeavour to shake,
He'll never, no never, no never forsake.'

10

AS A SCREAMING VULTURE

What did an Israelite learn when he brought his animal to the altar of sacrifice? He learned that sin is a very expensive thing, that sin is a killer. He sees the animal slain and he hears the fire on the altar roar as the priest lays the lamb in the fire. He sees the animal take his place. Sin is, I repeat, a very costly thing.

It is so hard to remember this. Sin at the start appears to be so charming, as soft and attractive as a dove but before it is finished it will pick at your very bones like a screaming vulture. Sin never runs out of ideas and slays the strongest of men and women. It has awful consequences. Meditate long, long, today

February

on what I am saying and as you think on the Lamb of God, remember the frightening price of Calvary's love. God is angry with sinners every day and he still feels as deeply about sin in the 20th century as ever he did in B.C. 2,000. Let us flee the very appearance of evil as we go through the coming hours.

11 ─────────────────

WHAT IF I SIN TO-MORROW?

How meagre was the message of the Old Testament sacrifice symbols of the tabernacle in comparison to what the Lord Jesus does!

What does an animal know of moral law? It lives by instinct. The Lord Jesus fulfilled all moral laws and choose to die for us. A sigh of relief went up from an Israelite when the sacrifice had been made yet he could not go out free because if he asked 'What happens, priest, if I sin again, tomorrow? What then?' The priest would answer, 'Then you must come again with another sacrifice. I am never finished my work here'. There were, in fact, no chairs in all the tabernacle structure, outside in the court or in the tent itself. There was no opportunity to sit or rest, anywhere.

But this man, Christ Jesus? 'This man, after he had offered one sacrifice for sins for ever, sat down at the right hand of God'. There is no more sacrifice for sin because there need be no more. You are forgiven, christian! If that doesn't make your day, never to speak of your eternity, what will?

12

THE INCORRUPTIBLE WOOD

I have a feeling that someone will think the gruesome fires and gory sacrifices of Israel that I am writing about at the moment were thought up by a people steeped in superstition. People will say God is a God of love and the prodigal will find his way back to God eventually.

Let me tell you God is unchanging. He doesn't grow feeble and relax his standards. The more a doctor loves his patient the more he will hate the disease that kills him. A doctor who says that diease doesn't matter has ceased to be worthy of the name of doctor. A God who says sin doesn't matter would cease to be God.

In the altar of burnt offering those folk learned something of the love of God. It was made of wood covered with copper. Trees to a Hebrew mind were examples of different kinds of individuals. The altar of burnt offering was made of Achachia wood which was so hard that the Greeks called it 'the incorruptible wood'. What a lovely symbol of the sinless one who died for our sins. The copper which covered the Achachia wood endured the tremendous heat of the sacrifice fires and thus protected the wood. Copper typified the power to withstand. So it is that in Christ human and divine combine sinlessly. He could withstand all that Satan threw at him. If you are hiding in him you will have victory. You too will know how to endure all the onslaughts of the evil one through Christs power. What a Saviour! Is he yours today? If so, enjoy his friendship. If not, enter into it right now.

February

13

Redemption ground

Do you find it easy to get your christian friends in your local church to stand side by side in good order? All the time?

It was also quite a problem to get a system whereby the frames of the tabernacle would stand at the right angle and in perfect order to hold up God's testimony. How did you get a frame fifteen feet high to stand up in the first place?

Every frame had a tenon which were small projections at the lower end of the frame to sink into sockets to hold the frames in place. The fascinating fact is that the sockets were made of silver. The Israelites got the silver from the ransom money at the census when Israelite males came to have their names enrolled in the citizens lists and census of Israel. Each man had to pay a ransom for his soul. Now get it straight:

'We are not redeemed with corruptible things like silver,' wrote Peter, 'but with the precious blood of Christ as of a lamb without blemish and without spot'. That is how you have unity in the church to begin with. It is first essential if men and women are going to stand together to give practical expression to the unity of the Spirit that every single 'frame' must be personally standing on their redemption that is in Christ. If not then soon those 'frames' will be without foundation and wobble all over the place.

It is a sorry thing to encourage folks not truly

converted and who don't know the Lord Jesus personally to think that they are members of his church. From a practical point of view it won't work. The frames in the tabernacle had two feet and they stood on silver. The christian secret of standing on his or her two feet before God is on redemption ground. What a place! May you know the assurance of it today.

14

THE RIGHT ANGLE

Did you get yesterday's message on the unity of the tabernacle frames? Good. Now let me point out that it wasn't enough to have each frame standing on a solid silver foundation. When they came to put the whole thing together the angle had to be fixed. This was done partly by the corner frames.

So it is that christian lives who form the dwelling place of God are fixed in the angle they live at by the corner stone of the church of Christ. As Peter put it 'You also, as living stones, are being built up as a spiritual house, a holy priesthood, to offer up spiritual sacrifices acceptable to God through Jesus Christ. Therefore it is also contained in the Scripture, "Behold I lay in Zion, a chief corner stone, elect, precious, and he who believes on him will by no means be put to shame." Therefore to you who believe, he is precious; but to those who are disobedient "the stone which the builders rejected has become the chief corner stone". (I Pt. 2 : 5-7).

It is vitally important that if we want to be a spiritual temple for the Lord we must let ourselves be fitted to Christ the corner stone. We take our angle from him. 'Coming to him as a living stone, rejected indeed by men, but chosen by God and precious'. The church is a spiritual building and it is not made with dead stones but living ones. As we constantly come to him so we constantly get adjusted. Come to him in a fresh way and get the angle set for your day ahead.

15

DON'T SAY A WORD

You know how it is: you drive up to someone's house and you look for signs of them being at home. There is your friend's car or his 'light' is on or whatever. We all know the signs of someone being at home.

A cloud rested on the tabernacle above the place where the ark stood. The cloud clearly indicated that God was present. The cloud also functioned as a guide when the people of God were to move on again (Ex. 40 : 36-38).

I wonder what signs indicate that God dwells in the temple which is your body? Are there tell tale signs that indicate to others that you are a christian? The way you react to a frustrating business deal? The look in your eye when you are deeply hurt but your lips remain shut? The quietness you show when everyone else around you is tearing someone else apart with words and you are all picture and no sound? Perhaps the presence of God in our lives is often as powerfully reflected in what we don't say rather than by what we do. A young christian

handed me the following little poem, once, and I
pass its message on to you today:

> Are you nervous and blue?
> In doubt what to do?
> Misunderstand, too?
> Don't say a word.
>
> Is business so bad?
> It's hard to be glad?
> Inclined to get mad?
> Don't say a word.
>
> Are things awry?
> Does it seem vain to try?
> Must you worry and sigh?
> Don't say a word.
>
> Climb bravely life's hill,
> Seek only God's will,
> Trust Him and be still —
> Sh! Don't say a word.

Anon

16

DEEPER DOWN THAN THE TITANIC

I like the little magazine called 'The Gideon News'
because it contains one of the most fascinating
'Letters' section of any magazine I read. From hotel
suites to prison cells people write in to Gideons to
say how they have been converted through reading
the Scriptures. The thing is, tremendous.

February

It makes me think of the bronze laver which held the water in the tabernacle. God required that priests serving him in the tabernacle were to wash their hands and feet before every service for him at the laver otherwise they risked the penalty of death. Yet, for all the instructions given about the laver you will look in vain for its measurements (Exodus 30 : 17-21). As I see it the laver with its water represents the Word of God (see Ephesians 5 : 26). When you have been to Calvary, the blood of Christ cleanses you from the guilt of your sin but as you continue the christian life constantly reading the Word of God it constantly cleanses those dirty feet and hands of ours which get defiled as we pass through this world.

As the laver was measureless so the cleansing from the Word is measureless too. How many thousands of times have you been diverted from a wrong path by a verse of Scripture? How many times have you been checked in your reactions by a riveting Word of God? Scripture is measureless in its influence. Dr. Ballard could descend 2½ miles into the Atlantic in a tiny submarine to explore the wreck of the Titanic. But no machine will ever be able to calculate the depth of the Word of God. For about 20 years I have taught Scripture weekly, and, often nightly and daily; I feel but a little lad with my bucket and spade digging on the seashore of an ocean. Even then my analogy breaks down for as far as Scripture is concerned there is no shore! It is measureless.

Don't debate the Bible, don't dispute it, live it — stand fast!

MORE THAN A SPARKLER

The wedding guests had all been seated for some time before I noticed it. The light caught the diamond on the ladies finger and the brilliance of it dazzled even my eyes. Why do I say 'even my eyes'? Because I wouldn't normally know a real diamond from a cheap one in a jeweller's window most days of the week. It was the way the light caught that diamond: there was no escaping that it was fabulous. Subsequent, gentle enquiries proved that it was!

Precious stones are some of the most beautiful products of the earth and are often of immense value. The High Priest in the Old Testament wore some precious stones on his right and left shoulders. Six names were engraved on each stone making up the exact number of the tribes of Israel. He also wore a breastplate on which were set in gold twelve different precious stones. In each one a separate name was engraved. The shoulder stones represented the nation as a whole, the breastplate stones represented each tribe individually.

So it is that the Lord looks upon his people as his jewels (Malachi 3 : 17). He carries the church on his shoulders and also knows each member individually. You may not be known on earth, christian, but I can tell you that you are well known in Heaven. Borne on Christ's shoulders, borne on Christ's heart: what have you got to fear? Consider, today, the High Priest of your profession. It is always a beautiful, heart warming consideration. It helps you see the wood from the trees in your life. It points your heart, life and spirit in the right direction. It puts an inch to your step and a glint in your eye. Bless the Lord, O my soul and all that is within me, bless his holy name.

18

INTO THE LOOKING-GLASS

It has been said that the greatest god ever raised to human beings is the mirror. You know that famous song about the girl sitting in the restaurant who thought she saw a woman outside staring in at her? She discovered the woman was only examining her own reflection in the restaurant window. We have all done it, though not necessarily out of pride but more out of a spirit of can-we-do-anything-about-the-apparation!

The material of the tabernacle laver was made out of the metal hand-mirrors of the women of Israel and showed up the necessity of cleansing. (Exodus 38 : 8).

It reminds us of the apostolic word from James 'But be doers of the word, and not hearers only, deceiving yourselves. For if anyone is a hearer of the word and not a doer, he is like a man observing his natural face in a mirror; for he observes himself, goes away, and immediately forgets what kind of man he was but he who looks into the perfect law of liberty and continues in it, and is not a forgetful

February

hearer but a doer of the work, this one will be blessed in what he does.' When you look in the mirror of God's Word don't forget what you see. It certainly will never flatter you but it will drive you to the one who can give you a beauty not your own.

19

QUIT FOOLING AROUND WITH WOOD, HAY AND STRAW

I always remember, as a lad, speaking at a children's service. A little girl came to talk to me about becoming a christian and I didn't know what to do because I was so shocked that the Lord had actually used something I had said to touch her life! I virtually ran, scared. Do you not feel the same when God takes something you have said or done and actually used it to help someone?

Yet, why should we run scared from being used? God WANTS to use you, today. 'See', said God, 'I have called by name Bezaliel . . . and I have filled him with the Spirit of God, in wisdom, in understanding, in knowledge and in all manner of workmanship, to design artistic works, to work in gold, in silver, in bronze, in cutting jewels for setting in carving wood and to work in all manner of workmanship. And I, indeed, I have appointed with him Aholiab . . . and I have put wisdom in the hearts of all who are gifted artisans that they may make all I have commanded you.'

Did only Bezaliel and Aholiab build the tabernacle? No, the lovely fact was that every Israelite could bring building materials and gifts and

February

contribute to the erection of the tabernacle (Exodus 25 : 1-9). So, today may the Lord use you to help in the building of the House of God on earth. The materials are available, 'gold, silver and precious stones' but the truth is that a lot of us are fooling around with 'wood, hay and straw.' Such will be the losers for 'The Day will declare it . . . if anyone's work which he builds . . . endures, he will receive a reward. If anyone's work is burned, he will suffer loss.' (1 Corinthians 3 : 10-15). The choice is yours.

'Deeds of merit as we thought them,
He will tell us were but sin,
Little acts we had forgotten,
He will tell us were for Him'.

20

A PICKET FENCE WITH A RAMBLING ROSE?

We are all looking for the Ideal Place. We dream and think that someday we will find it. If we don't find it for a fortnight on the Costa del Wherever next year, well, there is always the hope of that little cottage with a picket fence and rambling rose surrounded by quiet hearts and gentle people in retirement. Yes? Somewhere, sometime we feel the idyll will arise in front of us and we will have arrived at a spot where there is no hassle, no stress and no trouble.

It is of course, a lie. As Uncle Remus, whom I am very fond of quoting, said, and let me repeat it, 'You can't run away from trouble because there 'ain't no place that far.' No trouble-free zone exists.

February

It is true 'that a sparrow has found a home and the swallow a nest where she may lay her young' but what does the Psalm mean when it says 'My heart and flesh cry out for the living God . . . even your altars, O Lord of hosts?'

There were, of course, two altars. The first, the brazen altar of burnt offering which was in the tabernacle court, spoke of Calvary. Now there, there is a resting place par excellence.

'Sweet resting place of every heart,
That feels the plague of sin,
Yet knows the deep mysterious joy,
Of peace with God within'

Have you been there? Have you rested on Christ's finished work? From Calvary the famous spiritual 'Old man river' which speaks of the slave who was 'Sick o'livin and scared o'dyin' has no echo. Why? Because those who trust the Saviour find life worth living and dying, gain.

The second altar was the golden altar of incense which spoke of prayer and worship. Worship is the highest thing we can give. It begins now and it will never end. There is rest and refreshment in prayer and worship which no novel, film, meal, house, clothes, holiday, share, bank balance or human friendship can give. May your heart cry out for the altars of the living God, today. Stop whatever you are doing now and thank God for Calvary and worship Him. Go on. Do it now. Feeling better already?

February

21 _____

GOD IS NO MISER

You might forget a Charles Dickens plot but you will certainly never forget his characters. Take Scrooge, 'Nobody', wrote Dickens, 'ever stopped him on the street to say 'My dear Scrooge how are you?. When will you come to see me?'. No beggars implored him to bestow a trifle, no children asked him what it was o'clock, no man or woman ever once in all his life enquired the way to such and such a place of Scrooge. Even the blind man's dogs appeared to know him; and when they saw him coming on, would tug their owners into doorways and up courts; and would wag their tails as though they said. 'No eye at all is better than an evil eye, dark master!'

But what did Scrooge care! It was the very thing he liked; 'To edge his way along the crowded paths of life, warning all human sympathy to keep its distance was what the knowing ones call "Nuts" to Scrooge.' Unforgettable, yes? Yet, there is a Scrooge in all of us, God forgive us.

When God set up the fabulous tabernacle in the wilderness he was no miser. It was a House of Gold, it was the House of God. In nothing was God skinting, from the fabulous gold of the lampstand to the precious gold that covered the walls which formed the tabernacle, there was nothing cheap. So it is that we read of gold in the Garden of Eden in Genesis 2 and gold in the New Jerusalem of Revelation 21, the city which was of 'pure gold.'

February

Christ who was rich for our sakes became poor that we through his poverty might be made rich. Why, so often, are we less than generous and more than selfish? Why when God gave us his very best and redeemed us with something even more valuable than gold, namely the precious blood of Christ, do we react with such a miserly spirit when all around us are crying out for compassion and help? Why are we so reticent to allow the Lord Jesus to take up full possession of what is rightfully his?

A Korean Presbyterian church elder called Elder Kim was once asked to speak at the General Assembly of his denomination. He began modestly, reminding his hearers that he was no scholar and that he was neither going to preach nor attempt to teach them. What he wished to do was to put before them a great problem and to ask their advice for its solution.

'A year or two ago,' he began, 'I received a letter from a young dentist friend who wanted to establish a practice in my city. He wanted me to find a house for him, which I did. I explained that the house was in bad condition, in a bad neighbourhood and at a very high price. He sent me a telegram telling me to buy the house. A day or so later I received a cheque for several thousand yen for the down-payment so I signed the papers to purchase the house. Down-payment was made and the final payments were to be made in three days at which time the owner agreed to vacate the house. The payments were made but the owner asked for a day or two in order

February

to find another house. Six months passed and he was still there. The man who sold the house has bought new clothing for his family and they are eating polished rice instead of the cheaper grains. He knows that I am a christian and that in Korea we christians never go to court against other christians and we try not to go to court against unbelievers. He laughs at me when I come. What should I do?'

The General Assembly of the Presbyterian Church in Korea voted that Elder Kim had the right to proceed legally to have the man evicted.

'Thank you', said Elder Kim, 'but before I sit down, I wish to draw one conclusion. The Lord Jesus came down from Heaven to purchase for himself a dwelling place.' Then, striking his hand upon his breast, he continued, 'He bought this old shack. It was in a run-down condition. It was in a bad neighbourhood. He bought me because he wanted to take possession. He gave himself for me, and he gave me the Holy Spirit as a down-payment on my inheritance, bringing me innumerable blessings with his redemption. But I cling to my tenement and leave him outside. But now if you say that I have the right to seek the help of the authorities to evict a man who is occupying my friend's house, what shall you and I say of ourselves when we deny the Lord Jesus the full possession of that for which he gave his own life?'

I leave you to draw your own conclusions. Selah.

February

22

STROKE IT BETWEEN THE EARS

We have looked at some deep truths from the great Tabernacle over the past few weeks. Now I want to simply communicate a few simple pertinent things as we see February out. On the surface they may seem light but if you think about them you will discover they are not only profound truths but also useful.

The every day life of the British House of Commons is very noisy and often the language of Members of Parliament is vindictive, childish and even cruel. As for the behaviour, the Speaker of the House of Commons gets fifty or sixty letters a day complaining about it! How does he keep his House in Order? Mr. Speaker Wetherall says that he once got good advice from the Riding Master when he was in the 19th King George V Own Lancers. Speaking of handling a horse the Riding Master said 'If you have to use the whip, gentlemen, stroke it between the ears quick'. I reckon, with Mr. Speaker Wetherall, that the same applies to handling people.

23

AT HOME EVERYWHERE BUT AT HOME

Speaking of the problem of some christians who travel the world holding christian meetings, seminars, conferences, etc. Os Guiness has wisely said that they are often 'At home everywhere in the

February

world but at home.' I find his statement too close for comfort! How about you, preacher? If you had to sit in the local pews and attend all the local meetings of your local church for a couple of years without publicly participating I reckon you would be a bit easier on the folks who have to do just that for most of their lives. Are you at home, at home?

24 ————————————

Are you weighing your thumb?

A butcher was once asked the difference it made to him when Christ entered his life. He did not hesitate for one moment to give an answer: 'I've stopped weighing my thumb!', he said.

He then told how that in his unconverted days he put the meat on the scales in such a way that his thumb trailed down approximately the weight of an ounce. He had included that thumb in the weight of beef, pork, lard and every other item of his merchandise. After he came to know the Saviour he stood away from the scales and gave a full 16 ounces of meat. When he served customers whom he had formerly cheated he added an ounce to make up for his past cheating. 'He who walks blamelessly and works righteousness' says Psalm 15, 'Who does not put out his money at usury nor does he take a bribe against the innocent. He who does these things shall never be moved.' Tell me, are you weighing your thumb?

25

MR. JOHNSTON'S QUIP

Mr. Willie Johnston, much loved by many in our Ulster community once put out his two hands and quipped about spending money; 'If you don't have it in this hand,' he said 'don't hand it out with the other!'

26

THE PHONE

Not everything that cries the loudest is the most urgent thing in your life. Especially on the phone.

27

SPEND YOUR STRENGTH WISELY

Mrs. William Booth once wrote to her husband General Booth; 'Remember a long life of steady, consistent holy labour will produce twice as much fruit as one shortened and destroyed by spasmodic and extravagant exertion; be careful and sparing of your strength when and where exertion is unnecessary.' Selah.

February

28

IFU

There is nothing that seems so insignificant and yet there is nothing that impresses so significantly as IFU. What's that? Immediate Follow Up.

29

FASTER THAN A MAN CAN RUN

As we leave February I want us to think about words.

Eve used them badly and Adam fell. At Babel they said a lot of proud things and look what happened. Abraham told lies in Egypt and Pharoah threw him out. Miriam spoke jealous words and got leprosy for it. The children of Israel grumbled and provoked God to anger. Saul persecuted David with threatening language and ended a suicide. Sweet talking women turned the brilliant Solomon into an effeminate fool. Job's friends talked pious but broke his heart. The wise David was tricked into taking Absalom back into his court by a very clever talking widow and lost his throne.

Sennacherib boasted all over the place against the Lord but went out one morning to discover 185,000 corpses in his army camp due to one stroke of the angel of the Lord. It was Daniel who talked to God and not to men about his heart problems and the lions stopped talking. Belshazzar talked plenty with his enemies, concubines and lords. He took the gold vessels that had been in the sanctuary of God and as he drank out of them 'Praised the gods of gold and silver, bronze and iron, wood and stone'. His talk soon changed when the fingers of a man's hand wrote his future on the wall. That night his earthly tongue quit talking forever.

Herod didn't know how to handle a silent Lord Jesus. One word could have slayed the men who came to take Christ but it didn't come. Yet, the well meant words of Peter about never deserting his Lord soon turned into oaths and curses. The line that was to surely haunt him for all the days of his life 'I know not the man' could have been so different. It could have been 'I gladly know him well'.

Words. Words. Words. They go faster than a person can run. 'Study to be quiet' said Paul to Timothy. Are you ready to let rip against an individual? Sh! not a word. Are you ready to say 'I'm sick to death of my local church'? Sh! not a word. Are you ready to defend what you know is right before God but what others have twisted and misunderstood? Let them go. Sh! not a word. Do you watch others manipulate their way to the top in your business career over your head? Remember Joseph. Sh! don't say a word.

Remember that a tongue 3 inches long can kill a man 6 feet tall. When you have got a word on the tip of your tongue it is sometimes better to leave it there. There are many millions of people who can carry considerable weights but who have great difficulty in holding their tongue which in fact weighs so little. The truth is that the only part of the human body that never seems to get tired,

February

eventually, is the tongue. When a tongue is sharp it invites a split lip and its product, language, is in the strange world in which skating on thin ice can get you into hot water.

It has been said that the five most expressive words in English are 'Alone, death, faith, love, no': the ten most persuasive words in the English language are 'You, easy, money, save, love, new, discovery, results, proven, guarantee' and that the four letter words which change the world are 'Love, hope, care, heal, work, feel, duty, home, good, kind, pity, rest, seek, pray, God, the Lord Jesus, the Holy Spirit, live'. Watch how you use these words but never forget those very important occasions when the best word to use is no word at all. Let's speak less and listen more as the month of March approaches.

March

March if often a winter month with dull, damp days interspersed with rain, hail, sleet and even snow. In the woods though, the pale lime-yellow flowers and the wrinkled green leaves of the Primrose are beginning to lighten things and an early honey bee or two can be seen on the Coltsfoot in the thicket glades.

The jay is probably still feeding on the acorns it has buried for its winter store but the acorns it forgets become oaks! Incredible, isn't it, that the oak-wood that has made everything from Viking longboats to Nelson's battleships, from house beams, a thousand years old, to pulpits and pews was, in all probability, once little acorns the birds forgot to eat? There is a lesson in it because little acts you had forgotten, God will tell you were for Him. The results could surprise you a thousand years from now.

March

1

GROW UP, PLEASE

So, your parents were great. Wonderful. I know a fellow who at 45 years of age is still trying to live up to what his father's image of 'Wonderful' is. It has wrecked his gut, fused his nerves and turned him into the saddest, sickest workaholic I know. You want to see his drained expression.

'As I was with Moses, so will I be with you', said God to Joshua, 'I will not leave you nor forsake you'. Did that mean Joshua had to be Moses? They followed the same blueprint but applied it to different generations with different personalities. They were not created to be the same. Neither are you. Honour your father and your mother but don't try to be a copy. You can't be. You were never meant to be. 'Have I not commanded you? Be strong and of good courage, do not be afraid, nor be dismayed for the Lord your God is with you wherever you go', says the Lord. With a promise like that, grow up and don't wait until you are 45 to do it either. Please.

2

A LIGHT TO EVERY HUMAN BEING

I believe God crosses every person's life with spiritual light and some respond to it and some refuse to. Rehab the prostitute heard of the Lord's power among the Israelites and when the spies that Joshua sent came to her city she chose to follow the Lord. 'For', she said 'The Lord your God, he is God in Heaven above and on earth beneath'. Other people perished because they refused the light God gave them. Are you going to be one of them?

3

THE CORN FROM HEAVEN

Are you moving into a new area, changing jobs, going to a new school, moving to a new country or county? Maybe you are even moving to a long stay in hospital today. Are you frightened to leave all the security of past days behind? God is moving you on, the time of waiting is over and now a time of action lies before you.

The children of Israel had known manna to fall from the sky, daily, for 40 years. It was white, of delicious flavour and resembled seed of the coriander and was both tasty as well as nourishing. It was called 'Corn from heaven' and 'Angel's food' (Psalm 78 : 24-25). It must have meant great security for the people.

March

But when Joshua crossed over Jordan with the people 'The manna ceased on the day after they had eaten the produce of the land; and the children of Israel no longer had manna but they ate the food of the land of Canaan that year'.

If God dries up on one source of substance he will open another. You need not fear crossing over into your new surroundings. Do not be afraid to go into the future, God is already there.

4 ——————————

GOT THE KEY?

There lies a beautiful walled garden near my home and I used to take my children for walks in the park where it lay. The gate to the walled garden was always locked, though I discovered later that if you asked the gardener he would give you the key to get in.

Walls are formidable things and Joshua could ask no inhabitants of Jericho for the key to any gate through Jericho's walls. But God had the key and Joshua listened to him and the walls fell down flat. Yet the method God used to get Joshua through the walls certainly looked foolish. 'See! I have given Jericho into your hand, its King and the mighty men of valour.' Circling the city with the ark containing the law of God and the people and the trumpet blowing priests and a pre-planned shout must have had the inhabitants of Jericho 'guffawing'. But the walls came a 'tumblin down'.

March

Do you look foolish with your teaching of the Bible in godless days? Your worship of your Lord looks weak in comparison to Trident or Polaris or SS 20's. I tell you, the Word of God changes lives more than any other force? It influences minds like nothing else on earth. Even in this land of violence where I live the Scriptures get behind prison walls and sectarian walls and walls of prejudice and change lives like fighting never can. Often the Devil taunts me with the seeming ineffectiveness of God's key to getting through, then I remember that heaven and earth and barriers of men will pass away but the Word of God endures forever. I'm sticking with it, by God's grace. How about you?

_____ **5**

ATTACKED WHILE WAITING

Challenger fell to the ocean floor with its crew of astronauts when it should have been touching the stratosphere. Why? It seems that engine rings were faulty. Millions felt sick at heart and loved ones mourned.

A DC10 plunged to earth from French air space and lives were tragically cut off. The reason? A faulty aircraft door.

The Titanic sliced into an iceberg and as she sank the cry for help went out from her radio operator. Another ship only ten miles away failed to respond. The reason? Its radio operator was asleep. Over 1,000 lives were lost.

March

Recently an entire city underground transport system suddenly stopped. Men and women sweated in darkness. Children panicked. Everyone wondered. The fault turned out to be a Coca Cola tin which had short-circuited the system!

Little things can cause great problems. A man called Achan once stole a beautiful garment, made in Babylon. He picked it up along with some gold and silver when the children of Israel went into the city of Jericho after the miracle of the tumbling walls.

It only seemed a tiny incident in a huge and successful operation. What did it matter? It mattered when 3,000 men put their lives on the line at a place called Ai. Thirty-six men died immediately and 2,964 of them were chased. The entire nation of Israel panicked.

Israel's leader, Joshua, was a man long-famous for his faith and his patience in waiting for God. He and his friend Caleb were the only two people of the entire generation that came out of Egypt to get to the promised land. It was, of course, because they had been prepared to wait for God to fulfil his promise.

Joshua must have seemed a fool to walk around the city of Jericho with his army once a day for six days. You can reckon on the comments he would get from the other side of the wall, not to speak of his own side!

Imagine the comments when he went around seven times on the the seventh day! It was embarassing to the flesh but it brought about the most famous demolition act in history.

Joshua, by long practice, turns to wait upon God again. He falls on his face before God until it is evening with dust on his head. He is in real trouble. He even doubts the guidance he has been given. Israel is running before their enemies. The Lord's name is in disgrace. He should have been content to stay on the other side of Jordan, his mind suggests.

The mind, even while it waits before God, can be attacked by Satan. Have you not found that? You can sit as a Christian in God's presence as you break bread and drink wine at the Lord's table and what happens?

The filthiest thoughts can invade your mind. Words can surface into your mind you never thought possible for a Christian. The Devil torments you into thinking you are not a true believer and so you do not concentrate on what you are doing and your remembrance of your Saviour's death is ruined.

Satan makes you think that the thoughts are yours whereas, in fact, they are his. They are called 'fiery darts' in the Bible. Recognise them as such, quote a promise from Scripture at Satan and he will flee from you.

There is a time for waiting on God but there is also a time for action. As we have seen in this book so far, sometimes you can do both at the same time. 'Get up', said God to Joshua, explaining that there was sin in the camp. 'Up! Sanctify the people'! Joshua obeyed, Achan's sin was put away. Ai was conquered and much more besides.

The lessons are clear. We must watch the little things. We must keep short accounts with God. In all situations, embarassing to the flesh or not, we must wait for God. A whole nation's progress may depend on it.

March

6 ———————————

A TRIP TO SPACE MOUNTAIN

It was called Space Mountain and your Irish writer, naturally, thought it was all about space. He clambered into a little moving car. The huge crowds of Disneyland were soon left behind as the little car climbed a steep gradient.

He was waiting to be taken through a world of space modules, of astronauts and fabulous pictures of earthrise, but he was in for a very rude shock!

Suddenly, he was rocketed into darkness and discovered he was on the most horrific, frightening, stomach-turning ride of his life.

This was no NASA presentation, this was a roller coaster that did not coast.

He can report that the ride exercised his prayer life dramatically. What a ride!

We have all known experiences in life which words fail to convey. We try: 'Never seen anything like it!' we gasp. 'Fantastic!' we shout. 'Unbeatable!' we insist. Often we are exaggerating.

The Bible never exaggerates but it does enthuse. If anything, the sacred Scriptures are the master of quiet, confident, incontrovertible fact. When you come across a verse like I did the other day, it certainly makes you think, but its claim is no exaggeration.

The verse reads, 'There was no day like that before it or after it.' What is it describing? Let me tell you about it.

March

Five kings and their armies ganged up to destroy Israel. It was a formidable sight but the Lord said to Joshua, 'Fear them not; for I have delivered them into your hands.'

The enemy was duly defeated but Joshua wanted the day to remain a little longer so the enemy could be thoroughly crushed. He went about it in a very matter-of-fact way.

He said, 'Sun, stand still upon Gideon; and moon, in the valley of Aijalon. And the sun stood still and the moon stayed until the people had avenged themselves upon their enemies . . . and there was no day like that before or after it that the Lord listened to the voice of man: for the Lord fought for Israel.'

I am not advocating the initiation of longer working days or more sunshine through prayer for recreation days but you have to admire the faith of Joshua. This man had waited for God to fulfil promises made at least 40 years before.

The hour for those promises to be fulfilled had come and as Victor Hugo said, 'Like the trampling of a mighty army, so is the force of an idea whose time has come.'

So sure was Joshua that the Lord was with him, even the sun and moon in space became but faith's tools in accomplishing God's will.

Joshua climbed no Space Mountain in a recreation park of the 20th century; he prayed and his faith invaded the very real world of actual space and held up the sun and moon in their tracks.

Sometimes when I see young people doing their dissertations at university for their PhDs or

March

whatever, I long to encourage them to do a study on the promises of God in Scripture. There are thousands of them.

What about a promise like 'Prove me now herewith says the Lord of hosts . . . if I will not open the windows of heaven and pour out a blessing such as there will not be room to contain it.'

Against such promises I would urge them to write the letter 'T' in the margin of their Bibles, asking God to fulfil the promise to them.

When the promise is accomplished I would urge them to put the letter 'P' under the letter 'T'. What is the code? It is simple. 'T' means tried and 'P' means proved.

If every believer did it we would have a generation of Christians of whom it could be accurately stated. 'There was no generation like them before or after.'

The fact remains, as Joshua proved in his day, God never made a promise that was too good to be true. Try it and prove it.

7

A FEW THOUSAND AT 5.30 A.M.?

I often imagine that if I had money stacked in bundles, one bundle of several thousand pounds for each person and it could be collected some morning at 5.30 a.m. outside a church building, how far would the queue stretch?

'But there remained among the children of Israel seven tribes which had not yet received their inheritance. Then Joshua said to the children of Israel; 'How long will you neglect to go and possess the land which the Lord God of your fathers has given you?'

Imagine having an inheritance and not possessing it? Is it not true that some folk would die at the stake for the Bible but they never read it! Should I give you several thousand pounds some morning it would soon disappear but your soul would still be hungry for spiritual food, wouldn't it? Get into God's Word, christian, and draw from the incalculable wealth of its pages. Don't, on pain of spiritual poverty, neglect it. Possess your possessions.

8

THE INNOCENT SMILED

I remember hearing the story of the local church in my own country which was behaving very badly. A group of men had lorded over God's heritage and were breaking the hearts of others in the local fellowship. Quietly one Lord's Day morning one of the quietest christian men in the fellowship rose to speak at the morning service. He spoke from a passage of Scripture which was on his heart and which had nothing to do with the current crisis in his local church. Yet, the men who were splitting the church thought that the quiet christian's message was an omen of a coup d'etat. They panicked and left the church. That local church had peace at last and the innocent man must have smiled.

March

That true story reminds me of Joshua's last message to the children of Israel. 'One man of you shall chase a thousand, for the Lord your God is he who fights for you, as he has promised you'. Feeling alone in a situation? Feeling isolated as though a thousand were against you? One with God is a majority. Keep on going on and wait for God at the same time. A rout is on the way. You'll see 2,000 heels soon!

9

FOR THE LOVE OF A LADY

The Irish have their own way of doing things. Take David Marshall, for example. The 26 year old David ordered a chaffeur driven vintage car to pick up his girlfriend early one morning recently at her home at Dundonald. She was then whisked off to the spot where she and David had first met to find David on bended knee waiting for her. He proposed to her on the spot and when she said 'Yes' she found herself having a very special breakfast at one of Northern Ireland's top hotels, surrounded by red roses! Ah, the Irish.

'For the love of a lady' has covered a multitude of actions and the Scriptures highlight them quite frequently. I particularly like the story of Othniel. When Israel started to possess the land God gave them Caleb, one of Israel's great heroes, said 'He who attacks Kirjath Sepher and takes it, to him I will give my daughter Achsah as wife'.

March

Now Kirjath Sepher was a place full of giants but it did not trouble Othniel. For the love of Achsah he took the city. Achsah also had land which was her inheritance but it was a very dry inheritance. She asked her father Caleb to give her the upper and lower springs and he did!

While this couple lived for the Lord the children of Israel lived for themselves and other gods. While Achsah turned Othniel's heart even closer to the Lord the men of Israel's hearts were turned away from following the Lord by the Canaanite girls they married. God is a jealous God and he refuses to allow his own to flirt with or follow other gods without action on his part. He would not be God if he turned away from such a thing. 'Therefore the anger of the Lord was hot against Israel, and he sold them into the land of Chushan-rishathaim of Mesopotamia; and the children of Israel served Chushan-rishathaim 8 years.

Think of it! Long years before God had called Abraham out of the sophisticated society of Mesopotamia to follow him to a city which has the foundation, whose builder and maker is God. The Mesopotamians lived under the philsophy that things are an end in themselves and that there is no transcendent Lord above and separate from his own creation. They worshipped the elements not the Lord of Lords. Abraham had gone out of it all, by faith and now his children were in bondage to what he had left. For 8 years they had been held captive by the King of Mesopotamia.

The lovely thing in the story is that when the Lord sent them a deliverer the man he chose to do so was

March

Othniel. 'The spirit of the Lord came upon him and he judged Israel'. He went out to war, and the Lord delivered Chushan-rishathaim King of Mesopotamia into his hand; and his hand prevailed over Chushan-rishathaim. So the land had rest for 4 years.'

I love to think of Achsah having a profound effect on her husband for good and he, in turn, had a profound effect under God over Israel.

The lesson of Israel's captivity under the King of Mesopotamia, his name means 'double wickedness', is very relevant to our generation. The Prince of this world has brought people, sadly, in our country to think that throwing out their mother and father's God will bring them freedom. They say morality doesn't matter. So you get Christopher Reeves, the Superman hero, who has lived with the former model Gae Exton for 11 years, with her two children saying 'Marriage isn't important for the sake of the children. We have a most comfortable life, and we are tremendously happy and enjoy great security.' You get Peter Ustinov the brilliant raconteur setting aside truth saying that everybody is basically good, 'they are only made bad'. Gifted gentle giant that he may be he is way off the mark in denying original sin. All around us we see this breaking away from the transcendent Lord and look what is happening to us. Divorce rates are soaring. Homosexuality is rife. Ours is a cut flower generation. When a sign of life remains we cut ourselves off from our bibical roots and the petals are beginning to droop and fall. We are fast becoming a society without standards. One young rock star summed up his generation well when he said recently 'I believe absolutely nothing'.

Even within the life of the church the second generation syndrome is getting to us. The parents fervour for the things of God becomes the dry formalism of the children and the apathy and indifference of the grandchildren. A second generation experience is often a second hand experience.

Maybe in the midst of it all there is an Othniel and Achsah of our generation. Maybe there is a young couple who will put God first in their village, town or city and turn their generation back to the Lord. Has Othniel and Achsah's God changed? Now that they are through, why not you?

10

ARE YOU LEFT HANDED?

It must be difficult in life for people who are left handed. Scissors cut the wrong way and watches wind the wrong way. Violins are made for right handed people and so are can openers. Even record players are for right handed folk.

Think of a cricket match where the entire field has to change position every time a left handed person comes into bat. Yet in sport left handedness is fascinating. Neurologists claim that left handed people adjust more readily to underwater vision. So Mark Spitz won seven Olympic gold medals. The Prince of Wales is left handed and plays a tremendous game of Polo, forty percent of the top

March

tennis players are left handed, including Laver, Connors, Villas, Navratilova.

Have you noticed in the world of politics that handedness has connotations. Cold hearted Conservatives are called right wingers and dreamy Liberals are called left wingers.

Let no one ever claim that left handedness is an obstacle to brilliance. Some of the worlds most creative people have been left handed and that includes: Michaelangelo, Leonardo de Vinci, Picasso, Hans Holbein, Charlie Chaplin, Jim Hendron, H. G. Wells, etc.

One of the most fascinating facts that has emerged about people who are left handed came when NASA went searching for imaginative, super reliable, multi talented people to be astronauts and to explore the moon. One out of every four Appollo astronauts turned out to be left handed — a figure 250% greater than statistical probability!

There can be absolutely no doubt that God can use a left handed person just as much as a right handed person. Probably the most famous of all left handed people used by God was an Old Testament judge called Ehud.

The state of the children of Israel at the time was that for 18 years they had been in captivity to the King of Moab. Moab's history had been exceptionally sad. Originally Moab was the incestuous son of Lot and as the Moabites grew in number their worship of their idols involved, by definition, sexual impurity. In Ehud's time they were epitomized in the King of Moab who was called Eglon. The Bible describes him as a 'very fat man'. He lived in great ease in Jericho and there can be no doubt that he represented all that the sins of the flesh and self indulgence can be.

There is no doubt that the christian in the modern 20th century has great problems with the flesh. Even the great Paul was moved to say 'O wretched man that I am! For I know that in me that is in my flesh, dwelleth no good thing . . . for the good that I would I do not but the evil which I would not, that I do . . . who shall deliver me from this living death.' Thank God that when a person comes to know the Lord Jesus that person is no longer rooted in the flesh but is rooted in the Spirit. But there can be absolutely no doubt that a christian can be tempted to follow the sins of the flesh. There are very serious consequences for those who do. We are told to wage an unceasing war against the sinful activities of the flesh. Arrogance, pride, self indulgence and carnality are to be abhorred in the christian life.

The man who got rid of the King of Moab was Ehud. He came to give the fat Moabtish King his tax. But Ehud felt in the name of God the time had come when he had had enough of giving him his tax. Giving Moab a little didn't get rid of him it only perpetuated his rule and dominion.

The Bible tells us that Ehud made himself a dagger of two edges. Notice he did not use a great battle sword. May I say that you and I need to make of the sword of the Spirit which is the Word of God a few small 'daggers' which we can have at our command to use from time to time for the glory of God. How sad it is that when we go to witness sometimes we fumble to find the verse we need to back home a truth we are trying to present to others.

March

The Bible says 'He put his dagger on his right thigh'. It was a providential mercy that the man was left handed. Ehud had a private audience with the King of Moab and said to him clearly that he had a message from the Lord for him. The message was the judgement of God for he took his dagger and rammed it through the man's belly right through to the other side. The Bible does not spare us the details. If Ehud had gone in with his dagger on his left thigh the King would have seen the move. But when he moved with his left hand the King would have thought he was brushing off a mosquito or something and would never have suspected him. So was the judge Ehud used by God to bring judgement upon the evil of his day. Such an action is not allowed within the christian church for our swords must be put away as Peter knew to his cost. In the day of the judges Israel was under Theocracy, God-in-parliament used men like the judges to execute judgement upon evil.

It is fascinating to read in Scripture that Ehud's campaign against evil had its turning point when 'He himself turned back at the carved images that were by Gilgal'. The wrong use of the knife had produced the carved images at that place. Let it never be forgotten that it was at Gilgal that Joshua had circumcised the children of Israel. The right and the wrong use of the knife was clearly seen at Gilgal. The Bible is adamant that it was at that very place that Ehud turned to go to put a knife into the flesh which was to lead to 80 years of peace for the people of God in the land.

Is it any wonder that Paul thunders in Philippians 3 that he has no confidence in the flesh? He warns us that there are even professing christians 'Whose end is destruction, whose God is their belly'. He describes them as people who set there mind on 'earthly things'. Thus do the Scriptures teach us that the judge Ehud subdued the enemy so Paul tells us in Philippians 3 : 21 that Christ 'Is able even to subdue all things to himself'. With all my heart christian I plead with you to wage an unceasing war against the sins of the flesh and carnality in your christian life. Get that small dagger out and ram the flesh right through. Do not say to it 'This is going to hurt, I'm sorry.' Make no excuses, slay it by the power of the Holy Spirit in your life and you will have blessing everywhere you go. Sow to the flesh and you will reap the flesh. Sow to the Spirit and you will reap the Spirit. The man who was left handed stands as a memorial to the fact that the flesh can be overcome. Let no one despise those left handers because God can use them as much as any other to his glory.

11

A WOMAN IS NOT A DOLL

In Korea, I discovered, if a man has a daughter he can have a divorce from his wife. I have read words which say 'A Hindu husband regards himself as lord and master of his wife who must ever dance attendance upon him'. In SURA 4 of the Koran entitled 'Women' the instruction is given that 'Men have authority over women because Allah has

March

made the one superior to the other . . . as for those from whom you fear disobedience admonish them and send them to beds apart and beat them . . .' Some Jewish men have been known to thank God in their prayers every morning that they were not born a woman.

One could not be blamed for assuming that for millions of men a woman is not a person but a thing. The whole feminist movement feel great hurt and one can understand their rage at how women have been treated. Male chauvinism has driven Germaine Greer to write of a women that 'She is not a woman . . . she is a doll . . .' The way a lot of women are treated, especially in the Western World, shows that they are viewed by many men as a mere sexual object, an idol.

When woman sinned in the garden part of God's judgement was God's word to the woman 'Your desire will be for your husband and he shall rule over you'. How men have exploited that judgement! Do men fulfil their 'ruling role' responsibly? A lot of men, for example let their wives do the ruling, particularly over their children; many husbands are passive when it comes to applying discipline in their home. They don't wish to be unpopular with their children so poor Mum has to do the unpopular things.

Rule? Let me ask you, husband; 'What are your wife's greatest needs at the moment emotionally, spiritually and practically? What are you (or I) doing at the moment to meet those needs of our partners?' The teaching of Scripture on the headship of the man was never intended to break a woman but to provide a secure area for her own particular gifts and role to flourish.

Husbands are exorted in Scripture to love their wives as Christ also loved the church. How did Christ love the church, his bride? He loved her to the point of giving his life for her. Does Christ abuse his church, sarcastically dominate his church, suppress his church? Certainly not. Neither should a husband do such things to his wife. To rule is a position of great responsibility requiring, particularly, initiative. Millions of men have failed in the area of initiative. Like Mr. McCawber they still await 'The ship' coming in and God knows their wives are all too aware of their ever-waiting-on-the-pier existence. Initiative means, under God making the very best of what we have around us at this time. The plain fact is that if you don't find pixies on your doorstep you will never find Fairyland.

I came across a fascinating little verse in Judges the other day. You know how the very sophisticated Canaanites rose and brought the Israelites into captivity under Jaban and his Commander-in-Chief, Sisera? They had learned how to smelt iron and had 900 chariots of iron which was the most sophisticated weaponry of any army in the then known world in its day. In those days Deborah arose and, believe me, there were few like her before or since. Getting a message from the Lord she told Barak to go up Mount Tabor with 10,000 men and then to attack the enemy. He was to 'Lead captivity captive'. (Psalm 68 : 18). The Lord sent a flash-flood and Sisera and his 900 chariots got stuck-in-the-mud and a great victory was achieved for the Israelites.

March

12

KEEPING THE FOOD SUPPLY GOING

Have you ever come across a spiritual nomad? You know the type. They want spiritual food but they are not prepared to go to the bother of getting it for themselves. They go around churches, raiding them and taking what they can get for nothing. They cause arguments and division and then they are away, leaving a wilderness of trouble behind them. They will never be permanent, anywhere, and have no notion of settling. They are nomads.

In the Bible there were a group of nomads who came up to the land flowing with milk and honey and took the milk and honey away. They didn't plough, nor did they sow seed with the sweat of their brow but waited for the Israelites to have all that done and then at harvest time they came up like locusts and stripped the crops and left 'No sustenance for Israel'. This went on for years until God chose Gideon to stop it. Why Gideon? Because the very first time we meet him he is threshing wheat in order to hide it from those raiding nomads, the Midianites. That's why God chose him. He was the man who kept the food supply going no matter what else happened. 'The Lord is with you thou mighty man of valour!', he was told. He had the right strategy because one of the strongest principles to remember for any army when facing a battle is that any army marches on its stomach.

March

God's army is no different, so if you can possibly do it, christian, feed them despite internal argument and external raiding nomads. You'll eventually win a great battle. You'll see.

13

PEACE IN A LAND OF TROUBLE

Having a rough time? People criticising you? People saying that you have not got what it takes for the work you are attempting? Surrounded by misers? Sickened by selfishness? Feel like Dean Jonathan Swift who had his ficticious character Gulliver go out and talk to the horses in the stable because they behaved better than humans?

Gideon could have been but in the middle of everything that was wrong in Israel he built an altar to the Lord and called it 'The Lord is peace'. What? Peace in the middle of an 8 year war? Of course. You too can know that peace which passes all understanding. A few days ago cruel men murdered a young man who lived a few doors from my home. Last night a bomb rattled my window panes at around supper time. In the last few days I have talked with christian women whose husbands have regularly beaten them up. I could go on and on but what are my trials in comparison with yours? Few, I reckon. But, christian, learn it and learn it well; you can know the peace of God intimately and exult in him today though the very earth is scorched under your feet. Gideon tells me so.

March

The little verse that fascinates me was regarding Barak's response to Deborah's order. He said 'If you will go with me, then I will go, but if you will not go with me, I will not go'. So she said, 'I will surely go with you; nevertheless there will be no glory for you in the journey you are taking, for the Lord will sell Sisera into the hand of a woman'. Another translation puts it 'Because of the way you are going about this, the honour will not be yours for the Lord will hand Sisera over to a woman'. It seems very plain to me that Barak missed the blessing because he would not fulfil his God given role to lead.

It is a man's place to lead but because of the way he often goes about it honour is not given to him. How much more honourable we men could be if we sought to fulfil the role God has given to us more carefully, sensitively and wisely. Think of how much more glory could be brought to God and what a blessing it would be to those around us.

Regarding our state in Christ there is no difference for there is neither Jew nor Greek, slave or free, male or female. In our roles there is a very real difference between male and female and although a woman is every bit a sinner as any man, sinners saved by grace will be given grace to fulfil the role God has designed for them. Let us then, fellows, not fail in the God given role that is ours. Lead means lead not laid-back passivity.

IN YOUR OWN BACKYARD

O.K. So Gideon kept the food supply going and fed both his family and the Lord, but was that it? Did the enemy fall down dead? You didn't think it was as easy as that, did you? You are right. Before any great influential and widespread victory can be achieved for God you have to deal with the enemy in your own backyard. Gideon did just that because the Lord told him to haul down the altar to Baal which his father had built and to cut down the totem pole representing the Canaanites goddess of fertility. He obeyed God but please notice that he did it at night when his father couldn't see him, 'Because he feared his father's household and the men of the city too much to do it by day'.

Faith, you see, is not demonstrated by fearlessness but by obedience. So you are fearful as you witness for the Lord Jesus at home or at your daily place of work? That in no way means that you are faithless. Gideon obeyed the Lord despite his fears and the results were great. Let's do the same, should our very knees knock as we do it.

15

A NICKNAME

The results from Gideon's obedience to God in tearing down his father's altar to Baal were three. First, the men of the city were ripping mad and

March

wanted to kill him and the men of the city were Israelites! How far can a people go? Maybe because of your obedience to the Lord you face great opposition from those who ought to know better around you. So what? If you please God he will make even your enemies to be at peace with you. Look at the second result, Gideon's father, Zoash, became Gideon's greatest defender. He whom Gideon had feared most came round to be at peace with him. He basically said 'If Baal is all that he is cracked up to be, let him defend himself!'

The third result was that Gideon's father gave him a nickname. He called him Jerubbaal meaning 'Let Baal plead' which came to mean the 'Baal conqueror'. Every time folk looked at Gideon they saw the weakness of Baal and the power of God. Obey the Lord in that matter he is challenging you on. Don't look to the right or to the left. Obey and wait and see the results. You may even get a nickname which will go down in history. God's history.

16

FOOD FOR THE LORD

Wasn't it a lovely thing that when the Lord came to talk with Gideon that he had food to feed him with? Not only did Gideon have food for his family, he had food for the Lord. 'The meat he put in a basket, and he put the broth in a pot; and he brought them out to him under the Terebinth tree and presented them'.

March

Tell me, waiting one, have you got food for the Lord today or could it be that all we have for the moment is a headful of thrashy novels and T.V. soap operas not worth a button of our time? Could you or I go to the spiritual pantry of our hearts and give the Lord something from the store we've got there from fellowship and prayer with him and from reading his Word? Israel had no food for God because they were at that time, disobedient. Gideon was different. He had plenty for God. Have we?

17

DEW CONTROL

The fleece that Gideon put out as a test to discover God's will for his life has caused a lot of discussion. Was it a sign of lack of faith on Gideon's part? Is it right to try to put God in a corner and say, for example that by 10.00 p.m. you want the Lord to do something. If that thing happens at 9.59 is it the Devil who did it?

For 7 long years the Midianites had simply come and taken from the Israelites what they wanted. But not this time; Gideon and an army of 32,000 were waiting to be committed to battle. As Gideon waited for God he certainly needed to know if God was with him in the coming conflict. So the farmer decided to see if he could control the dew by his prayers. Why the dew? A friend of mine once pointed me to Psalm 133 for the answer. 'Behold how good and how pleasant it is for brethren to dwell together in

March

unity! . . . it is like the dew of Hermon, descending upon the mountains of Zion; for there the Lord commanded the blessing — life for ever more.'

David saw dew as representing unity among God's people. Gideon was no fool. He needed dew-control and so do we. When we go through life do we leave behind us a certain feeling of refreshing in the hearts of folk? Do they feel that some of the heat and weariness is gone? Can they now see the wood for the trees since you came into their lives? Do you unite or divide them? It all depends on dew-control doesn't it? Make me as the dew, Lord.

18

BIG IS NOT NECESSARILY GREAT

'The people who are with you are too many for me to give the Midianities into their hands, lest Israel claim glory for itself against me', said God to Gideon.

In two separate tests God whittled Gideon's army of 32,000 down to 300. It seems incredible that with just that small number of men he had to face an army of 135,000; he was out-numbered 400 to 1. Less than 1% of his original group were left!

Think well on what I am about to pass on to you as you pass on in your day or roll over to sleep. 32,000 men originally turned up to fight for Gideon. There can be no question that they were faithful. The problem with them was that although they were faithful they were scared. When God said all who were frightened were to go home I am sure that Gideon never dreamt that 22,000 men would leave.

March

That left 10,000 men who were fearless. Yet even that was not what was needed to fight the Midianites as far as God was concerned. The test of those who would lap water and those who fell down with their faces in the water to drink it was to prove one thing; only 300 men were careful enough not to put their own personal need before keeping an eye on the enemy. Those who lapped water out of their hands were the best soldiers but they were more than that. Not only were they faithful to fight, and fearless in their attitude to fighting; they were in fact fervent. In God's army in which category are you? Faithful? Fearless? Fervent? How about being all three?

19

THE LIGHT IS THE THING

The story of Gideon's attack with torches and cries of 'The sword of the Lord of Gideon' has often intrigued me. Strategically what was the significance of the torches?

Imagine yourself going down a road at night and along comes a car. You see lights but you cannot immediately identify if the car is a Porche or a Mini-minor! The light is the thing. When the Midianites saw 300 torches they couldn't see what was behind them and fled!

So you may feel depressed today about the seeming insignificance of your witness for Christ? You may be filled with self doubt (I'm plagued with the wretched thing) yet if only one person this year,

March

this month, this day catches a sight of something different about you, namely the presence of the light of the world in your life and is led to come to know that light in their darkness does it matter if they cannot see you and your weaknesses for the light that is shining through you? The light's the thing, discouraged one, the light's the thing.

20

DID MARY PETERS RUN TO LOSE?

She did indeed. I heard her say so. Her problem was that some of the great athlete's friends got jealous of her winning streak so she came second to lessen their jealousy.

One day after a competition her coach warned her that if she did not stop trying to please others and go for the winning tape she would need to find a new coach. Mary listened to his advice and became the greatest all round athlete in the world at the Munich Olympics.

The Ephraimites were jealous of Gideon. 'Why have you done this to us by not calling us when you went to fight with the Midianites?' Gideon was a wise man for he did not stop pursuing the enemies of God's people in order to placate the jealousy of some of the Lord's people. He reminded the Ephraimites that they lived in a more luscious part of the country than he ever did and anyway had not God delivered the princes of Midian, Oreb and Zeeb into their hands? 'And what was I able to do in comparison with you?', he added.

March

It seems to me that Gideon knew the difference between jealousy and envy. Envy begins with empty hands mourning for what it doesn't have. Jealousy is not quite the same. It begins with full hands but is threatened by the loss of its plenty. Envy has a screwed-up narrow gaze. Jealousy has a squint. Gideon reminded the Ephraimites that their hands were full and that they had no need to feel threatened. So are ours and neither need we. Put out that hell spark of jealousy in your heart in a sea of prayer today.

21

HOW AN APRON BECAME A SNARE

I was once taken to see the fabulous treasures of the Czars in Moscow. I shall never forget looking on the women's dresses with pure gold thread running through them. The riches of the Russian court of past days was incredible.

When Gideon and his men brought back plunder from the Midianites we are told that Gideon made an ephod from '1,700 shekels of gold, besides the crescent ornaments, pendants, and purple robes which were on the Kings of Midian and besides the chains that were around their camels necks'. This was a kind of apron which he probably wore on ceremonious occasions. The Bible distinctly declares that 'It became a snare to Gideon and to his house'. Isn't it incredible that although Gideon refused to be made the king of the Israelites because he wanted the Lord to have all the glory, the apron that he made to wear became a snare to the people of God because they started to worship it? Imagine worshipping an apron, even though it was gold studded.

I wonder what you and I worship today? Have you expected too much from your marriage? Have you expected too much from that date you were going to have? Were you looking forward to going to that college and are disappointed? Did that ski trip that you took leave you cold from dashed expectations long after you left the slopes. Did you hope for so much from that local church and you were disappointed? Are you like me? Are you tempted to worship your expectations instead of the God who never disappoints? Whatever it is you worship if it isn't the Lord, abandon it, this very moment. You will not be sorry.

22

THE UPSTART

There was a man called Abimelech who set himself up in the days of the Judges as a ruler of God's people. 'Rejoice in Abimelech,' the proud, selfish upstart said to Israel. He would teach us one very solemn lesson; far from delivering Israel from the enemy he became the enemy from which Israel needed to be delivered. That's what pride can do to you.

THE SNITCH

Have you ever read Jotham's fable in Judges chapter 9? It tells the fable of the trees of the wood trying to make a king. The olive tree refused because it felt it was doing a good enough job serving God and men by giving oil. The fig tree refused to be king of the wood because it didn't want to stop giving sweetness from its good fruit to go and hold sway over the other trees. The vine when asked refused to become king because its wine cheered both God and men. Low and behold a snitch of a bramble when asked was absolutely delighted to become king and told them that if they did not lie down under the shelter of his shade then he would devour by fire the cedars of Lebanon.

The fable has its modern counterpart for often there are reigning in industry, commerce, politics and other corridors of power snitches of brambles who give neither shade nor shelter and who without a moments notice devour the mighty cedars of our society that have taken hundreds of years to grow. Let God be truly king in our lives and let us go on with the work to which he has called us. Enough of brambles!

March

24

Down at a little place called Ballycopeland there stands one of Ulster's only windmills. Knowing that the famous Christian writer, Amy Carmichael was born nearby I mentioned to the curator of the windmill that the initials 'R.C.' which I noticed on a grindstone in the mill probably stood for 'Robert Carmichael' who had owned a mill in the district. The curator was fascinated not knowing anything of any of Amy's family history.

I may be right or I may be wrong about the Ballycopeland grindstone but I can tell you that Abimelech the 'bramble' king of Israel knew very well who owned the grindstone that brought his selfish, godless life to an end. One day on his way to do a very evil deed against the Lord's people a woman standing on a height noticed him passing beneath her and the Scriptures say that she 'dropped an upper millstone on Abimelech's head and crushed his skull'. The Bible tells us that 'He called quickly to the young man, his armourbearer, and said to him, 'Draw your sword and kill me lest men say of me 'A women killed me'. So his young man thrust him through and he died. I reckon there is many a woman across the country who would dearly love to drop a grindstone on the head of some false leader of God's people to bring the misery he is bringing to an end! The story would remind us of the words of Christ warning us that if we stumble even one of his little ones it were better that a millstone were hung about our necks and we were drowned in the depths of the sea.

25

ROYAL QUIP

'People', commented the Duke of Edinburgh, 'would rather be bored than embarrassed'.

26

WHAT I CALL A FRIEND

One whose grip is a little tighter.
One whose smile is a little brighter,
One whose deeds are a little whiter.
That's what I call a friend.

One who'll lend as quick as borrow,
One whose the same today as tomorrow,
One who'll share your joy and sorrow.
That's what I call a friend.

One whose thoughts are a little cleaner,
One whose mind is a little keener,
One who avoids things that are mere,
That's what I call a friend.

One who has been fine when life seemed rotten,
One whose ideals you have not forgotten,
One who has given you more than he's gotten.
That's what I call a friend.

Author Unknown

March

27

THE MOCKERS

One of the most formidable enemies that Israel ever had were the Ammonites. Again and again in Scripture the Ammonites try to make the people of God look stupid. The condition for a treaty the Ammonites wanted to make with Israel was that the Ammonites be allowed to put out all the right eyes of all the Israelites! It is little wonder that they didn't agree to the condition. We read that when David sent some of his men to the Ammonites they actually shaved their beards off and cut their clothes until they were scantily clad indeed. The men returned to David ashamed. That is exactly how the Ammonites wanted them to feel. You remember Tobia the Ammonite mocked Nehemiah and those who built the wall of Jerusalem with him. 'Even that which they build if a fox go up, he shall even break down their stone wall', said Tobia.

It seems to me the Ammonites are by no means dead. There are those around who still try to mock the people of God. They say that christians nowadays are too narrow for an age of pluralism. They say we are too humiliating for an age of self sufficiency. They reckon we are too demanding for an age of permissiveness. They would try to mock the great doctrine of justification by faith alone, the efficacy of the precious blood of Christ shed at Calvary to cleanse from all sin, the authenticity of the virgin birth, the inerrancy of the Word of God, the reality of a lake of fire for Christ rejectors and a

Heaven for Christ acceptors. They try to make christians out to be narrow minded sectarians who know no love in the truest sense. You think I exaggerate? Take the words of Sir Alfred Ayer 'Christianity is the worst of the great religions of the world, because it rests on the allied doctrines of original sin and atonement which are intellectually contemptible and morally outrageous'. I am glad that the Judge Jephthah stood up to the Ammonites and was not duped by their mocking for he knew very well that at every opportunity they would seek to take away the inheritance of the people of God. Let us not be duped by those who would try to disinherit us of the beautiful and eternal doctrines of the christian faith. We say to our lovely Lord Jesus today 'Lord, to whom else shall we go you have the words of eternal life'. They mocked him when he was here on earth and we who seek to sincerely follow him need not be amazed when we receive the same treatment.

28

ONLY REGRET

There is a very great difference between regret and true repentance. A christian lady once visited a man in jail and said to him 'I hope you have repented of what you have done so well as not to make the same mistakes when you are released'. The prisoner replied 'No mam, I won't. Next time I pull a job I'll be sure to wear gloves!' That is regret, not repentance!

March

When the Israelites faced the Ammonites they cried to the Lord in their distress but they had only regretted their backsliding and had not repented from it. They had for years been serving other gods and only turned to the Lord God because they were in need. The Lord did not at that time deliver them but said 'You have forsaken me and served other gods. Therefore I will deliver you no more. Go and cry out to the gods which you have chosen; let them deliver you in your time of distress'. It was the best spiritual medicine they could have for we read that the children of Israel then said to the Lord 'We have sinned! Do to us whatever seems best to you; only deliver us this day, we pray'. They put their foreign gods away from among them and served the Lord and the Bible says 'His soul could no longer endure the misery of Israel'. God's heart was touched and moved and grieved and in turmoil over what Israel was suffering. So the Lord raised them up a deliverer called Jephthah.

May we not just turn to the Lord our God when we are in need but turn to him at all times and when we sin may we not turn to him just with regret but with true repentance. When there is true repentance he will certainly deliver us.

29

No TALE OF TERROR

I love the story of the Soviet christian who was asked as to how he survived 32 years in a Soviet labour camp. The man did not burst out into great anger nor was there any trace of bitterness in his words. He did not tell some gruesome tale of terror. Rather he quietly answered, 'Brethren, even a desert looks like a flower garden when you are in communion with the Lord'.

We read that Jephthah was put out of his home by his half brothers because he was the son of a prostitute. His father had allowed him to stay in the home but his father's sin left a huge scar on him socially. He went to the land of Tob on the northern frontier of Israel as a social outcast. It was there that the Lord trained him to become the great Judge who was to deliver the children of Israel from the plague of the Ammonites. No place is too obscure for God to do a great work in your life. Like our friend from the Soviet Union even a desert can look like a flower garden when you are in communion with the Lord. Please meditate today on the thought that although your circumstances may be very difficult and obscure all the time God is training you for a greater work that lies ahead. Don't be afraid to wait for God. He never made a mistake and he's not going to start with you.

30

DOWN WITH SHIBBOLETH'S

After Jephthah had defeated the Ammonites we read that the Ephraimites came up with their old practice of being jealous. Unfortunately Jephthah did not react to them as Gideon had done years before him. Jephthah and his men seized the fords

March

of the Jordan before the Ephraimites arrived. And when any Ephraimite who escaped said 'Let me cross over', Jephthah's men would say to him 'Are you an Ephraimite?' If he said, 'No', they would say to him, 'Then say, Shibboleth!'; because he was an Ephraimite he couldn't say Shibboleth but only Sibboleth, for, he could not pronounce it right. The Bible tells us that they then took him and killed him 'at the fords of Jordan'. Unfortunately 42,000 of them were killed in this way and the great Jephthah, who with diplomacy and courage had fought and defeated the Ammonites ended up fighting his own people because they could not say the word Shibboleth properly. The sickening truth of the story is that Shibboleth and Sibboleth both mean the same thing!

Could it be today you are warring with some fellow christian over your own Shibboleth. See them for what they really are and turn away from your warring to concentrate on the true enemy that faces you both. Let us destroy our Shibboleth's and then turn and seek to destroy Satan's power in our area and in our hearts by the power of God.

31

No need for rash vows

As we close March and move to April, let us make one final point about the judge Jephthah. The Bible tells us that he made a rash vow and said that if God would give him victory over the Ammonites he would sacrifice as a burnt offering the first thing to come out of his house. We know those graphic verses in Scripture which say that the first one to come out of his house when he came back victorious after the battle was his own daughter. Did he offer her as a burnt offering? It is a very difficult point and Bible commentators have differed on it for centuries but all in all it seems to me as if the emphasis seems to lie upon the fact that she was given into Tabernacle service and never married. Judges chapter 11 : 30-40 emphasise over and over that he had only one daughter and that this daughter never had any children. In no way do I agree with Jephthah's rash vow but one thing is very clear from the passage; it was not the day for turning a deliverer into a monument, still less into a dynasty. Jephthah had earlier made it very clear that he did not want to become King of Israel and having no children apart from his daughter, who had no children herself, the line came to an end at Jephthah's death. No royal line of Jephthah was ever begun. Jephthah wanted the Lord alone to be king and in this, at the end of a busy month, you and I are in full agreement with him.

APRIL

Native pinewoods are very special in Scotland and survive in about 30 glens, isolated from one another in the Highlands. The very finest stand in the strathes of the Spey and the Dee, near Ballater. Scots pine get its name from the fact that although once native all over the British Isles it now survives in strength as a wild tree in the Highlands of Scotland. In April its buds break and soon the pine scatters clouds of golden pollen on the wind.

Travelling one day near Ballater with my friend Mr. Stephen Cordiner he told me of the days when his father had owned forests in the area, and, pointing to a thickly wooded hill he said: "My father owned that hill". Then he burst into laughter: "Come to think of it", he said, "My Father owns all the hills!" Every christian would heartily agree. May you enjoy many a good walk this April across a few of them in this lovely Springtime.

April

1

SECRETS

When God wants to do a great thing with a person, he very often begins with that person's parents. The life of Samson is typical of such a principle. The angel of the Lord visited Samson's parents and when asked his name replied 'Why do you ask my name seeing it is secret?'

The incomprehensibility of the name is the seedbed of Samson's life. Again and again in Samson's incredible career we come up against secrets. The Philistines were dead set on finding out Samson's secrets from the riddle he set them to the reason why he had such supernatural strength.

The whole point of Samson's life was that he was to 'Begin to deliver Israel from the Philistines. The angel laid emphasis on the word "Begin" to Samson's parents before Samson's birth. He was not to lead a great deliverance but he was to begin to do so. Samson was to begin to make a difference that was to be obvious between the god of the Philistines and the God of Israel. Everybody would see that difference.

Tell me, honestly, as you set out on another day, or roll exhausted into bed, does your christian life and witness show that there is a difference between the God you worship and the god's of this Century that are all around you? Does your God DO anything? If not you are worshipping a God of your own making. You are no better off than the Philistines.

2

DOES YOUR GOD CARRY YOU?

What kind of an enemy did Samson have to face? The Philistines worshipped a god called Dagon and, once, he fell of his plinth and broke his head and arms. What on earth do you do with a god who has broken his head and arms? You stick them on again! And they did. The fact was that, as with any god of earth, when you hit upon trouble, he doesn't carry you but you carry him!

Isaiah had warned of this years before Samson and he mocks those who have to lob their heavy gods into the back of their waggons as they try to flee their enemy and instead of their gods helping them they cause their waggons to stick in the mud! "Listen to me", writes Isaiah, speaking of the Lord who says "Even to your old age, I am he and even to grey hair I will carry you and will deliver you". That God carried Samson, despite his faults and he will do the very same for you today. He will not only carry you, he will never, ever drop you. Trust Him.

April

3

PUPPY LOVE

Gift and grace are two very different things. You can have a person who has no outstanding gift and they can be an extremely godly person and you can have a very gifted person who behaves like a scoundrel, at times. Samson was the latter.

We read that Samson ordered his parents to arrange a marriage to a woman of Timnath with the cheeky and selfish words: "Get her for me for she pleases me well". There was not a hint of waiting for the Lord to guide him. She looked good to Samson and that was all that mattered. That her treachery and unfaithfulness were to bring him hurt and anger he couldn't see; she looked good, that's what he saw, alone. That the Lord used the marriage as an occasion against the Philistines was not because of the marriage but in spite of it.

Bitter, bitter will be your harvest, if you marry that girl merely because she looks good to you. Tears will flow, if you marry that chap just because he is handsome. Do not be unequally yoked together with an unbeliever. Even apart from that solemn truth always beware of puppy love for it may lead to a dogs life!

4

CHECK THE CREATOR'S HANDBOOK

Samson found that out-of-bounds honey was very sweet. Before he was through he found eating it brought consequences that were as bitter as gall. He fooled his parents with the honey he brought to them but he did not fool God. Neither can you. Better to stay with the honey God allows you, than to dab with out-of-bounds kind. Know the difference, be a connoisseur; your spiritual effectiveness and spiritual health depend on it. Don't just go by what the label says. Check with the creator's handbook of real honey. The creator knows what is best and sweetest and just the right amounts necessary. As the handbook says, 'Eat honey because it is good' but remember it also warns; 'Have you found honey? Eat only as much as you need, lest you be filled with it and vomit'. Careful, now.

5

WOULD YOU GO THROUGH FIRE FOR HIM?

Samson set a riddle at his wedding feast which went 'Out of the eater came something to eat, and out of the strong came something sweet.' The solution was of course, the fact that he had eaten honey out of a lion he had killed. The lion's carcass was out-of-bounds for a Jewish person to touch.

April

Samson's Philistine wife nagged at him; 'You only hate me! You do not love me! You have posed a riddle to the sons of my people, but you have not explained it to me.' She 'Wept on him the seven days while the feast lasted'.

Now it is true that the people threatened to burn her alive if she did not find out the solution to Samson's riddle, but would love not have found a way to be faithful to her husband's secrets and not betray him? Michal, King David's wife made a dummy for his bed and helped him escape despite the fact that her father wanted David's head! Why did she lay her life on the line for her husband? The Bible tells us that she loved him. The threat of fire tested Samson's wife's love and she was found wanting. True love would go through fire itself for the loved one, if necessary.

Say, lady, do you really love your husband? The fire of testing may come your way today. Be ready for it.

6 _____

CREDIT LIMIT

'There is no limit to the good I can do if I don't care who gets the credit.'

7

LEARN BEFORE IT'S TOO LATE

Why, oh why didn't Samson go home after the death of his wife (she was burned to death by the Philistines) and breathe a sigh of relief that he had been spared? Why did he not learn from his bitter experience? Why did he not go on to be a consistent blessing to others?

Let's not be too hard on him. Are we not often a long way into life before we begin to learn the principles that make for lasting good? Life sometimes seems to be nearly over before we begin to learn, if we learn at all. Then it is too late to recapture all those wasted years.

Are you in the midst of a storm in your life at present? Learn from it. There has got to be some lesson God is trying to teach you. Samson was stubborn and learned so little. Don't you be the same. Please.

8

DEFINING THE ENEMY

'We have come to arrest you', they said to Samson. Were those the words of Samson's enemies? Not at all they were the words of the men of Judah who had come to bind Samson to hand him over to his enemies. Samson had been upsetting the establishment! 'Do you not know that the Philistines rule over us,' they said.

April

The fact was that the children of Israel were supposed to be in possession of the land God had given them but have now become so compromised in their position that it had become known as the land of Palestine. Palestine means 'The land of the Philistines', not Israel. The men of Judah did not like Samson making a distinction and identifying the enemy!

Are you defining the enemy today? Are you upsetting things for the enemy and are you the target of those who don't like their compromise exposed? Good on you. As the French say 'Vive la difference!' Such Samsonomics we exalt.

9

ARE YOU GUNS POINTING THE RIGHT WAY?

Was there not a touch of irony in the statement of Samson to the men of Judah when they came to bind him and take him to the Philistines? 'Swear to me', he said, 'That you will not kill me yourselves'. Ironic indeed, for he could easily have split their skulls by the thousand had the notion taken him. He was gentle with the people of God, even though they had behaved disgracefully. Samson concentrated on the main enemy and slew a thousand of them instead of a thousand of the Lord's people.

Methinks, in the spiritual battle, that the church of Christ are like the British guns at Singapore during the last war. When the enemy arrived, the powerful British guns were useless. Why? Because they were pointing the wrong way! They were pointing out to sea and the enemy came by land. Selah.

10

ENJOY YOUR ICE-CREAM

When Samson had a great victory over the Philistines he asked God to give him a drink of water. He got it. Sometimes it is not a sin to prefer a cup of cold water at a given moment to your prayers. One is as vital as the other.

George Harper, a very well known Bible Teacher across the United Kingdom for over 50 years, once sat at my table and gave me a profound piece of advice. 'If you are standing at the side of the road eating an ice cream,' he said, 'Enjoy your ice cream!' He knew from experience that some folk would hardly let you enjoy a moments break. So it is that we read that 'God split the hollow place that is in Lehi and water came out' and Samson drank and 'His spirit returned, and he revived'. Learn the simple lesson that God is no killjoy.

11

LUST TODAY — GONE TOMORROW

When Samson entangled his life with a prostitute at Gaza the Scriptures say that the Gazites were told of his presence in their city and 'Surrounded the place and lay in wait for him all night at the gate of the city'. They were quiet all night saying 'In the morning when it is daylight we will kill him'.

But Samson did not stay with the woman all night. The Bible says that 'He arose at midnight' and left the woman. Immorality carries with it no promise,

April

no lifelong, never to speak of nightlong, commitment. Sex without love and the commitment of marriage is one of the loneliest things in the world. Samson's experience at Gaza could have one thing written over it; it was 'Lust today and gone tomorrow'.

12

THE TRAGEDY OF A SELFISH EVENING

Again and again in the life of Samson we read the words 'And the Spirit of the Lord came upon him'. When he faced the lion, when he was at Ashkelon, when he slew a thousand with the jawbone of an ass, the spirit of the Lord came upon him. But when Samson left the prostitute at Gaza and 'Took hold of the doors of the gate of the city and the two gateposts, pulled them up, bar and all, put them on his shoulders, and carried them to the top of the hill that faces Hebron'; we do not read that the Spirit of the Lord came upon him. It was an incredible fete for it is 38 miles from Gaza to Hebron. Yet, he did not carry them, it seems to me, in the strength of the Lord, but, in his own strength. He was not guided of the Lord to do it.

Everytime someone uses a gift that they have from God does not necessarily mean that they are guided of the Lord to do what they are doing nor does it mean that they are necessarily doing it in His strength. They could be doing it on their own. The end results will not bring glory to God but to themselves. Mark well that fruitless evening that Samson spent at Gaza and the equally fruitless walk home.

Teasing can be lethal

If we have a moral compromise in something it always leaves us very vulnerable. When Samson got involved with Delilah and she plagued him for the secret of his strength he should have sensed danger and fled from her. But Samson compromised and the resulting tragedy came as a direct result of that compromise. If he had left Delilah he never would have lost his two eyes. Notice how he toyed with her when she plagued him for his secret and had a lot of fun in teasing her as to what was the secret of his strength. He snapped the seven fresh bow strings and he broke the new ropes and he pulled out the batten and the web from the loom into which he had tricked her to weave the hairs of his head. It was all a lot of fun as far as Samson was concerned. How very sad to see a great man of God play and have fun with a sacred gift given to him to use for the glory of God.

I wonder if someone reading this little book is doing the same thing with the sacred gift that God has given to them? Be very careful my friend. Flee from what you are doing and that bad company and rededicate your gift to the glory of God. Samson went once too far for the Lord and God took his strength from him and he became the sightless, bald headed clown of Philistia. Do not fool around with sacred things.

April

14

WHEN GOD SHOUTS

When the Philistine lords gathered a great crowd together to offer a sacrifice to Dagon their god, the cry soon went up 'We want Samson!' The drink flowed freely and their hearts were merry and they had a field day of sport with the sightless judge of Israel. What they did not know was that Samson's God is a God who can restore his fallen children. We read that 'The hair of his head began to grow again' and this symbolised the fact that Samson had been restored to his Lord. Samson had not listened to the Lord when he whispered to him in love but it seems very clear that he had listened to God when he shouted to him through discipline and chastisement. Notice the amazing fact that God even used his blindness to get him to a pillar where he could execute a great victory for God over the enemies of the Lord's people. The Bible teaches that Samson said to the lad who held him by the hand, 'Let me feel the pillars which support the temple so that I can lean on them'. Little did that lad know that God was using Samson's great weakness to bring about God's great strength.

Have you been chastened by the Lord because of sin in your life and you feel that God will never use you again? Let me tell you heartbroken one that although the consequence of your sin will remain with you all the days of your life God can bring about good and use you mightily again despite the evil you have done. Notice the consequences of Samson's sin was that he lost his eyesight and although his hair grew again he did not get his eyes back. What he did get back was the strength and power of God to bring glory to God once more in his life. There is great sadness when we read that 'He pushed with all his might and the temple fell on the lords and all the people who were in it. So that the dead that he killed in his death were more than he had killed in his life. And his brothers and all his father's household came down and took him and brought him up and buried him between Zorah and Eshtaol in the tomb of his father Manoah'. Yet, tucked into that Judges chapter 16 despite its sadness is the mighty grace of God. Never before have we read in the life of Samson that he ever prayed before he attempted to do something for the Lord. This time in his restored state he had and a great victory ensued. Reach out, backsliden one today, return unto the Lord and He will abundantly pardon you and use you once more.

15

THE FINAL ANALYSIS

What is your opinion of Samson? Do you really feel he was an immoral, foolish, ill-disciplined lout? Do you feel that his life should sink without trace? Do you reckon that all of his strength was absolutely wasted and that he contributed nothing to the work of God on earth? That may be your opinion but it is not God's.

We read in God's ultra select list of 14 men of faith in Hebrews chapter 11 that Samson is among them.

April

Despite all his faults Samson made a difference between the uncircumcised Philistines and the chosen people of God, Israel. As the angel predicted before his birth to his parents that he would 'Begin to deliver Israel from the Philistines', so it had happened. He could have done a lot more if he had been disciplined and if he had fled from temptation. Yet let it never be forgotten that Samson made his mark despite his incredible faults. He had on occasions exercised faith in God and God had honoured his faith on those occasions. Would to God he had exercised more faith. The challenge is there for you and I to respond to in our generation. As Hudson Taylor put it 'All God's giants have been weak men, who did great things for God because they reckoned on his being with them'. Will you be one of those giants?

16 ───────────────────────

ONE SOLITARY LIFE

Have you ever come across a quiet, bubbling stream in a forest? In the heat of the day you might have got caught in brambles and briars and nettles, even your walk on the clearer woodland paths might have wearied you but, there, is the stream.

The Book of Ruth is like a quiet, bubbling stream between the Book of Judges and the two Books of Samuel. On either side is war, jealousy, envy, murder, deceit, immorality, pride; the quiet stream that is the life of Ruth is so refreshing between them.

I love those opening words of the Book of Ruth,

April

'Now it came to pass in the days when the judges ruled'. As we have seen together in past readings those days were exceptionally troubled but now comes the lovely story of Ruth in the midst of those turbulent times.

It proves you don't have to live in quiet times to live a life that is effective for the Lord. Who would ever have thought that Ruth's quiet and beautiful life would have been noted amid the fierce feuding and slaughter of war that marked the age in which she lived? Your life is also being noted. No life ever lived for the Lord is wasted. Be that 'quiet stream' in the midst of all the turbulence that is going on around you. May, as Jesus put it, your life be as 'A well of water springing up into everlasting life'.

17

THINGS ARE NEVER AS THEY SEEM

How the world about us loves success stories. Newspapers, television, theatres, films, novels, thrive on what the world counts a success story. The story of Ruth certainly did not begin with what the world counts success.

Ruth's husband had just died. She was surrounded in the land of Moab where she lived with a famine. The mother in law that she loved was about to return to her native Israel and pled with her to stay in Moab. 'Turn back' she said 'Go your way'. But Ruth did not want to go her way. 'Entreat me not to leave you, or to turn back from following after you; for wherever you go I will go', said Ruth. 'And

April

wherever you lodge, I will lodge; your people shall be my people, and your God my God. Where you die, I will die and there will I be buried. The Lord do so to me and more also, if anything but death part you and me'. If you and I happened, by chance, to come walking past these two women we would have walked on. Just two women talking by the side of the road; the wind blowing up dust as usual, the sun bearing down on the quiet countryside. But things are never as they seem. In the heart of that beautiful girl there struggled the biggest decision in her young life. She had discovered the true God and was she going to go back to the worldly substitutes in Moab that never satisfy? The loneliness of an alien land, the future seemingly blank, with little chance of gaining a husband, or the ease of familiar things, its the old and endless question. God calls, we hear and respond negatively or positively. Who would ever have thought as a result of the decision Ruth made that from her womb, down the line of generations was to spring the Saviour of the world? Do not fear to respond to the way God is calling you today the world may yet know incredible blessing as a result. The Lord help you, as he helped Ruth, to decide.

18

Two questions to ask

So, out of the blue there comes showers of blessing for Ruth? She finds wealth, happiness, and her man? Not so fast. God is never in any hurry. To find and to do God's will is not accomplished all in one day. He spent forty years training Moses after he yielded to His will. David fought a lion and a bear before he faced Goliath. Amos was first a shepherd in Tekoa. John lived in the wilderness before he blazed a trail for God at Jordan. Peter had to learn his own weakness in the judgement hall before he led 3,000 to His Lord at Pentecost. Paul went first to Arabia before he went to Jerusalem. When you are under God's training the hardest lesson of all is to wait for Him. Work for Him, pray to Him, read about Him, but wait for Him, there is the rub. To find the will of God for one's life is probably the most difficult task in christian existence. The search for it is not to degenerate into the merely interesting, or the pretty. There is blood and iron in it. Ruth had to first glean corn before she was ever to fall in love with the man who owned the field she gleaned in.

The greatest guiding line to follow when faced with the decision as a christian, I have found, is to shut your door. Get the influences of life out of the way and explain everything in secret to your heavenly Father. Acknowledge Him. Then go out and act in a common sense manner according to your abilities and limitations. When you acknowledge Him He then directs your paths. Ask two simple questions, 'Is it right?' and 'Is it necessary?' If there is no cloud between you and your Lord, go ahead. It was right and necessary that Ruth should look after Naomi. She acknowledged the Lord in all her ways. God acted. He was, by promise bound to. Just like my friend, David who was almost killed in a terrorist bomb explosion. The bomb had injured

April

him in the face and weeks after the deadly hour I was overhauling the universe with him around a blazing fire. What was his reaction to the whole thing? Quietly looking at me he said: 'If God can bring order out of the chaos of the cross, he can bring order out of the chaos of my face'. Those words are alive in me even now.

19

WHEN YOU FALL IN LOVE

I love the words of the Authorised Version describing how Ruth first found the field belonging to Boaz. The Authorised Version says that 'Her hap was' to light on a part of the field belonging to Boaz who was a relation of Elimelech her dead father in law. There is enough in that phrase 'Her hap was' to keep me writing until the end of this book. Aparently, by chance, Ruth came to glean corn in a section of the field belonging to that mighty man of wealth. The phrase 'Her hap was' shows clearly that she did not understand the full significance of what she was doing. There is the secret. She acknowledged the Lord, and it was no happening that she walked into Boaz's field, though at the time she thought nothing of it. The simple fact is that in ten years time you may look back and find that the most important thing you did this year was to open a book, walk across the street or bump into a friend. Little things have fascinating reprecussions. A word here, a word there, can ripple through eternity.

April

Watch the little things.

> 'How much of our life resembles
> Time lost in going upstairs;
> What days and weeks seem wasted,
> But we're climbing unawares.'

I strongly suspect that Boaz was deeply in love from the very first glance he had of Ruth. From his enquiry 'Whose young woman is this?' to his immediate provision for her immediate needs of food, drink and work, love was his motivation. Is there anything wrong with that?

> 'Though cities bow to art, and I am its own true
> lover,
> It is not art, but heart, which wins the wide
> world over.'

Dr. Boreham once wrote of an eminent pianist whose recitals crowded the most spacious auditoriums in Europe with ecstatic audiences. Yet there was just one thing lacking in his life. This brilliant pianist was a lonely, taciturn man and a certain coldness and aloofness would steal into his playing from time to time. At that moment there also lived another much older pianst whose name was a household word in musical circles the wide world over. One day this person laid their hand upon the shoulder of the brilliant young performer and said; 'Will you let me tell you, my boy, that your playing lacks one thing. So far you have missed the greatest thing in the world. And, unless you fall in love, there will always be a certain cold perfection about your music. Unless you come to love another human being passionately and unselfishly, you will never touch human hearts as deeply as you might'.

April

We sometimes take it for granted that we serve the Lord because we love Him; I simply want to ask is this assumption always safe?

20

HERE AND NOW

The yesterdays I cannot readorn
Or bygone years I never can relive;
And future happenings are yet unborn,
But now is ever here with much to give.

L. M. Clay

21

THE LINEA BLOOMA

There can be no doubt that Ruth did not set out to help her mother in law with Boaz in mind. He came into her life as a result of God's blessing upon her life and he fully understood the spirituality of the girl that he had fallen in love with. 'The Lord repay your work,' he said to her 'And a full reward be given you by the Lord God of Israel under whose wings you have come for refuge'. Ruth had taken the lowly place and God had noticed her humility and blessed her.

Are you being despised by someone because they think you have been given an insignificant role in your christian life? You know that you have been given that role by the Lord and nothing that He gives us to do is insignificant. Yet you may be smarting under the problem of being despised by others because you have taken, gladly, the humble place. Could I quote to you a beautiful piece of writing which means a lot to me?

'I was tired and sat down under the shadow of the great pines in a Swedish forest, glad to find such cool retreat from the broiling sun. I had not been there long before I noticed a fragrant odour and wondered what it could be and where it came from.

No Marechal Niel rose grew on that barren soil, nor could the sun penetrate the shades of the forest to extract its perfume even if it had; I looked round, and found by my side a tiny flower about half the size of an ordinary daisy, nearly hidden from view by the moss. It was the little 'Linea Blooma'.

O how fragrant it smelt! Again and again I held it near my face, enjoying the perfume, and then I looked up and thanked God for that tiny flower — so insignificant, growing in a wild, almost untrodden forest, yet bringing cheer and refreshment to me.

I thought why is it so obscure, when it is a flower with such fragrance, and surely worthy of a place in the most stately grounds? I learned a lesson by it, and it spoke powerfully to my heart.

I thought, if I cannot be a pine in God's forest, I may be a tiny flower to send forth the fragrance of Jesus in this world of sadness.'

April

22 _____

Ruth was nervous. Boaz was in love with her but there were problems in the way. She was agitated and moving around. She couldn't sit down for a minute. Would the problems be removed? Did a mother in law ever give a daughter in law better advice? 'Sit still, my daughter, until you know how the matter will turn out; for the man will not rest until he has concluded the matter this day'.

Ruth's mother in law was simply reminding her that if Boaz said he would take care of her concerns, then he would do just that. So it is that if God says he will save you if you trust His son, then he will do just that. If God says 'Delight yourself also in the Lord and he shall give you the desires of your heart', he will not rest until it is done. While we stumble and stray the Lord never rests working for us. While Ruth worried, Boaz was in the city busy knocking down the problems, one by one! Away with your doubting! Did Karl Marx ever reach down and give you peace? Have exsistentialists like Jean Paul Satre ever given you one minutes rest of mind and heart? You can philosophize, argue, worry and doubt but one thing I know — once I was restless, purposeless, empty, and lost, and now I have the Lord Jesus. Like you, maybe I too have sat listening to hundreds of lectures given by the greatest minds, but they never, never, gave me what I got through the victory of Calvary — a Holy Spirit to guide me, and a Christ to redeem me. I do not understand all this; do not begin to understand it; never expect to understand it. Yet I realise that it meets the deepest needs of my heart. For a thousand reasons I feel I am but a little child, and need a father; I am a sinful man and I desparately need a Saviour; I am troubled and heartbroken, and I need the Spirit, the Comforter. If He shall not rest, day or night working at God's right hand on our behalf, then what cause have we to fear? Sit still!

23

THE STONE WITH A BROKEN HEART

Why, before God could bring Ruth to the place of security, rest and happiness did she have to go through so much? Ellice Hopkins once put it this way: 'Do you know the lovely fact about the opal? That, in the first place, it is made only of the desert dust, sand, silica, and owes its beauty and preciousness to a defect. It is a stone with a broken heart. It is full of minute fissures which admit air, and the air reflects the light. Hence its lovely hues, and that sweet lamp of fire that ever burns at its heart, for the breath of the Lord God is in it.

You are only conscious of the cracks and desert dust, but so he makes his precious opal. We must be broken in ourselves before we can give back the lovely hues of His light, and the lamp in the temple can burn in us and never go out.'

April

24

Ruth, the Moabitess as well as Naomi, her mother in law, were concerned with a field. If a kinsman was to redeem the field then that involved marrying Ruth, the widow of a childless kinsman in order to have a child to carry on the inheritance. In other words if the kinsman was to buy the field then he must in addition provide for Ruth. Boaz was a kinsman of Ruth and Naomi but there was another kinsman nearer to them than he. Before ten elders at the gate of Bethlehem Boaz put the problem before the nearer kinsman.

The nearer kinsman was certainly ready to buy the field without marrying Ruth, and, indeed, he may well even have been ready to marry Ruth without buying the field. What he could not face was doing the two things. It would mar his inheritance. 'I cannot redeem it', he says. I leave you to conjecture why. He certainly was not willing to redeem all that she was and had.

By this time quite a crowd had gathered for all the world loves a lover. The nearer kinsman, according to ancient custom drew off his shoe and handed it to Boaz to indicate the withdrawal of his claim to redeem and inviting Boaz to take it up. What a moment it was when Boaz happily indicated that he wanted not only the field but Ruth as well. That is what true love is all about. Boaz was not just interested in a field he was interested in Ruth. God is not after us for what he can get from us, he loves us as individuals. You lose a sense of his love for you today and you will lose your balance and equilibrium in your christian life. With all my heart and soul I remind you today that God loves you. Go out and live in the joy and knowledge of that today.

25

WHAT'S IN A NAME?

What's in a name? Before a great crowd Boaz gave a tremendous speech in Bethlehem. 'You are witnesses this day that I have bought all that was Elimelech's and all that was Chilion's and Mahlon's from the hand of Naomi. Moreover, Ruth the Moabitess, the wife of Mahlon I have acquired as my wife, to raise up the name of the dead on his inheritance, that the name of the dead may not be cut off from among his brethren and from the fate of his place. You are witnesses this day'. Think of all those names that Boaz mentions. Elimelech means 'my God is King'. In that Hebrew name we have God's purpose for man. We are born to let God have supremacy in all things. Elimelech married Naomi which means 'pleasure'. Man in the garden did that very thing by obeying his own desires rather than God's and it very quickly turned to Mara which means 'bitterness'. They had two sons whose names mean 'sickness' and 'pining away'. Yet man was stiff-necked because he went on stubbornly like Orpah which means 'stiff-necked'. Then came Ruth which means 'beautiful' who obeyed God and

April

through Boaz, which means 'strength', we hear him redeeming all that was Elimech's, Mahlon's, Chilion's, Ruth's and Naomi's. What a circle! But it is not complete yet.

Boaz married Ruth and they had a little son whose name was Obed. Some render the meaning of Obed as 'servant', others render it 'worship', but both give the idea of humility and obedience. The amazing fact is Obed had a son called Jesse and Jesse had a son called David. What is so amazing about that? David was — the King! What a circle from the first tragedy of Elimelech, 'My God is King' in famine and death to David the King. As for God, His way is perfect, for in that very town centuries later David's greater son came to redeem not only all that was Elimelech's, Mahlon's, Chilion's, Naomi's and Ruth's but to you and me and all men, women, boys and girls who will put their trust in Him. God always brings beauty out of ashes, something beautiful always comes out of the tragic, if God is trusted. Ruth had certainly been wise to say 'Your God shall be my God'. She may have seemed peculiar to her friends, but better a thousand times effective peculiarity than uneffective ordinariness. Her complete subordination to a single aim was absolute. No person who goes for that aim with single heartedness can fail. God promises, repeat, promises, that 'Those who honour me, I will honour'.

WILL NOT THE END EXPLAIN?

It is absolutely true that the Lord often chastens His own. There is no question that He had chastened Naomi but the end product brought through the life of Ruth was the thing that mattered. So it is with us that when God chastens us the end product is the important thing. Try to remember that as you go through pressure today.

> Will not the end explain,
> The crossed endeavour, earnest purpose foiled.
> The strange bewilderment of good works spoiled,
> The clinging weariness, the inward strain, will not the end explain?
>
> Meanwhile he comforteth,
> Them that are losing patience
> T'is his way;
> But none can write the words they hear him say
> For men to read; only they know he sayeth
> Sweet words, and comforteth.
>
> Not that he doth explain,
> The mystery that baffleth; but a sense
> Husheth the quiet heart, that far, far hence
> Lieth the field set thick with gold and grain
> Wetted in seedling days by many a rain;
> The end — it will explain.

Amy Carmichael

April

27

QUIT GLEANING

I sometimes think about Ruth and her marriage to Boaz. Could you imagine Ruth going out to glean corn now that she had the hand of the man who owned the whole field? It would have been ridiculous for her to do so. Sometimes do you not think that we christians wander about the world trying to glean a little here and there rather than truly putting our hand into the hand of the one who owns it all? If you know Him, my friend, go and enjoy all the privileges that are yours — go to His storehouse, of which you are a joint heir in Christ, and see if He will not open the windows of Heaven and pour you out a blessing that there shall not be room enough to receive it. It certainly involves your whole heart but it ends far from gleaning alien corn. Quit gleaning and enjoy a full harvest.

28

FAITH

Faith came singing into my room;
Other guests took flight.
Fear and anxiety, grief and gloom,
Sped out into the night.
And I wondered how such peace could be,
Faith said gently, 'Don't you see?'
They really could not live with me.

Anon.

A NEW BABY

When Ruth bore her little boy Obed the women of Israel said to her mother in law 'Blessed be the Lord, who has not left you this day without a near kinsman; and may his name be famous in Israel and may he be to you a restorer of life and a nourisher of your old age; for your daughter in law who loves you, who is better to you than seven sons, has borne him'. It is absolutely incredible how that a little baby born into a family can bring new life to the older members of that family. I am always intrigued with the famous 'This is your life' television programme. When all the strands of the life that have been highlighted are drawn together at the end of the programme it is usually the grandchild that the camera concentrates upon and the sheer delight in the face of the grandparent or parent. In spite of all the successes of even famous lives it is the little ones who bring them the greatest joy.

So it is in the christian church whenever new babies are born into it. They bring a freshness and a special touch that those who have been members of the church for so long don't have any more. Pray that there will be many new births in your local church this year. There is nothing like it to bring new life to every part of its work.

April

30

A MARK OF GOD

So we have come through the fierce years of the Judges to the quiet life of the beautiful Ruth. Soon we shall be back into the fray again and on to the fierce years of war with the Philistines with Saul and David. Yet, there, in the middle of it all was the quiet life of an obedient and godly young woman which was to influence a history of the world. Think of it; one solitary life.

So I challenge you, as the fresh woods of bluebells blossom this April, to think about that one solitary life of yours. Where is it going? What is it doing? What will be your epitaph? I plead with you to live your life with eternity's values ever before you. It will not be easy, and often it will certainly not be popular. Yet may your epitaph be of one who left, like Ruth, their mark for God on all succeeding generations.

> 'Let thy mind still be bent, still plotting where,
> And when, and how thy business may be done.
> Slackness breeds worms; but the sure traveller,
> Though he alight sometimes, still goeth on.
> Acting and stirring spirits live alone;
> Write on the others, Here lies such a one.'
>
> George Herbert

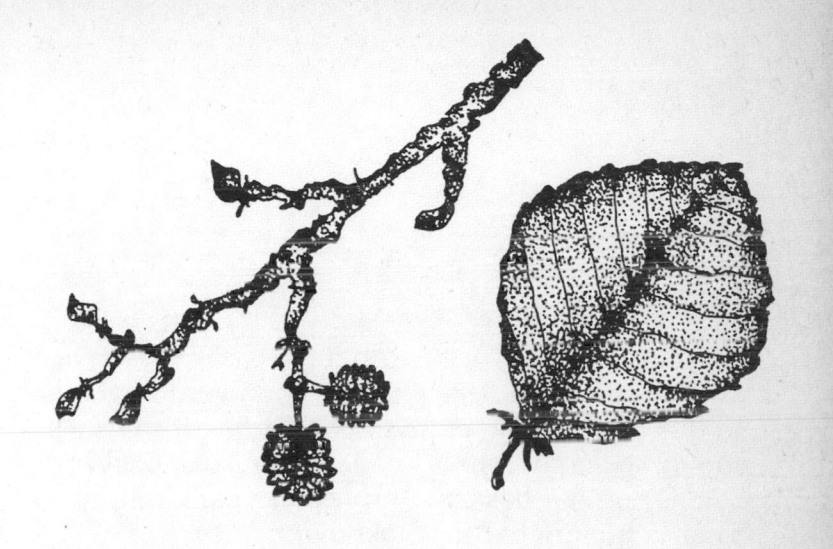

MAY

Cowslips, Mouse-ear Chickweed, Germander Speedwell and the little mauve puffs of Lady Smock appear in May. On the woodland borders the Red Campion blooms and Bluebells crowd the thickets. And there by the gurgling woodland stream is the Alder tree.

Nearly always found on the banks of streams, rivers and lakes or in places where water formerly stood or ran the Alder tree produces its tiny seeds which are water-borne by little floats. Alderwood makes soles for wooden clogs, excellent broomheads, and, when turned into charcoal, first rate gunpowder! Amazing how a little tiny floating seed could be, one day used to clean and brighten a house or blow it apart. So with our lives.

May

1

In every age there have been homes where no childish romp has changed the routine and where no bits of potato lie on the best carpet. In childless homes an alarm clock is needed to waken people up in the morning because the regular early morning cry of a hungry baby is unknown.

The saddest of all children is the child that is not. He is the saddest for he is the child of the imagination, the child of longing and Hannah knew all about him. 'Now there was a certain man of Ramathaim Zophim of the mountains of Ephraim and his name was Elkanah . . . and he had two wives; the name of one was Hannah and the other Peninnah. Peninnah had children but Hannah had no children. This man went up from his city yearly to worship and sacrifice to the Lord of Hosts in Shiloh . . . whenever the time came for Elkanah to make an offering, he would give portions to Peninnah his wife and to all her sons and daughters. But to Hannah he would give a double portion, for he loved Hannah, although the Lord had closed her womb.'

The childless Hannah had a husband who loved her. His name meant 'acquired of God' and Hannah was sure that as his name, so was he. There is usually no problem in singling out men who love

156

their wives. Notice, when in the company of a couple who love each other, there is no stale familiarity between them. Watch the men who love their wives show deference to the woman of their hearts, even when in a crowd. They show deference in opening a door for them or even in sitting down last! They give themselves away in the little things they do. With Elkanah it was the way he offered his peace offerings before the Lord. Tell me, husband, could others tell by the way you behave that you truly love your wife? Show some deference to her to prove it today.

2

SATAN IS A DIRTY FIGHTER

Mark well those moving words that describe Hannah's childlessness in Scripture; 'The Lord had closed her womb'. There is great comfort for all who are childless in these words. The Lord had made Hannah childless and nothing but his action could change her condition. The will of God is our only safety and God never makes any mistakes. If childlessness is our condition rest assured that it is for the best. God will not begin to make mistakes with us. Hannah's problem of childlessness was certainly hard to bear but what was to follow made it even harder. She became subject to the most unbelievable cruelty. As Hannah worshipped the Lord with her husband in Shiloh every year another Jewess, unnamed, but simply called her 'Rival' broke Hannah's heart. The Bible says, 'Her rival also

May

provoked her severely, to make her miserable, because the Lord had closed her womb'.

In life it is pretty amazing the people Satan gets to do his work for him. Just as Satan used one of the children of Israel to hurt another, we all find that his tactics do not change through the centuries. We are warned in Scripture not to be ignorant of his devices, so, we must not be surprised if Satan uses those people in our lives whom we least expect to break our hearts. They can say cruel things behind our backs. Their cruelty will be used by Satan to wreck our path of faithfulness to our Lord Jesus and steer us as far away as possible from believing that all things work together for good to them that love the Lord.

That person may be someone you work with, or, even, the seemingly 'ever so nice' person at our local church or even a member of our own family circle who will provoke us sorely. Don't be shocked when it happens. Through Hannah's life we have been warned.

3

BEETHOVEN WENT STONE DEAF

As we saw last month so we will now see in the life of Hannah that despite all the suffering that came along, she endured. There is a great undercurrent of blessing which runs right through her story. It is a fact that adversaries or rivals, tragedies or heart-breaks can be turned into blessings. Have we not found it so? It is a fact of life.

May

Who in history, composed our greatest symphonies? Beethoven, Handel, Schubert, Chopin, Schuman, Debussy, Tchaikovsky and Dvorak are amongst our greatest composers. A look at their lives is a very illuminating experience; a little research leaves the researcher gasping. Beethoven spent his youth in poverty and misery. As he grew older he was generally referred to as an ugly man. Tragedy of tragedies for him, he went stone deaf. It was a terrible thing to happen to a musician and yet it was after this that he wrote some of his most wonderful music — music which he never heard himself. He never stopped producing masterpieces; 9 symphonies, 32 piano sonatas, 17 string quartets amongst a list of other works. The last twelve years of his life were lonely and unhappy and after four months of intense suffering from lung inflammation he died in December 1827 in the midst of a thunderstorm.

Handel first had to play the clavichord in an attic in case his father discovered him! Later in life after many adventures he composed his most widely popular work 'The Messiah' under a cloud of misfortune and bitter disappointment. His last two operas had failed, largely through the plots of opponents who even hired ruffians to prevent people reaching the building where the operas were being performed. Later in life Handel went blind but he refused to give in, playing from memory and giving sound to the endless and wonderful music passing through his mind. Tomorrow we will continue with our research into the lives of great composers who composed from the midst of

May

unfortunate circumstances. One thing is for sure from Hannah to Handel our sweetest songs have always come from saddest thoughts. Do not despise your circumstances today. They will be the making of you.

TCHAIKOVSKY MARRIED THE WRONG GIRL

The Scriptures tells us that Elkanah, Hannah's husband said to her 'Hannah, why do you weep? Why do you not eat? And why is your heart grieved? Am I not better to you than ten sons?' Poor Hannah her grief could not be pacified even by the kindness of her husband. Who would ever have thought that such great blessing came from so many tears?

Let me continue with our theme of yesterday. From Hannah's wonderful burst of praise, which was to come from the victory God gave her, to the most beautiful music still around in the world today, the circumstances that brought it out have always been exceptionally difficult. Schubert was, they say, a physically squat, stout, clumsy little man with an unhealthy complexion and round shoulders. Yet, music simply poured out of him.

Chopin was plagued with ill health all his life and he had to fight constantly against disease. In later years his life was one long struggle against comsumption. It was said 'He came into the room bent double and with a distressing cough . . . but when he sat down to the piano he played with extraordinary strength and animation'. He died at the age of 39.

May

Ilich Tchaikovsky had moods that alternated between happy exuberant spirits and black depression. (Who of us hasn't?) He married a girl whom he did not love because he was afraid she would commit suicide if he refused her. After nine weeks they separated and Tchaikovsky suffered such mental torture he became unconscious. Although he said he was 'worn out' and 'done for', he was conceiving in his mind a haunting and beautiful 'Pathetique' Symphony. He unfortunately drank some unboiled water which brought about a fatal attack of cholera.

Dr. M. R. De Hann once calculated that if all the tears shed in the world could be barrelled and poured into a canal such a waterway would stretch from New York to San Francisco. He maintained that it would make a river in which barges could be floated. Few would doubt him. Yet God can turn tears into incredible joy. Even yours. Don't despise them for they could water seeds which will grow into incredible blessing as Hannah was soon to find out.

5

DON'T BE DIVERTED

Learn a very simple rule in the face of adversity which I learned from a Scotsman once. Talking with Alex Easton one evening as we went for a stroll together, and discussing the adversaries one found in the Lord's work he turned and said, 'Don't be diverted!' It is an excellent rule. No matter what our

May

circumstances, nor how dark our path, nor how great the provocation given by our adversary don't ever let Satan divert us. If he can cause us to veer off the path of God's will then his deadly work is done. Let's always remember in the darkness what God taught us in the light. Let's not be diverted into some foolish action but press on with the immediate work that lies to our hand, even though our hearts may be heavy. Even though, like Hannah, we may actually have lost our appetite because some cruel person used their tongue against us or gave us the hard look. Do not despair. In our story God is about to change the history of a nation through a brokenhearted, childless, sorely provoked and fretting Hannah. He can do the very same through us, if we let him.

6

INFLUENCE

Every journey begins with the first step. That initial step may seem insignificant but as Neil Armstrong pointed out on the moon, what is a small step for a man can become a giant leap for mankind, influencing millions. With Hannah the first step towards spiritual blessing is described in quiet measured tones. 'So Hannah arose after they had finished eating and drinking in Shiloh ... and she was in bitterness of soul, and prayed to the Lord and wept in anguish'. It is obvious that the great religious gatherings at Shiloh did little for Hannah.

May

Gatherings for worship do not always turn out to be spiritual gatherings. The facts were that Israel was far from God and evil priests had 'made the Lord's people to trangress'. Sin and genuine worship never go together. There at Shiloh they had an outward form of godliness but they denied the power of it.

Can you not see them? Plenty of gossip and chat. 'Did you see so and so and did you hear about . . .?' Too well we know such gatherings. It left poor Hannah sick and lonely at heart. She knew in her heart that something must be done. 'So Hannah arose', would to God that an army of men and women in the church of Christ would do the same. Little did Hannah know that as a result of her earnest and eager step toward the place of prayer and her Lord, millions were to be influenced. The influence of her prayer became infinite in its scope.

Influence? Who can begin to estimate its power? Hannah had Samuel, Samuel judged Israel and annointed David and David became Israel's beloved King and David's 'greater Son' conceived of the Holy Spirit, was, and is, the Saviour of the world. Influence! Who can measure the influence of your prayers this day? Find a quiet spot and steal away and talk to your Lord in prayer.The results could influence the history of the world. Not only will it do that but two minutes spent face to face with your Lord, heart to heart with him will infinitely influence your day.

May

7

WATCH THOSE SNAP DECISIONS

In life things are never as they seem. It is a fact that is learned the older we grow and the sooner it is learned the better. The experience of discovering things being the opposite to what they seem, can be shattering. For example, a friend proves that all the time he was a critic and an enemy, leaving a broken heart behind. The seemingly prosperous business project is discovered to be fraut with fraud. An often sworn lover is found to be a faithless braggard. A high Priest, chosen of God to lead the House of Israel, proves to be one who is so far away from God he cannot even distinguish between someone who is drunk and someone who is praying. 'And it happened, as she continued praying before the Lord, that Eli watched her mouth. Now Hannah spoke in her heart: only her lips moved, but her voice was not heard. Therefore Eli thought she was drunk. So Eli said to her, 'How long will you be drunk? Put your wine from you!'

It seems an incredible thing to believe that a great so-called spiritual leader could have made such a mistake, though he was probably well used to drunkenness around him for even drunkenness was mild to what sometimes took place at the door of the tabernacle of the congregation. Another translation reads Eli's stinging words as 'How long will you go on, you drunken creature? Away with you, go and sleep off your drunkenness.'

May

Snap decisions! The woman was crying and her lips were moving so she must be intoxicated. It was a misjudgement. How many times have we made hasty judgements? It appeared to be so, therefore it must be. How many lives have been wrecked by the unthinking mind and the tongue which reported something exactly as it appeared and forgot to take the second look? Innocent individuals do not escape the maliciousness of tongues. Why, how many times has some poor innocent fellow, merely passing the time of day to some girl of his acquaintance, arrived home to hear the he is engaged to be married to her! Never, ever judge things by their appearances.

8

HE DIDN'T TAKE A SECOND LOOK

It has been said that decisions made in the heat of an emotion usually turn out to be the wrong ones. If this is true then decisions made on mere appearances turn out to be disasters. Eli should have known, as Samuel later learned when trying to find a king to lead Israel, 'The Lord does not look at the things man looks at. Man looks at the outward appearance, but the Lord looks at the heart.' As one who has been constantly involved in the spread of the Gospel of Christ it has been a privilege to see people respond to that message and become believers in Christ. Yet, how many stories could be written of those very people returning with heart-breaking stories of disillusionment with Christian

May

leaders? Perhaps some problem has come up and they have gone to find help from some 20th century Eli, only to find that he was so hasty in judgement that he strained at a midge and swallowed a camel! Don't let you and I, by God's grace, ever be like him.

9

DON'T WALK OUT!

In the face of Eli's cruel and heartless accusation the reaction of Hannah was amazing. If ever a woman had been insulted Hannah was that woman. If ever any person had the right to walk out of a place of worship and wash her hands of the leaders there, Hannah measured into such a right. To her eternal credit Hannah stood firm and looking into the face of that lazy, miserable priest of Israel said, 'No, my lord, I am a woman of sorrowful spirit. I have drunk neither wine nor intoxicating drink, but have poured out my soul before the Lord.'

Where did Hannah get the strength to stay rather than walk out? It is all in the fact that she had just been in the Lord's presence, she had just been in prayer. Being filled with the strength the Lord had given her, Hannah was not put off by Eli's accusation. She knew that God knew her plight. When we pour out our soul before the Lord a whinning, holier-than-thou 'spiritual' leader cannot stand in our way. The lesson is that we should pour out our soul before him oftener.

10

FRANCIS ASBURY

When I think of Hannah facing her accuser I always think of the story of Francis Asbury, the great preacher, when he received an abusive anonymous letter. In his journal he wrote about it with these words: 'I came from my knees to receive the letter, and having read it, I returned whence I came'. It is the way to react to all abuse. Eli wilted before it and answered Hannah's faith by saying 'Go in peace, and God of Israel grant your petition which you have asked of him'. Carnality flees in the face of faith.

11

REACTIONS CAUSE REACTIONS

This famous incident of Hannah's humiliation by Eli is recorded for us by God in order that we might know that although Satan may even use those we would least expect to dampen our faith, we must go on relying on God. The heartening statement that follows shows clearly that Hannah was already well on the way to greater and higher things; 'So the woman went her way and ate, and her face was no longer sad. Then they rose early in the morning and worshipped before the Lord, and returned and came to their house at Ramah'.

Think of how different things would have been had Hannah reacted naturally. She would have risen the next morning filled with depression and

May

bitterness. She would perhaps have been cursing God for the fact that she had no child in her womb and railing against the deadness of the spiritual leadership in the land. She still had no child and Eli was a 'spineless' man but Hannah was now 'worshipping the Lord' and was 'no more sad'. Everything depends on how you react to situations as they arise throughout the day. If you react in an unspiritual way it will have deep consequences on how the rest of your day will go. Remember reactions cause reactions.

12 ——————————

SHOW ME HOW TO LIVE

Hannah prayed for a little boy and vowed that she would dedicate him to the Lord 'That he may appear before the Lord and remain there forever'. As parents we should let Hannah's example inspire us to pray earnestly for our children. Even before they are born. God will not desert us; he will answer our prayers, somewhere, sometime. Even if you have had that sickening experience of having to gaze into your own child's grave, all I can say is that you will know God's compensations in a way that those of us who have never had to go through such an excruciating experience will never know. If God spares your child to you all the days of your life then he will also give you strength to face all the responsibilities that that brings.

Hannah prayed and Samuel came. Elijah prayed again and the drought disappeared. Moses prayed and God rained down angel's food. David prayed and Goliath fell. Samson prayed and the temple crashed around him. The christians were praying at Jerusalem when the Holy Ghost came. Paul prayed three times for the removal of his thorn-in-the-flesh. God let the thorn-in-the-flesh remain but sent him His grace. A prayer meeting of Jewish women by a river was the start of Christianity in Europe. At the prayer meeting Paul spoke to the Lord Jesus and Lydia's heart was opened. Her heart was the highway to God for Europe and its millions.

Joni Earickson prayed for death after breaking her neck in a crippling dive into a deceptively shallow Chesapeake Bay. Death didn't come. 'God', she pleaded, 'if I can't die then show me how to live'. The word quadriplegic will never be the same again to millions who have read her story of learning to trust God. It is never a waste of time to pour one's soul out before God in prayer. That particularly applies when we pray for our children.

13

PRAYER IS GOOD FOR YOU

You may say that you do not always feel like praying. True enough. It would seem that Hannah prayed only out of great bitterness of soul to begin with. Prayer is never easy. You may not always want to pray but pray you must to know spiritual blessing. The woman we are talking about was no joyous, buoyant, never-so-happy-in-my-life woman. She was bitter in soul.

May

It is a miserable state to be in. God knows that with all that goes on amongst so called believers today, it is no wonder the church has its fair share of bitter-in-soul folk. 'Why go on?' says Satan. Yet, once that sacred face which was so marred more than any man's is sought in prayer, a sweetness begins to fill your life, a peace that passes all understanding guards your heart and mind. You cannot come away unaffected. How did it affect Hannah? 'So the woman went her way and ate, and her face was no longer sad'. Her being with the Lord changed the very expression on her face.

How can a person dwell in the presence of the Lord Jesus and come away bitter in soul? How can one sit at His feet and listen to His Word and not be strengthened? It is impossible. They that wait upon the Lord shall renew their strength. The very expression on Hannah's face was changed and her appetite returned. Prayer is good for you! She walked away from her encounter with the Lord and back to Ramah, unwearied. May you go back to your tasks today after having sought His face with an extra inch to your step.

14

ALL DRESSED UP WITH NOWHERE TO GO?

I am always aware that I can never tell into whose hands this book will fall. Perhaps you are a wealthy person and live in sophisticated surroundings in some beautiful mansion on some hill somewhere. Rich, but sad. Society and its whirl you enjoyed but only for a season. The bubble you chased has burst. You feel like Charlie Chaplin, the great comedian who said 'I am all dressed up with nowhere to go'. With all my heart I advise you to go to the Lord Jesus for salvation and forgiveness. 'Believe on the Lord Jesus Christ and you will be saved'. Perhaps you live in great poverty and consider yourself a failure. All of life's prizes seems to have passed you by and you are at Wit's End Corner. Rise up and go to the Lord Jesus. There are worthwhile and eternal riches in Him. Perhaps you are a baffled church elder dealing with the endless problems of people. You, who have comforted so many are yourself in great need of comforting. There is none like the Lord who understands and who endured, like you, the sting of ingratitude.

Perhaps you are a young christian, a few days or weeks in Christ. You have a lot of hard questions to ask about a thousand and one things. Do not be afraid to come to the One who is greater than Solomon. Call on Him, tell Him all. Pour it all out before Him and you will not be sorry.

Perhaps you are the victim of extreme violence today and you are losing faith in God. One of the most moving stories I have ever read was of the guards at Auschwitz. He first tortured and then hanged a young boy who had a refined and beautiful face. Just before the hanging someone was heard to whisper 'Where is God? Where is He?' Thousands of prisoners were forced to watch the hanging (it took the boy half an hour to die) and then those prisoners were forced to march past and look the child full in the face. Before the hanging

May

someone was heard to whisper 'Where is God? Where is He?' After the hanging the same voice was heard to ask 'Where is God now?' Should that person but have realised the story of the gospel he would have seen that God too, in the person of His Son was once on a gallows. They crucified the Lord of glory and they hung Him on a tree. There has never been any sorrow like His sorrow and it is to such a God I would urge you to turn today.

15

I ASKED THE LORD FOR HIM

How must Hannah have felt, when many months later, the Lord answered her prayer? The look on her face must have been incredible the day her little baby boy was born. Her thoughts were later put into prayer and it is one of the most moving prayers recorded in Scripture: 'My heart rejoices in the Lord; my strength is exalted in the Lord. I smile at my enemies, because I rejoice in your salvation. There is none holy like the Lord, for there is none besides you, nor is there any rock like our God. Talk no more so very proudly; let no arrogance come from your mouth, for the Lord is the God of knowledge; and by Him actions are weighed . . . the Lord makes poor and makes rich; He brings low and lifts up. He raises the poor from the dust and lifts the beggar from the ash heap, to set them among princes and make them inherit the throne of glory'.

And she called the little fellow, Samuel, saying 'Because I asked the Lord for him'. Indeed, she had

May

Did you ask the Lord for something a while back? Has He given it to you? Did you wait for God and God has in his own time and place answered your prayer to a far greater extent than you could ever have dreamed. Have you, like Hannah returned to give thanks? If not do it now.

_____ **16**

WHERE LIFE MAKES UP ITS MIND

When Elkanah went up on the year of Samuel's birth with his family to offer the annual sacrifice to the Lord at Shiloh the Scripture tells us that 'Hannah did not go'. What about her vows? It was because of those very vows that she stayed at home. She said to her husband 'After the boy is weaned, I will take him and present him before the Lord, and he will live there always'. So the woman stayed at home and nursed her son until she had weaned him. To raise children properly seems, to those who have never experienced parenthood, ridiculously simple. It is not so simple and to do it properly will require the very best we can possibly give in time, patience, effort and financial resources. Many christian mothers, (and fathers too) will find that they have to sacrifice many things in order to look after their toddler or toddlers at home. This may mean that parents often have to deny themselves full attendance at the local church services and other gatherings for mutual christian fellowship. Hannah in her turn stayed at home to 'wean' her child. She

May

did not go up with Elkanah to Shiloh to worship until her child was able to live independently of his mother and this could have meant anything up to a period of twelve years.

It has been proved again and again that home is the place where life makes up its mind. The shaping of a child's mind and will is accomplished in the very first few years of its life, particularly in the first two years. The showing of firm discipline and deep affection in these few years sets the sails for the voyage of the child across the sea of life. Mothers in particular who make the sacrifices necessary to stay close to take care of their children in those early months and years are doing the greatest work in the universe. All those weary 'walks' and gropings in the dark and dead of night to answer a child's needs will not be in vain. She who rocks the cradle rules the world. Train up a child in the way it should go and when it is old it will not depart from it. Part of the problem of mothers who get frustrated when they can't get out to worship because of the responsibilities of children is that they do not understand that service is part of worship. It is, in fact, a very significant part. Hannah was worshipping the Lord as she looked after Samuel at home every bit as much as her husband was worshipping the Lord up at Shiloh.

STATE SECRETS FOR A LITTLE BOY

It could be that some little boy or girl is reading today's entry. Notice, children that the Bible says that when Samuel was serving God in the temple at the beginning 'He did not yet know the Lord' (1st Samuel 3 : 7). This clearly shows that even a careful, godly upbrigning does not make the child of any home the Lord's child. In our day, being born into a christian home, attending a place of christian worship does not make a person a christian. As with Samuel, so with us: there must come a moment when we personally respond to the Lord's call and put our faith and trust in Him. This is called the new birth (John 3 : 7). To all who, as a definite act, receive the Lord Jesus as their Saviour, to those who believe on His name, He gives them the right to become children of God. Have you received the Saviour as your Saviour?

'Speak', said little Samuel on the night the Lord called Him, 'For your servant hears'. Quietly the Lord revealed to that little boy news which he said would make the 'ears of everyone who hears it . . . tingle'. God revealed secrets of the state of Israel to a little boy which he did not reveal to the so called spiritual leader of the country. Here is a lesson for us adults. As it was in the days of Samuel so it is in our day that often God has hidden things from those who may have years of experience but who are not as open to His voice as a little child can be. May we always have childlike openness to our Father's call.

May

18 ───────────────

Some people have the idea in their minds that Samuel was sent off by his mother as a child to Shiloh, and, apart from those yearly visits, when Hannah made him a little robe and brought it to him, she never saw him again. In point of fact Samuel was not a monk. We read that his permanent house was eventually made in Ramah where his mother lived and it is interesting to read that despite his many travels 'he always returned to Ramah for his home was there. There he judged Israel, and there he built an altar to the Lord'. (1st Samuel 7 : 17). Could Hannah credit it? Her little boy had now grown to be a judge and prophet and was disciplining and judging a nation in righteousness from the very town where she had trained and disciplined him!

Many a woman living in obscure circumstances has ruled the world through the child in which her noblest self has been reproduced in masculine or feminine deeds and words. Think of Rachel in Jospeh; Jochabed in Moses; Elizabeth in John the Baptist; Monica in Augustine; Suzannah in John Wesley etc. Hannah stands for all that God can do in and through a mother dedicated to him. Let us see what history says of her. Let's walk into that great Hall of Fame that is Hebrews chapter eleven and look at the portraits of the men and women of God displayed there. Listen to the words of the guide who conducts us through: 'and what more shall I say?

For the time would fail me to tell of Gideon and Barak and Samson and Jepthah, also of David and Samuel and the prophets'. Ah! Samuel and the prophets; he is, among the prophets, singled out for mention. 'Who,' adds the guide, 'through faith subdued kingdoms, worked righteousness, obtained promises.' What God promised, the forlorn Hannah had believed in prayer on that heartbroken day so long ago. So it will be with us. If we believe God.

19

JUST TO PLEASE THE BOYS

When Samuel grew up and became a prophet in Israel he had a huge amount of trouble from someone who was outstandingly handsome and decidedly ugly. Who was he? Well, he was a giant and a dwarf. He was a hero and a rebel. He was a king and a slave. He banned occultism and he dabbled in occultism. He began with a blessing of God on his head and he ended as a suicide. His name was Saul.

When Saul set out as a young man he had every opportunity to leave a trail of spiritual blessing behind him. He was surrounded, the Scriptures say, by a group of men whose hearts the Lord had touched. He was shy and modest. He was also very generous of heart. How, then, did such a great man become such a fool? How could a great leader slide through a succession of incidents into a suicide's grave? The answer is that Saul did not wait for God.

May

On one occasion he was leading his army, and the enemy was arrayed against him. He had been specifically told by Samuel the prophet not to go into the attack until Samuel himself arrived on the scene. Saul waited for some time, but slowly his men began to slip away from him. Their leader seemed far too hesitant. Were not the enemy mobilising before their eyes? Saul's men began to panic and desert.

Just to 'please the boys', Saul said, 'Bring a burnt offering and peace offerings here to me'. With a flurry of activity to impress his men he offered the burnt offerings, and as soon as he had finished Samuel came. It seems such a tiny act, and yet no act in all his life cost him dearer. 'What have you done?' said Samuel, and Saul poured out his reasons. 'You have done foolishly', said Samuel. 'You have not kept the commandment of the Lord your God, which he commanded you. For now the Lord would have established your kingdom over Israel forever. But now your kingdom shall not continue. The Lord sought for himself a man after his own heart, and the Lord commanded him to be commander over his people, because you have not kept what the Lord commanded you'. (1st Samuel 13).

Let us be warned! Advantages in themselves are not a guarantee of success. Opportunities in themselves are not enough to give life its highest fulfilment. A moments disobedience to God's will through impatience can lead to incredible disaster. Better is the New Testament's Saul's epitaph which said so profoundly 'For me to live is Christ and to die is gain'. Which Saul would you rather be? When

May

David, God's saviour of Israel, came and slew the giant Goliath, Saul was delighted. It was lovely. He gave the youth top priority. He even gave him his daughter in marriage. He made him a captain in his army. It was peace in Israel alright. David even played him lovely songs. All seemed fine.

Yet, slowly, it began to dawn upon Saul that this David was God's annointed saviour and king. He was no ordinary youth. Saul realised that if David became king then he would no longer be king. It must be very hard to stop being a king once you have been one, I imagine. Top orders no longer come from you. You have to take a subordinate position. You become more of a servant than ever before. Saul didn't like it.

So it was that Saul set out to kill Israel's saviour. He tried to get his daughter to kill David but he had a problem there, for Michal positively loved him. She arranged for David to escape. He tried to get his son Jonathan to join him against David, but Jonathan read the score very early on and laid his regalia as king-designate at David's feet. On and on the stubborn Saul hunted the young David; again and again David gave him opportunity to repent and accept God's will but he refused. There was 'a great space between them', says 1st Samuel 26 : 13. Indeed there was and soon it was unbridgeable. Saul was found with the witches of Endor dabbling in the devil's powers. Trying to find out the future. The future proved to be suicide. It is a very serious thing to refuse the kingship of God's Saviour, it has great consequences, for, to go out into eternity without Him is to go out into unalleviated darkness.

May

Did not Herod realise immediately what the young Saviour of Bethlehem meant and he too decided to kill God's Saviour. Where are Herod's palaces now? Mere Mediterranean rubble. The kingdom of David's greater son will have no end. Crown the Lord Jesus king of your life today and stop trying to be king yourself. It is not easy to hand over the reigns of kingship to him but it is eternally worth it.

20

TRAGEDY AT NOB

After the Falklands conflict the British Army buried its dead. The cold winds of the South Atlantic blew across the bleakest of cemeteries carrying the sounds of that funeral service to the waiting microphones and television cameras which beamed it to the watching millions across the world. Those mourners sang the 23rd Psalm and I thought of David. Musician, military strategist, king and poet. If you ever meditate on the fact that there was a giant who chased David during his life time; the giant was called Panic.

King Saul had determined to kill David and when he moved against him David found that panic had ceased his heart and mind. Panic is in fact a very hard giant to shake off because he tends to cease, particularly the mind of his victim, so that he cannot think rationally. I am chased by him often.

The last thing Panic's victims tend to think about is waiting for God. Even the author of the most famous Psalm in history fled under Panic's influence to a town of priests called Nob, just north of the city of Jerusalem. There he met Abimelech, lied to him that he was on the King's business and asked for a sword. The tabernacle stood at Nob at this time and asking Abimelech for a sword was something akin to going to the local preacher or christian leader nowadays and asking him for a gun. 'We have no sword here but Goliath's', answered Abimelech. The great symbol of David's faith had been carefully kept as a trophy at Nob. 'There is none like that', answered David. 'Give it to us'. Panic had him by the mind and David, famous for his faith in God, now puts his faith in Goliath's sword.

Does it really matter that panic chases us now and again out of the will of God? It certainly does. When Saul eventually found out that David had been to Nob he came and the entire priestly community was exterminated. Only one man escaped and he fled to David who was hiding in a cave. Panic is serious and who of us have not known it tempting us to refuse to wait for God? Let's remember that other people are inextricably involved in the consequences of our deeds. Let's go carefully into the coming days. Sadly, David had not gone watchfully and prayerfully into his.

21

WHEN BEAUTY AND BRAINS COMBINE

We used to have in Ulster a Presbyterian minister called Marshall who wrote in one of his most famous poems of a woman who had a face like 'A jail door with the bolts pulled out'. Such a comment makes me think of a lady who said, 'I'm tired of all this nonsense about beauty being only skin deep. That's deep enough. What do you want — an adorable pancreas?'

Other views of beauty aside, the Bible describes a famous lady called Abigail who became David's wife as 'a woman of good understanding and beautiful appearance'. Beauty and brains are a rare combination. Abigail was used by God to change the very course of David's life. You do not need to be beautiful to be good looking as far as God is concerned. There is a beauty that he can give you and an understanding which Estée Lauder and Laura Ashley combined could never give you. You can have a mind like Christ's and be dressed in a beauty not your own, but His. What a combination! (If you don't believe me check out 1st Peter 3 : 3-5 and James 1 : 5).

22

AIDS CAN BE AVOIDED

There is a verse of Scripture which always haunts me. Let me tell you about it.

I once watched some young people being interviewed on the subjects of AIDS. A camera went amongst the crowd of young people in their early twenties and the interviewer asked if they would take any protection in their sexual relations from the plague that is breaking out across this often promiscuous nation. Not one showed the least inclination to do so. I was astonished. Not for one moment do I think that every young person is like them but the plain fact is that too many are. The clear evidence put before them was that 'sleeping around' could kill them. They didn't seem to care. I reckon that the plain boundary set by Scripture on sexual matters would not bother them either. That marriage is that sacred boundary is ignored by millions.

King David of the Bible had the same problem. One day, when he relaxed on a rooftop in Jerusalem David saw Bethsheba and committed the sin of his life. The alarm bells of his conscience must have been screaming but he refused to listen. One brief spell of passionate indulgence and then his character was blasted irretrievably, his peace vanished, the foundations of his kingdom were threatened and a great opportunity was given to his enemies to blaspheme. David, man of God, sensitive poet, dedicated shepherd, spiritual giant, leader of God's people, man after God's own heart; how could you? But he did and war never left his home after it. Whether it is AIDS that follows or endless feelings of guilt or whatever, the chasing of sexual pleasure outside of the boundaries God has set for it to keep it sacred and wonderful, spells trouble. Moments of leisure are more to be dreaded than moments of toil. Middle life, for David was more than fifty years of age, has absolutely no immunity from the temptations that face young people. The verse that haunts me from David's tragic episode with Bethsheba records what the prophet Nathan said to him when sent by God to confront David with his sin. 'Then Nathan said to David, "You are the man!" Thus says the Lord God of Israel; "I annointed you King over Israel, and I delivered you from the hand of Saul. I gave you your master's wives into your keeping and gave you the house of Israel and Judah. And if that had been too little, I also would have given you much more!" God had more for David but he couldn't wait. David had to reach out and take for himself that which belonged to another and disaster came. A monogamist relationship for men and women was God's ideal from the very start of creation. David was warned by the law of Moses not to multiply wives, never to speak of taking someone elses. David's habit of sensual indulgence pre-disposed him to the evil solicitation of that evening in which he fell.

I was pleased to hear a medical Professor say on the T.V. programme about AIDS that the disease could be avoided by a simple solution. The solution was a monogamist relationship; one partner for life. If you could talk with David now, even though AIDS was not his immediate problem, the Professor would have, I reckon, one person who would wholeheartedly agree with him. Don't let experience have to teach you to agree with him too.

23 ───────────

THE HEART STEALER

He didn't steal their money. He didn't steal their cities or towns. He stole their hearts. If a man or woman's heart be stolen then they will be deeply influenced by the thief and Absalom was an expert heart stealer.

'Whenever anyone came near him to bow down . . . he would put out his hand and take him and kiss him. In this manner Absalom acted towards all Israel who came to the king for judgement. So Absalom stole the hearts of the men of Israel'. David's son was a smooth operator; slick, silver tongued and handsome. 'In all Israel there was no one who was praised so much for his good looks, from the sole of his foot to the crown of his head there was no blemish in him'. When such a character starts talking, people listen and it was not long before his winsome ways had stolen a nation of hearts.

His public relations exercise in Israel was not only to greet and win the favour of everyone who came to his father with a problem, but he knew how easily folks were impressed with outward appearances. He got himself horses and chariots and fifty men to run before him. People by the million, in all ages fall for the old trick that, 'the medium is the message'. That the man had treason in his heart and could not wait for God's time for him to have a position of influence in the land, never dawned on them. That a man's life does not consist of the abundance of the things he possesses did not occur to them. That a hypocrite preaches by the yard but practices by the inch was hidden to the nation by, 'just-look-at-all-those-chariots-and-footmen'.

Absalom was in a hurry and God was not even in his reckoning, but God the great heart seacher soon destroyed the heart stealer. Caught by the

May

very hair of which he was so proud in the thick boughs of an oak, Absalom was killed by his enemies. He became a monument of warning to all of us not to be taken in by what seems great. God does not primarily ask for our money, our home, or land, or hands or our feet. 'My son, give me your heart', he whispers. Let him have that and he has all. Let any other false king reign in your heart and you will be as Israel found to their cost, disillusioned. Beware of heart stealers. They abound.

24

THE BLESSING OF A FRUSTRATED DESIRE

David's life was over. His years of leadership and service were at an end. At the conclusion of the journey, he had the opportunity of looking back and asking himself how much of his life had been permanent, vital and effective. As he looked back he recognised he had only one thing to face — his accountability before God. The summing up had come. It was a tremendous moment in David's life and it will be an equally great moment in your life when it comes, as it will for all of us, sooner or later. Wouldn't it be good if you and I just took the opportunity now to ask ourselves a few questions? I believe that now would be a golden opportunity. Let's reflect then for a moment and look back on our lives. Has your life, my life been worthwhile? Has it brought Heaven any nearer for someone? Has it made the Lord Jesus Christ more real and precious to others? How much of my work can stand the test of judgement before a Holy God? Those are solemn questions but I think it's good to reflect on them while there is still time to make an adjustment in our lives and ministry.

David told his people how he wanted to build a great house for the Lord. But God said 'No'. What did David do in the face of a life-times ambition that was shattered because it was not God's will? Did he become sour? Did he resign and give up? Did he allow his frustration to turn him away from God's work? No! The truth is that he gave himself more completely to serving the Lord in His will.

Maybe you have pictured yourself as the great successful servant of God, a missionary, christian leader, Bible teacher, a powerful preacher, an evangelist, a christian writer, much used by God. But somewhere along the line, God has said 'No'. God has chosen a different sphere altogether for you. If you are living with a frustrated desire, an ambition which God has cut right across, what have you done about it? Hard to give up a cherished ambition, isn't it? It's hard to die to ones own desire and accept God's will. It is cruel to the flesh. There's something in everyone of us that the Bible calls self which always wants to initiate something. But God says 'I don't want you to initiate anything. I want you to be a channel through which I am going to do everything'. Have you accepted the blessing of a frustrated desire? David did and gave a solemn charge to Solomon his son giving him the plans for the courts of the house of the Lord. 'All this', David said, 'the Lord made me understand in writing by his hand upon me'. All the work was to be done

May

according to the plans. David became a man who understood the mind of God, and it was accomplished in writing by the hand of God upon him. So it is that God has done the same for us and given us His written Word. I love the quote of the famous preacher A. W. Tozer when he said many years ago 'I did not go through the Bible. The Bible went through me'.

'Know the God of your father', David charged his son. He didn't say 'Solomon, know the God of Abraham, Isaac and Jacob'. One day, perhaps, you will have to say goodbye to your children for the last time, until you meet them in Heaven. I wonder will you be able to say 'Know the God of your father?' Above everything else, this is what mattered most to David. He had learned to know God, intimately, and to praise him superbly. The man passed, but his work remained. He didn't owe his immorality to the fact that he was a mighty king, but to the fact that his praise and knowledge of God surpassed his kingdom. David left bare the depths to which all humanity can sink, but he was not left at the bottom of the pit with no hope. There was a way out for him, for he knew that 'God did not despise a broken spirit, or a broken and contrite heart'. David learned that the 'steps of a good man are ordered by the Lord . . . though he fall, he shall not be utterly cast down'. May we live with such an attitude. May we pass on such a heritage. In the days that remain to us, let us do our part in the building of God's church, which is His body. May we, like David, be called men and women, boys and girls, after God's own heart.

ABOVE THE SUN PHILOSPHY

There was once a couple who went on a cruise and literally lived from one meal to the next. They had retired and had plenty of money and were constantly angry with the stewards for not giving them super-service. They seemed to be afraid that they might starve between courses. Their physical appetites seemed the one thing that mattered to them. They never read a book or paper.

One night they were sitting between meals, staring out blankly when a bright idea flashed across the dull brain of the man. He went to the mantlepiece and picked up some vases, looked into them and returned to his wife with the news; 'They're empty!'

A christian who had been observing the couple came very near to laughing and later wrote; 'The souls and brains of both of them were empty. They had much in their purses but nothing in their persons; and that was their punishment. They had security with boredom; no adventure. They had expanding girth and narrow horizons'. We read in the Scriptures that David's son Solomon investigated the question 'What are we living for' as no one else has ever done. He went after humour and concluded 'It is madness'. He drank wine, built houses, planted vineyards, made gardens and orchards, made water pools, got servants, accummulated livestock, collected silver and gold and treasure, and hired singers backed up by

May

musical instruments of all kinds. 'Whatever my eyes desired I did not keep from them,' he commented. His conclusion? All was vanity and grasping the wind. There was no profit under the sun'. In that little phrase 'no profit under the sun', Solomon gives us the secret of what is really worth living for. If we want lasting and true profits we must look above the sun. We must look beyond to God for our true peace and satisfaction. We were made to glorify Him and Him alone. We can never know true satisfaction until we know and serve God.

I remember a University professor who used to undermine my faith with his comments. One day he was holding forth about the fact that there were no lasting values and no lasting morality on earth. 'So', said a fellow student to the professor, 'if there are any lasting values they must come from outside the earth. Right?' The professor nodded. 'But that is where Jesus came from!', said my fellow student. I can see the old professors's face even now as I write! It was above-the-sun theology indeed.

26 _____

WHAT MONEY CANNOT BUY

'There is nothing better for a man than that he should eat and drink and that his soul should enjoy good in his labour', says Solomon in the Book of Ecclesiastes, 'This also I saw was from the hand of God'.

John D. Rockefeller was earning approximately one million dollars a week towards the end of his life. Sadly he did not enjoy the ability to eat much food. For breakfast one of the world's richest men was only able to have a drop of coffee, a spoonful of cereal, a forkful of egg and a bit of chop the size of a pea. The fact is that money cannot buy you even the enjoyment of a good breakfast. Remember that and don't despise even your everyday blessings.

27

ETERNITY IN OUR HEARTS

Solomon once wrote that God has 'Put eternity' in our hearts (Ecc. 3 : 11). It has been pointed out that God has provided a lot of lovely things for us to enjoy along life's journey but he has taken great care to see that we do not mistake any of them for home.

28

THE POOR WISE MAN

'Now', says Ecclesiastes 11 : 14-15, 'There was a little city with few men in it; and a great king came against it, beseiged it, and built great snares around it. Now there was found in it a poor wise man, and he by his wisdom delivered the city. Yet, no one remembered that same poor man'.

The more I think about this statement the more I would like to be as that poor wise man. Wouldn't you? Who cares about being remembered if the city is delivered?

29

CONTENTMENT

Fanny Crosby was blind from birth and she lived to be 90 years old. Consider the poem she wrote when she was only 8 years old.

> Oh! what a happy child I am
> Although I cannot see
> I am resolved that in this world
> Contented I will be
>
> How many blessings I enjoy
> That other people don't
> To weep and sigh because I'm blind
> I cannot and I won't.

If such a child could grow up to set the christian world singing by her beautiful hymns, how are you getting on with the advantage of your two perfectly sighted eyes. I'm not suggesting that you start writing hymns, necessarily, but have you been so foul tempered over the last day or two that you have caused someone to cry instead of sing? God forgive you.

30

INSIDE OUT

A new outfit without a new infit is a misfit.

Hank Mweder

THE HOUSE WITH 10,000 WINDOWS

Her name was Sarah. She was a young widow and her husband had left her 20 million dollars. He had been a rifle manufacturer called William Winchester and his untimely death seemed to haunt his widow constantly.

Could it be, she feared, that she and her infant daughter were suffering from 'the vengeance of the dead'? Their family fortune had been made through the manufacture of firearms which would have been used in the slaughter of possibly millions of people. Sarah's fears became greater. She had no peace. In desperation she sought help from the words of a medium and asked how she could find 'eternal life'. 'Yes, it's true,' the medium said, 'the family is being haunted by the hosts of people killed by the Winchester repeaters. It's true that the spirits have placed a curse upon you, but there is a way out. You must move West, buy a house and build more rooms. Listen to the spirits, they will tell you what to do'. In this way she was told, perhaps she could find eternal life.

Sarah arrived in San Jose in 1844. She bought an eight room farm house and this was the start of a frantic building project which continued without ceasing for the next 38 years until Sarah died. She had a staff of 22 carpenters working steadily 24 hours a day without drawings. By the time she died as a black veiled old lady of 82 the rambling building, now a major tourist attraction, had 467

May

doors, 10,000 windows and 40 stairways, some of which led to nowhere, 6 kitchens, 47 fireplaces and 3 lifts. All of this was in search of eternal life.

Solomon found it absolutely pointless to find lasting satisfaction in any thing this world had to offer. For as he said, 'the race is not to the swift, nor the battle to the strong, nor bread to the wise, nor riches to men of understanding, nor favour to men of skill; but time and chance happen to them all'. The Scriptures show us very clearly that in fact eternal life is possible to have in this life. If Sarah Winchester had come to know the Saviour (whom to know is life eternal) she would not have had to spend 38 years frantically building all those rooms seeking for eternal life. The medium's advice was from the prince of evil. For 'the gift of God is eternal life through Jesus Christ our Lord'.

Do you know the Lord Jesus as your Saviour? If you do, you need have no fear coming from the past, the present or the future. If you do not know Him why not trust Him as Saviour right now?

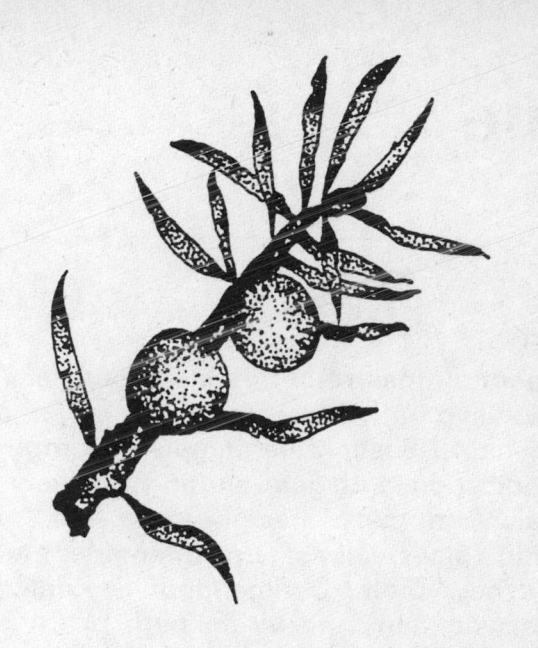

JUNE

June is a month filled with scents in the woods. The scent of Water Mint mixes with the heavy perfume of hawthorn blossom. If you are fortunate you may even see a few Southern Marsh Orchids. The massed pink and white flowers of the Dog Rose make a glorious show in the thickets. Perhaps you may even find a few Juniper trees with their sharp resinous scent.

The Juniper tree bears in summer days, juicy berries which can be distilled to yield a fragrant, strongly flavoured oil of juniper which is used in making perfume. No wonder the dejected Elijah lay down under the juniper tree! May our lives through June days send out the fragrance of the Saviour we ve trusted.

June

1

MORE THAN A VOICE

Desperate times require special people. To say that we live in desperate times is an understatement. AIDS is threatening plague proportions. Drug addiction and glue sniffing are new gods. Television morality has become the nations morality; plays, films, documentaries are the nations new Bible. Christendom is riddled with leaders who deny the virgin birth of Christ, the inerrancy of the Bible, the necessity of the new birth, the deity of the Saviour and vicarious atonement of Calvary's finished work. Divorce is rising to swamp family life and even the word 'family' is now under threat with the huge proportion of one parent families within our society. The nuclear arsenal is massive. Stress is the biggest threat to the nation's health. 'God' and 'Christ' are the two most popular swear words in Great Britain at the moment. Maybe they are in your country too. In the midst of it all the professing church is split and divided into fragmentation that must grieve the heart of its Lord. We have become a fen of stagnant waters.

Israel at the time of Elijah was also in a desperate spiritual condition. Suddenly a man appeared who, although described in Scripture as a man just like us was marked with great jealousy for the Lord God With single minded devotion he was used to tu the nation round. Fearlessly his voice rang out 'If the Lord is God follow Him; but if Baal, then follow him'. Because of his clear, decisive witness hearts were turned back to worship the Lord. But Elijah was more than a voice, he became the epitome of one who was determined to prove to a nation that his God was a living God who intervenes in human affairs, who can be known and who cares. Why not let your life be the same?

2

MADE FOR THE TIMES

We all have a plain choice in life — either we are made by the times or we are made for the times. Our relationship with God determines which we will be. Elijah was certainly made for his time. Are you?

3

BE WHAT YOU ALREADY ARE

According to Scripture there had already been a drought for six months before Elijah went to King Ahab with the devastating news that there would be no more rain until he said so! (1 Kings 18 : 1, Luke 4 : 25). What was more, he informed the king there would be no dew either. It must have taken a lot of moral courage to say such a thing but then Elijah had already had an answer to his prayer six months before he got to Ahab. Those who have proved God find earthly power trivial in comparison. No matter

June

how formidable the foe, the person who has tasted the sweet victory of answered prayer is not afraid of what man can do when compared with what God is doing. Notice those very vital words in his message to Ahab 'As the Lord God of Israel lives, before whom I stand, there shall be no dew nor rain these years except at my word'. Elijah was deeply aware that he was living his life before God. He was consciously aware that God's eye was upon him.

Behaviour on a motorway is greatly influenced when traffic passes before a stationary police vehicle, the pupils behaviour is influenced by the headmasters presence, conversation is influenced in a drawing room between two people when a third party comes in. Our God is not a policeman, nor is he anything like a headmaster, he is beyond human comprehension in the fullest sense but he is our Heavenly Father. We do not wish to grieve him, we want to obey his word and bring pleasure to his heart so whether it is 'pillow talk' or 'public talk' let us remember he is listening. Whether we fly to work on Concorde or take the No. 28 bus we will live our lives before him. It is not just when we meet together to worship that we act 'before him', it is in private as well. It seems to me that Elijah knew and proved God in such a way that when he burst on the public scene he epitomised the little phrase 'Be what you already are'. That's why he had power.

4

COMMITMENT

A great principle now came into operation in the life of Elijah because God always rewards obedience. 'The Word of the Lord came to him, saying get away from here and turn eastward and hide by the brook Cherith, which flows into the Jordan'. This was no easy command to follow but because the Lord went with him that was all that mattered. Cut off from friends and relatives, facing solitude and loneliness, Elijah proved to be more than a voice; 'He went and did according to the Word of the Lord for he went and stayed by the brook Cherith which flows into the Jordan'. Notice those words; 'he went and stayed'. Many of us have accepted the fact that God wants us in a certain place for a specific time but when we get there do we stay there? Commitment is not a thing the latter part of the 20th century majors on. It certainly did not seem to be the kind of place for Elijah to prepare for a national spiritual awakening but that is exactly what it was. Are you committed to the will of God for your life?

5

SERMONS FROM BIRDS

I remember a man from Liverpool once telling me how that Elijah was fed by 'waiters with black tails'. He was of course absolutely right for God had said 'And it will be that you shall drink from the brook,

June

and I have commanded the ravens to feed you there'. The ravens brought Elijah bread and meat, morning and evening. Humans carrying him food would have given away his hiding place, even a dog going back and forward every day would have aroused suspicion but ravens seemingly carrying to their young would not have caused anyone to follow them to their destination. So God had his servant covered.

Shall I ever forget walking through a busy Manhattan Street amid chock-a-block traffic and teeming New York crowds one summer's day? I had a lot on my mind. Suddenly I heard a sparrow chirping and couldn't believe my ears. Yes, there he was on top of a traffic light while the frantic, hurrying 20th century rushed by. It didn't seem to worry him at all as he chirped away contentedly. Famous words of the Lord Jesus flashed into my mind; 'Are not two sparrows sold for a copper coin? Not one of them falls to the ground apart from your Father's will do not fear therefore; you are of more value than many sparrows'. I stopped on the street with the thought of it. 'I saw it "hit" you', said a Welsh friend walking beside me for I had said nothing. 'The same thing happened to me during the awful depression of the thirties when I was unemployed, only God sent a sparrow to land on my foot!' We both worshipped God on that Manhattan Street together.

GOD SOLD THE CATTLE

I love Professor Howard Hendrick's story of the famous Dallas Theological Seminary, which shortly after it was founded in 1924 came to the point of bankruptcy. All the creditors were going to foreclose at 12 noon on a particular day and that morning the founders of the school met in the President's office to ask God to intervene and provide. The famous Bible Teacher Dr. Harry Ironside was there and when he came to pray he said 'Lord, we know that the cattle on a thousand hills are thine. Please sell some of them and send us the money'.

While they were praying a tall Texan with boots on and an open collar walked into the business office and explained that he had just sold some cattle in Fort Worth and had been trying to make a business deal go through which wouldn't work. He didn't know whether or not the Seminary needed money but he felt God was compelling him to give his 'cattle money' to the Seminary. The little secretary took the cheque, thanking him for it, then went and timidly tapped the door of the President's office. When she finally got a response she handed the cheque to the President, Dr. Chafer, who recognised the cheque's signature as the name of the cattle man from Fort Worth. 'Harry', he said turning to Dr. Ironside, 'God sold the cattle!'

June

7 ———————————

FAITH MUST BE TESTED

But Elijah's brook dried up. 'It came to pass', says one translation, 'after a while', says another, 'At the end of days', says the A.V. margin, 'The brook dried up'. Everything is transitory, even water. Cherith would not flow forever, not even for a prophet. You can't run away from trouble in this world because there is no place that far. Faith must be tested. The ravens would still have come but a human being cannot last long without water.

I can see him yet, that friend of mine, as I poured out my troubles to him. My brook was drying up and I was desperate. With a glint of Irish fire in his eyes he turned to me; 'You're being tested', he said 'God is testing you'. The scene changed and I sat in the home of a Scottish christian leader. The sheer loneliness of living for God was getting to me. It is often a very lonely path to follow the Lord. I moaned by his fireside. 'And did you think you would escape?' he said leaning forward, 'Your Lord did not escape loneliness and did you think you would?' I blushed with shame. The drying brook, of course, was in God's plan for the nation. Elijah had prayed for drought and he must suffer the result but also notice he did not move until God told him to.

Are you unemployed? Frightened? Panicing? Do you have itchy feet? Are you 'raring' to go? Be careful. God had to train Elijah and he had to train him to trust. Trust he did for we do not read that he made any moves to go anywhere until he got instructions from the Lord. If God has promised to supply all our needs according to his riches and glory by Christ Jesus there is no point in our trying to find out how God will do this. Our responsibility is to believe that he will.

8

HE BENDS BUT NEVER BREAKS

'When God wants to drill a man, and thrill a man and skill a man, when God wants to mould a man to play the noblest part; when he yearns with all his heart to create so great and bold a man that all the world shall be amazed, watch his methods, watch his ways! How he ruthlessly perfects whom he royally elects! How he hammers him and hurts him and with mighty blows converts him to trial shapes of clay which only God understands: while his tortured heart is crying and he lifts beseeching hands! How he bends but never breaks when his good he undertakes; how he uses whom he chooses and with every purpose fuses him; how every act induces him to try his splendour out — God knows what he's about.'

9

'NARROW FIRST: WIDER LATER'

Put yourself in Elijah's position. What would you have done? Most of us would have scrambled up the sides of the river Cherith, left the vicinity as quickly

June

as possible, muttering in our hearts. 'I must do something'. The plain fact was that the dried up Cherith was an answer to Elijah's prayer. If Elijah had cried 'What on earth are you doing to me Lord?', the answer would have been, 'I'm answering your prayers, Elijah! You asked for no rain and that's why the brook is drying'. We may have asked for strength so God sent us circumstances that made us feel weaker that we might prove his strength. You may have asked for wider circumstances, larger coasts to sail along, bigger pools to fish in, higher mountains to climb, a wider view from your front window but God put you in even more restricting circumstances that you may learn more of Him; you and I must learn how wide He is, how deep He is, how broad a view He has of history and the future. One day your Mount Carmel experience will come but for the moment you must go to your Zarephath in order to have your mountain top experience.

10 ⎯⎯⎯⎯⎯⎯⎯⎯⎯⎯⎯

WE KEN HIS FAITHER

Zarephath! Why, Zarephath was not even in Israel! It was the city of the Phoenicians between Tyre and Sidon on the Mediterranean coast. The ruins of the ancient town still survive about eight miles south of Sidon and fourteen miles north of Tyre. What is more, it was the country and town of Jezebel, the wife of king Ahab, Elijah's enemy. Hard enough to travel an almost 100 miles journey, presumably on foot through drought stricken country; hard enough for a prophet of Israel to go to a Gentile town to be provided for by a widow woman of the town; hardet of all to go to the town of Israel's greatest enemy! The Saviour's comment on the event shows very clearly that God understood what it cost Elijah to go to Zarephath. 'Assuredly', he said 'No prophet is accepted in his own country. But I tell you truly, many widows were in Israel in the days of Elijah, when the heaven was shut up 3 years and 6 months and there was a great famine throughout all the land; but to none of them was Elijah sent except to Zarephath in the region of Sidon, to a woman who was a widow'. Think of it! Thousands upon thousands of widows purported to serve God in Israel but none of them could be trusted to recognise the gifted prophet and treat him with the respect he was due as God's man for the hour.

Have you not noticed that as soon as God begins to use someone mightily the people of their own town or village, city or country begin to cut them down to size? In Scotland they have a phrase for it; 'Sure', they say 'we ken his faither'. (We know his father). People chip in with comments about the person's childhood faults or teenage foibles. Honour is the last thing they will give the person being used by God. It seems very clear from the Saviour's comments that no widow in Israel would have given her last meal to the prophet from the hills of Gilead. A Gentile would, though. Let this be a lesson to all who serve the Lord; honour will come to you from sources you never dreamt of. Let this also be a lesson to all who would particularly seek to

June

encourage those who serve the Lord; if one passes your door, today, be kind. I would guarantee the widow of Zarephath was not sorry she helped a lonely prophet from Gilead.

11 ————————————

THE LURE OF SOFTENING THINGS

Let us never underestimate the greatness of Elijah in his similarity to Christ's great forerunner, John. Both these men were very similar in spirit and in their ministries. They were both anointed with the same Spirit and power. Both were familiar with deserts and solitude. They both wore the same kind of clothing and lived simply. Both were fearless and unafraid to rebuke things and were sought to be killed by kings. Both were prone to discouragement. Both were preachers of righteousness. Both incurred the enmity of a queen. Both were fruitful in their ministry. Both had a tremendous influence over Israel. The two men were both subjects of prophecy. Both had a lapse of faith but quickly recovered. Both were, of course, prophets. Would to God we had people with such great, determination and godliness today. We could all do with a stirring. Agreed? We have been lulled asleep by the lure of softening things. May the Lord deliver us.

12

THE REFINER'S FIRE

It is interesting to remember that Zarephath in Hebrew means 'the place of refining'. Refining is the process by which dross is separated from fine gold. It is a long process because impurities are many. Today rock is first broken and water has to be fed into the steel boxes where the rock has been crushed. This turns the powdered rock into pulp. The gold particles have then to be separated from the pulp by allowing them to flow over mercury. Mercury dissolves the gold which has to be heated to get the mercury to boil off. The gold is then cleaned with acid and melted into crude bullion but even then it is still impure and must be refined to purify it. Today this is done by electrolysis or by treating molten gold with chlorine gas which causes impurities to collect in a crust on the surface.

To bring such a crust to the surface in a believer's life is also a long process. The man who was to bring down fire from heaven by faith had to go through the refiner's fire himself, first. So will you.

13

AT BOTH ENDS OF YOUR LINE

To the average person the woman gathering sticks at Zarephath was merely a woman gathering sticks, but in fact, every bend of her back, every movement of her fingers was being directed by

June

God. God had said to Elijah 'Arise, go to Zarephath, and dwell there. See I have commanded a widow to provide for you. So he arose and went to Zarephath. And when he came to the gate of the city the widow woman was there gathering sticks'. Notice how God was working 'at both ends of the line'. The message came to Elijah at Cherith and when Elijah got to Zarephath God was working ahead of him.

Are you worried about what's going to happen next week? Does what next year is going to bring worry you as you head out to face your day or put your head on your pillow, now, to sleep? Don't let it frighten you, God is working at both ends of your line too.

_____ **14**

TRUST GOD IN YOUR HOME LIFE

It was a very difficult request that Elijah gave to the widow of Zarephath when first he met her. 'Please bring me a little water in a cup that I may drink', he asks. There was little water about, a drink of water was a very costly commodity in a severe drought, but the widow went to get a drink for Elijah. She did not ask him any price for it or was there any sign of a 'Who do you think you are' attitude. As she slipped away to get him the water the prophet then tests her to the limit; he asks her what in fact turns out to be a request to share her last meal with him. 'Please bring me a morsel of bread in your hand', Elijah asks. 'As the Lord your God lives, I do not have bread, only a handful of flour in a bin, and a little oil in a jar; and see, I am gathering a couple of sticks that I may go and prepare it for myself and my son, that we may eat it and die'.

As far as the woman of Zarephath was concerned it was the end. She felt her home was finished and maybe you do too. Maybe circumstances in your home are such that you think death through illness stares you in the face, that it will all be over in a week or two, or a day or two. Maybe divorce has ripped your home apart or is threatening to, maybe your business is collapsing through no fault of your own, maybe your home life is non existent because of the fury of your circumstances. Yet, this very woman and her very home was about to sustain one of the greatest of all prophets and was about to see one of the most memorable miracles of Old Testament times. God gave the woman a promise from Elijah that her bin of flour would not be used up nor would the jar of oil run dry until the day the Lord would send rain upon the earth. The woman acted on the promise of God and it was fulfilled perfectly. Are the promises of God not the same today? The woman passed the first great test of her home life and Elijah proved as full of gentleness in her home as he was full of faith and courage in the king's palace. It is a very heartening story for all of us as we face the future. May we too pass the great test of trust in God in our home life today.

June

15

BLAMED IN THE WRONG

The accusing finger went out to the man of God. 'Have you come . . . to kill my son?', said the widow of Zarephath. During the time that Elijah was staying with her, her son had taken sick and died. It must have been a very testing moment for Elijah and it was a very unfair outburst from the widow. Elijah was being blamed in the wrong after showing great kindness, but he did not react as most of us would have reacted in the situation. A kind action can assuage any outburst. He took the lifeless form of the child to his own bedroom. He took the load from her heart to his own and overcoming all prejudices of the country he lived in, Elijah stretched himself out on the child three times. The effectual fervent prayer of a righteous man availed much and the child came back to life and was returned to his mother.

As I have travelled through life I have from time to time come across the comments of cruel people who have wickedly accused another for a death that has happened in their home. The accusations were not accusations of murder but accusations of 'if you had taken her to such and such a doctor she would still be alive' etc. If you have received such assusations react to them with gentleness, compassion and courage. Don't let such hurtful accusations ruin your life. Elijah didn't and neither need you.

SWEAT THE SMALL STUFF

For 1,000 days Elijah waited for God. Tough enough to wait for God at home surrounded by the comforts of friends and family and the sights of familiar things or the smell of bread baked in your own home. Imagine waiting for God to give you a word of guidance while waiting for ravens to feed you beside an ever drying brook and then waiting for up on three years in the home of a poor widow and her son in a town outside of your own country and people. Elijah knew God would send rain but he had to wait 1,000 days for word of it. In those 1,000 days he proved that he could 'sweat the small stuff'.

The Wall Street journal in an article called 'Workmanship' described it in this way; 'Your true value to society comes when someone says, "Let me see your work". Your glib tongue may open a door or two and your artful use of the right folk may win an approving nod. But the real test of your worth can be measured by the care you give to the job in front of you; a budget to plan; a report to draft; a leaky sink that needs fixing. Next time you write a memo, make sure you get all the facts straight. Pay attention to those details. Sweat the small stuff'.

June

17

MAKE EVERY DAY COUNT

'Now it came to pass after many days that the word of the Lord came to Elijah, in the third year, saying, Go present yourself to Ahab'. Notice that God constantly emphasises the importance of days rather than years. 'Therefore do not worry about tommorow, for tomorrow will worry about its own things. Sufficient for the day is its own trouble', said the Saviour. 'So, teach us to number our days, that we may gain a heart of wisdom', wrote David. To the teenager at school, to the Prime Minister at Downing Street, to the Queen of Buckingham Palace, to the bus driver on your local route, to the pilot of a 747, to the broadcaster, to the doctor, whatever, there are 86,400 seconds of time, 1,440 minutes a day given to all of us. It was Emerson who said of days that they 'Come and go like muffled and veiled figures sent from a distant friendly party; but they say nothing and if we do not use the gifts they bring, they carry them as silently away'. Make every day count.

18

SILENCE

Eventually the great day of Elijah's challenge came. He faced Ahab with the stirring words 'Now therefore send and gather all Israel to me on mount Carmel, the 450 prophets of Baal and the 400 prophets of Asherah, who eat at Jezebel's table'. It must have been a great sight when eventually tens of thousands gathered from all over Israel, from Dan to Beersheba and there standing alone is Elijah. Where did he get such courage? How did he endure such pressures of crowds and tension? He endured as seeing Him who is invisible. By far the overwhelming majority as far as human eyes could see were gathered on Baal's side. When Elijah opened his mouth with his immortal challenge 'How long will you falter between two opinions? If the Lord is God, follow Him; but if Baal, then follow him'. There was not a sound from the people. Notice that. Not a sound. Not a 'Praise the Lord!' Not a 'Hallelujah!' Silence. 'But the people answered him not a word'. Was it any different when David walked down the valley to meet Goliath with all Israel's army watching on the sides? Silence! Was it any different for the Saviour of the world when he set off for Calvary via Gathsemane? As he prayed and battled with Satan the only sound he heard was the sleeping disciples. Was it any different as Paul lay in prison in Rome awaiting execution? All the christians in pro Consular Asia were silent. 'No man stood with me', says Paul. Not one to testify for him in a Roman court. Silence, 'Nevertheless', wrote Paul, 'the Lord stood by me'. He is enough! Elijah proved it as have all persecuted ones to this very day. Recently I talked with an Ethiopian christian who had been in prison for his faith. He told me he was very sorry when he was discharged, so great was the joy of the Lord in his life when in prison. John Bunyan, when in prison, had so experienced the blessing of God he said he would have asked for 'The greater sorrow for the greater mercy's sake'.

Elijah was a man who certainly did not please himself. He cared only for the glory of God. He knew he was right in the centre of God's will. He was a servant in God's sight. Show me an individual like that and there is nothing to stop that person experiencing great spiritual blessing. As strategy, such an attitude will keep that person humble and useable.

19

'ANY RIVALS?'

Eventually the prophets of Baal failed to bring any fire upon the sacrifice that they had presented to their god. It was Elijah's moment. It was his hour of triumph. 'Hear me', he cried 'O Lord, hear me, that this people may know that you are the Lord God, and that you have turned their hearts back to you again'.

God heard. The fire fell. The people fell on their faces and cried, 'The Lord, he is God! The Lord, he is God!' Why did God answer so dramatically? It seems to me that Elijah knew what we all need to know, that God himself powerfully uses a heart that no longer shelters rivals to himself within its borders.

20

'WATCH IT'

Elijah did not fear a nation but when Jezebel rounded on him after his victory at mount Carmel, he fled. Was it not fear that first made gods in the world? Nothing is so rash as fear. Watch it.

21

'STAYED UPON JEHOVAH'

Jezebel knew that she could not harm the Lord so she set out to harm his servant. We must not be naive to the fact that earthly hatred against God is often vented on his servants. Elijah should have recognised that this was an attack of Satan, through the guise of Jezebel, but Satan's attacks are not always so easy to recognise.

Did the mighty Noah see, when he planted his vineyard, that it was going to be used of the Devil to disgrace the dignity of his walk with God? Did Abraham see that the Devil could use the love he had for his beautiful wife to bring about the present Arab/Israeli conflict? Did Lot see that the luscious plain that lay before him was to be used by Satan to hew him out of the will of God into a den of homosexuals? Did Moses see that righteous anger against disgraceful unbelief and miserly moaning against God on the part of the children of Israel could be turned by Satan into downright bad temper which would bar him from ever entering into the promised land? Did David ever imagine that his day off from his heavy responsibilities and hectic schedule was going to lead to the blasting of his character? Did Peter imagine that behind the innocent question of a teenage girl lurked the power of Satan which enticed him into the sin of his life?

The scared hero of Israel sitting out in the wilderness under a tree praying 'It is enough! Now, Lord, take my life, for I am no better than my fathers!' is a warning to all of us as to how easy it is to get out of the will of God. Elijah's mind was not stayed upon Jehovah, it was stayed upon Jezebel. We are only kept in perfect peace when our mind is stayed upon God.

22 ——————————

'JUST WHEN THEY NEEDED HIM MOST'

There is a song which circulated around the Western world recently and its words filtered out through airport lounges, restaurants, waiting rooms or wherever. It was a song of lost love and one line of it caught the imagination of millions. It ran, 'Oh! You left me, just when I needed you most'. Elijah's flight and behaviour was not a flight from the responsibilities of a human relationship of love between a man and woman but it was certainly a flight from his responsibilities as one who loved his Lord and had a clear duty to the people of God. When Elijah moved on from under the tree to spend the night in a cave the word of the Lord came to him saying, 'What are you doing here, Elijah?' The emphasis is upon the word 'you'. God is saying, 'Is this a place for a prophet of the Lord? Is this the time for you to beat a retreat and leave the people of God, just when they needed you most?' Elijah answers that he has left them because 'The children of Israel have forsaken your covenant, torn down your altars and killed your prophets with a sword'. Yet there was no excuse for running because God on Carmel had opened to Elijah a marvellous door of opportunity and that particular opportunity never returned again. May the Lord not have to say to us today in our circumstances what he had to say to Elijah. May you not hear the word of the Lord coming to you today, with sadness asking 'What are you doing here?'

23

'ARE YOU DEPRESSED?'

It is true that Elijah made a false step when he ran from Jezebel, yet we must be very careful to show compassion to such a spiritual colossus as Elijah. How would we have faired under such conditions? We probably wouldn't have ever raised our heads to witness for the Lord in such a hostile environment in the first place. Let's investigate some reasons as to why Elijah ran away.

In my experience depression very often plagues my life after some great victory which the Master gives in His work. Ninety people might tell you they have been greatly blessed by a word given for the Lord in public but one criticism, one hurtful jibe, one withering look can throw you. That one jibe you

June

remember — the other ninety blessings you forget. Depression can follow. This is particularly true if you are physically and mentally exhausted. Raw nerves emerge in exhaustion and the ogre of spiritual depression can march in to demolish the citadel of peace in your heart and mind. 'Not one word you have said in seven years has meant anything to me', said a Satan goaded individual to a godly Pastor I know. The next opportunity he had to preach God's word he simply could not face. He very nearly left his ministry for God.

Maybe you are, though you may be the last to realise it, a first class mother. Some jealous tongue has risen to criticise your lifestyle and attitudes to your children and now you sit like Elijah, confidence gone, sparkle dampened, enthusiasm choked and ready to throw in your responsibilities at home. Your children just love you, your husband loves you more than his own life, but you think you are no good. Maybe you are an exhausted elder of the church, loved by a multitude of men and women who looked to you for spiritual help and were not disappointed; now you sit at home and 'mope', no longer is your voice heard in public prayer or ministry and you are in the 'I'm-no-better-than-my-father's' syndrome. You might be the president of a multinational corporation for all I know but, as we say in Ulster, 'You have tripped over a straw and a hen has kicked you!' Don't let that tiny straw trip you. See that hurtful word for what it is, the devil is behind it, and don't let it force you to leave the work God has placed in your hand to do. Let us be very careful the morning after a great blessing because in the cold light of dawn with the crowds gone, the spectacular finished and the nitty gritty of every day reality staring you in the face you will be wide open for the Jezebel's of this world. There are millions of them but God can defeat every single one.

24

THE SAME SIZE IN THE BATH

When God faced Elijah at Mount Horeb as he hid in his cave his answer shows he had a view of himself which was much too egocentric. 'I have been very jealous for the Lord God of Hosts . . . I, even I only am left'. He in fact repeated the statement twice before God. God showed him that there were, in fact, 7,000 in Israel 'All whose knees have not bowed to Baal and every mouth . . has not kissed him'. Elijah when he got down, got depressed and could see only himself but God could see 7,000. No matter how dark the age, the Lord has his faithful ones and let me never think that I am the only one truly faithful. Would you have thought that the seemingly harsh Govenor of Egypt was Joseph in disguise, or the brillant Nicodemus would stand up for the Saviour or the wealthy owner of the garden of Gethsemane would gently bury the Son of God? Let us be humble or soon we will be humble-come-tumble. Let us emulate the attitude of the miner's son, George Thomas, who rose to become Speaker of the British House of Commons. He was asked how he felt when he became the Viscount Tonypandy: 'I'll be the same size in the bath', he replied.

June

25 ————————————

GOD'S WRATH IS AS GREAT AS HIS POWER

'Go out', said God to Elijah, 'and stand on the mountain before the Lord'. One of the most outstanding of all parables then took place before his eyes. A mighty wind, we perhaps might call it a tornado, tore into the mountain and 'Broke the rock in pieces'. But the Lord was not in the wind. Then an earthquake shook the mountain but the Lord was not in the earthquake. Then came a fire, but the Lord was not in the fire. Suddenly there came 'A still, small voice'. Many people speak of this as representing God's tenderness and love but have you ever studied what God actually said to Elijah in that still small voice? He told him of some of the most dire judgements that were coming upon Israel in coming days. 'It shall be that whoever escapes the sword of Hazael, Jehu will kill; and whoever escapes from the sword of Jehu, Elisha will kill'. Just because God speaks quietly does not mean that He is weak. God's wrath is as great as God's power and the worshippers of Baal who had long insulted God were soon to find that the 3½ years of drought had been but a warning. We live in an age which is now virtualy given over to greed, pride, promiscuity and selfishness and the church which preaches the love of God forgets to balance its preaching with the fact of God's wrath. The subject of divine wrath is virtually taboo in modern society but there are, in fact, more references to the wrath of God in the

June

Scriptures than there are to his love and tenderness and Bible writers have absolutely no inhibitions about mentioning the wrath of God. Neither should we.

26

'SOMETHING MONEY CAN'T BUY'

Ahab was pouting. Very valuable property, a vineyard lay close to his palace and its owner Naboth wouldn't sell. 'The Lord forbid', said Naboth 'that I should give the inheritance of my father's to you!'

I reckon Naboth had played under those vines as a child and money would never compensate for losing what money couldn't buy; home. Sure, he would have had plenty of cash in his pocket but what is money compared to walking down your own path and working in a corner of your own vineyard, given to you by God? Another vineyard for Naboth might have been bigger and better but don't you think one ounce of what God gives to you is better than a ton of what the wheeling and dealing Ahab's of this world offer?

I know that money is useful. In fact I sympathise with the late heavy-weight boxing champion, Joe Louis, who said, 'I don't like money, actually, but it quiets my nerves'! Yet Naboth wasn't for giving up what was his godly inheritance, and I think he was a wise man.

June

27

DON'T MARRY THE WRONG WOMAN

Five or maybe even six years have passed and there is silence from Elijah's corner. Did he wonder if he would ever hear the fond accents of the Lord's voice again? Others held the stage in the intervening years, other prophets were sent to carry the word of the Lord (see 1 Kings 20). But now the judgement of God must fall upon Ahab and Jezebel who had murdered poor Naboth for his refusal to sell them his vineyard.

One wonders what Elijah thought as he went down to that vineyard with the message of judgement. This time he certainly did not fear the wrath of Jezebel for he entered the vineyard to face the king with the word of the Lord. 'Thus says the Lord, have you murdered and taken possession?. . . in the place where dogs licked the blood of Naboth, dogs shall lick your blood, even yours'. One after another, Elijah laid out the judgements God had in store for Ahab. 'I have found you', retorted Elijah, 'because you have sold yourself to do evil in the sight of the Lord'. It all came to pass and one day an arrow wounded Ahab and his blood fell into his chariot. When they came to wash it in the fountain of Samaria the dogs licked his blood as predicted. As for Jezebel, she outlived her husband by 20 years but her end came exactly as Elijah had foretold. Only fools flaunt God.

They were dire days, Elijah's days, but there stands one very powerful practical lesson from it all;

Ahab married the wrong woman. All that followed was linked with his union with that devious, godless, heathen idolator. A whole nation was seduced from the Lord because of her. Godly blood soaked Israel's soil as a result of her treachery. No good came as a result of that union between a believer and an unbeliever. The warning is clear and how well I remember sounding it out one morning before hundreds of young people at a Bible study in England. A girl walked out of that study and broke her marriage engagement at the door. When she told me of it, I thought her fiancee might very well break me if he found me! Yet, sentimentality, emotional involvement, physical attraction, seeming compatability, do not change the law of God; 'Do not be unequally yoked together with unbelievers. For what fellowship has righteousness with unrighteousness? And what communion has light with darkness? . . . or what part has a believer with an unbeliever'. I know only too well the loneliness that comes for millions as a result of obeying such a command but the rewards are incalculable. May you know them.

28

PRESSED?

For Elijah it was a lonely path but he discovered that God is the God of the valleys as well as God of the mountains (1 Kings 20:28). Elijah was pressed hard and while the rich around him tried to get richer, he allowed the pressures to bring him closer

June

to God and we can rejoice to know that God touched his life in the valleys with power and blessing. Think about this little poem.

'Pressed out of measure and pressed to all length
Pressed so intently, it seems beyond strength,
Pressed in the body and pressed in the soul,
Pressed in the mind till the dark surges roll,
Pressed by foes and the pressure by friends,
Pressure on pressure till life nearly ends.

Pressed into knowing no helper but God,
Pressed into loving the staff and the rod,
Pressed into liberty where nothing clings
Pressed into faith for impossible things,
Pressed into living a life for the Lord,
Pressed into living a Christ life outpoured.'

29

WHO AM I?

When I think of the great Elijah and how in the end, he became one of the greatest of all the prophets. When I think of what he suffered and particularly of the moods he went through during a lifetime of service to God it reminds me of the great Dietrich Bonhoeffer who described his feelings about his own identity during his long imprisonment at the hands of Hitler from which he was eventually taken and executed. Like Elijah he found the secret not only of overcoming suffering but of overcoming despair itself. The poem is called 'Who Am I?' and I give it to you today in prose form.

'They often tell me I would step from my cells confinement calmly, cheerfully, firmly like a squire from his country house. Who am I? They often tell me I would talk to my warders freely and friendly and clearly, as though it were mine to command. Who am I? They also tell me I would bear the days of misfortune equably, smilingly, proudly, like one accustomed to win.

Am I really then really all which other men talk of? Or am I only what I myself know of myself, restless and longing and sick, like a bird in a cage, struggling for breath, as though hands were compressing my throat, yearning for colours, for flowers, for the voices of birds, thirsting for words of kindness, for neighbourliness, tossing in expectation of great events, powerlessly trembling for friends at an infinite distance, weary and empty at praying, at thinking, at making, faint, and ready to say farewell to it all?

Who am I? This or the other? Am I one person today and tomorrow another? Am I both at once? A hyprocite before others, and before myself a contemptibly woebegone weakling? Or is something within still like a beaten army, fleeing in disorder from victory already achieved? Who am I? They mock me, these lonely questions of mine.

Whoever I am, thou knowest, O God, I am thine!'

June
30

DO THE DUTIES OF TODAY

The end explains everything. The Bible tells us we are to mark and look at an upright man, 'For the end of that man is peace'. It seems to me that Elijah knew he was going to be taken to be with the Lord on a certain day (2 Kings 2:9-10). He knew it would not take place until he had passed through Bethel, Jericho and crossed the Jordan, for the Lord had sent him to all of those places.

We cannot but be deeply impressed by the calmness with which the prophet approached his translation to Heaven. We learn one great lesson from all this; the person who really knows the Lord and who is living for him need make no extra preparation when the Lord summons them to the next world. The best method of awaiting the great exchange of worlds is to go on doing the duties of daily life. When Elijah got the final call we find him doing the work he had been appointed by the Lord to do in the very place where duty demanded his presence at that particular moment.

Let us remember that the school classroom, the hospital ward, the university lecture theatre, the farm, the factory floor are as near Heaven as any church building. Your God given task is just as vital a place to go to as was the Mount of Olives for Christ. We do not know the day when we will be taken to be with the Lord but the lesson from Elijah's last days shows us how we should live as if today were our last. Let us even remember that lesson as we now approach the time for holidays across the nation. It will curb our accesses and temper our joys and work for us an eternal wait of glory.

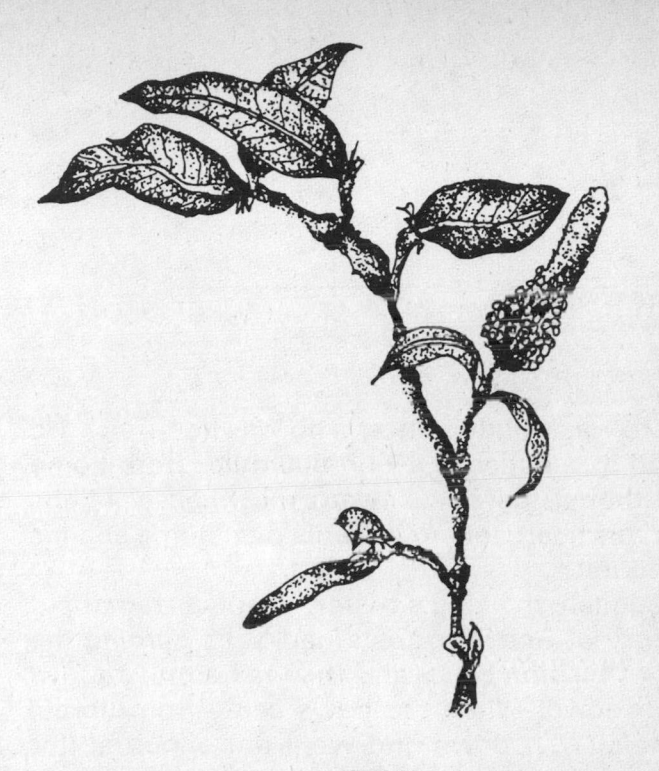

JULY

Pale green on the upper surface, covered with white down on the underside, the leaves of the beautiful white willow have a dazzling silvery appearance when the wind stirs them on summer days. And more: the white willow gives us the cricket bat. It's wood is very light and tough so that it is not liable to warp or split in the course of play.

God has his tough oaks but adds his light touch to his willows. Willow wood was long used to make bowls and plates and was used to make yokes worn by dairymaids when carrying buckets of milk suspended from their shoulders. May you know that Christ's yoke is easy and his burden light as you pass through summer.

July

1

WHAT THE BUTLER SAW

There was a butler, once, who was home sick. He worked as a butler to a king 800 miles from home and, although there never was a more conscientious butler, his heart belonged to his own home and his own country.

Nehemiah, the king's butler, deeply cared about the glory of God. Terrorists had been burning the gates of his home city and the wall around it was broken down. When the news came from home, Nehemiah 'Sat down and wept and mourned for many days'. He even went without food and gave himself to fasting and prayer about the situation. He pleaded the promises of God for his people and nation though physically far from both. Then, to his eternal credit, he waited for God.

For six months nothing happened. Those who wait for God seem to be initially weak and ineffective but, not for long. At the end of six months the king asked his butler why he was so sad. 'Why should my face not be sad, when the city, the place of my father's tomb lies waste and its gates are burned with fire!', he said. 'What do you request?' said the king. If ever there was a telegram prayer it occurred right then. 'So', said Nehemiah, 'I prayed to the God of Heaven and I said to the king'. What a lovely combination; he prayed and said! His answer contained a request for time off work to go and rebuild Jerusalem's wall. The king gave him more than his heart could have wished including passport, wood for the beams of the gates of Jerusalem and time off from his immediate employment to go ahead with his project. Think of it! A heathen king was the answer to Nehemiah's prayers. The lesson is straightforward; don't get a swelled head if the Lord uses you because he uses some mighty strange people!

What the butler saw at Jerusalem would have shattered even the most stout hearted but with resilience and faith Nehemiah rallied the despondent Hebrews and in 52 days the wall was completed.

At the Keswick Convention I was having breakfast with George B. Duncan. I shall never forget him giving me a summary of Nehemiah's life between pieces of toast! In three short sentences he epitomised the amazing feat of Nehemiah the great man of faith and action. 'First, Nehemiah took it to heart', said George. 'Second, he took it to God', he added. 'Third, he took it in hand', he concluded. Those simple headings of the great Bible teacher could well do as our guide posts for all the decisions we will make during this coming month.

2

A LITTLE ROBIN

A little robin comes to my study window regularly and I love to listen to him sing, for he sings whether

July

it be rain or shine. I was fascinated to learn from Mr. Chapman Pincher (Yes, it seems, he of the spy stories) that the red on a robin's breast will rub off! Enough to at least stain a handkerchief. I am not advocating you catch one to find out if this is true but it seems that it is.

The fascinating facts of nature around us make what seems very ordinary, incredibly wonderful. If you were to take a spoonful of seawater from near the surface and look at it through a microscope you would see a 100,000 living things moving around. Did you know that the lot lumped together is called plankton and one acre of the English Channel produces at least five tons of it a year? And take a limpet. It takes a force of 60 pounds per square inch to pull a limpet off a rock when it really puts its foot down.

Did you know that starlings and rooks fly faster than swallows? The starling knocks out 49 miles per hour, the rook 45 and the swallow only 39, though it goes much faster than this for short bursts.

Incidentially one oyster lays 60 million eggs a year but a mushroom only 3 inches in diameter drops 40 million spores an hour and goes on until it has 16 million! Interesting? I could go on but I reckon you are wondering what all these fascinating facts have to do with the subject of waiting for God!

The answer is they remind me of Job. You remember Job? Few men in history have suffered like him. Let us not go into all of his losses now but let us remember that in the end God spoke to Job. What did he say? Did he give Job a doctrinal explanation as to why he had allowed all the trials to sweep over his life? No. God, if I may paraphrase it, said to Job, 'Come for a walk with me'. There was no theology as such, or doctrine either, God just displayed to Job the wonders of nature around him. He gave him a conducted tour and pointed out the fascination of the sea, the snow, the hail, the rain, the stars, the mountain goat, the ostrich, the horse, the hawk, the locust, the eagle, the whale. From the natural world the omnipotence of God was revealed to Job in a way he never saw before. He became a new man. 'I know you can do everything . . . I have heard of you by the hearing of the ear but now mine eyes see you', he said to God. The lesson is clear; let's stop spending our time asking God 'Why?' Go for a walk today, wait and worship.

3

WHEN A TAN WAS UNACCEPTABLE

Millions of people across the country will, during this month, be looking for a tan. Some folk will even lie under sunbeds if the sun does not shine this month to keep up with those who have been able to get away to where the sun is! A tan is a status symbol in some circles but it was the opposite with a lady in the Old Testament. She is called the 'Shulamite', a term which comes, some suggest, from the town of Shunem on the edge of the plain of Esdraelon in Israel. The lady had a real problem. Her story is found in the Song of Solomon.

There was a row in her home. Her brothers were very angry with her and seemed to have banned her

July

from all housework. 'They made me the keeper of the vineyards', she said. It was hard work and as the Shulamite worked under the blazing sun she developed a very dark tan. She felt dishevelled — her hands probably got rough and she felt unkempt. She put it very succinctly; 'My own vineyard I have not kept'.

The Shulamite was brought into the king's palace by the king who thought her exquisitedly beautiful but she felt out of place. She made a strange request to the court ladies; 'Do not look upon me', she said, 'because I am dark because the sun has tanned me'.

It seems that we often, when called upon to wait in the presence of the King of all kings, feel the same as the Shulamite felt, only in a spiritual sense. We feel unworthy, spiritually dishevelled and, like Peter the fisherman, we cry, 'Depart from me for I am a sinful man, O Lord'.

Few of us would preach, pray or witness but that Satan would taunt us with thoughts about our sins, failures, disappointments, mistakes, faults or whatever he could throw in our pathway to prevent us waiting for God, from getting his instructions and going out to do his will.

As far as the one who loved the Shulamite was concerned he had no problems with her view of herself. He called her 'A lily among thorns' and like 'an apple tree among the trees of the wood'. He brought her into the 'banqueting house' and she tells how 'his banner over me was love'.

So it is with your Lord today. Because he has died for you and forgiven you you need not have any fears regarding how he feels about you. Like the Shulamite we need reassurance that we are accepted. Are we? We couldn't be more accepted for in Christ we have the word of the King that nothing can separate us from the love of God which is in Christ Jesus our Lord. So christian, if I may parody Sir Robin Day, 'sleep well!'

4

CURE FOR INSOMNIA

A businessman suffering from insomnia asked a friend how he managed to sleep so soundly every night. 'Don't you count sheep?' he enquired. 'No', replied his friend. 'I talk to the shepherd'.

5

DOES GOD FORGET?

I stood on a skycraper above Fifth Avenue in New York City and gazed down at the city traffic. Round me I could see the towers of the World Trade Centre and the Empire State Building. Over there was Macy's, there was the late Aristotle Onasis's headquarters, there was Broadway. But it was a little garden flourishing on the roof of a section of the skycraper that intrigued me.

The little roof top garden, hundreds of feet above the city, was beautiful. It reminded me of the hanging gardens of Babylon, one of the seven wonders of the world. The gardens consisted of terraces supported on huge masonry arches on which the carefully tended gardens were visible

July

above the tops of the buildings and provided a welcome contrast of greenery against an otherwise unrelieved background of white roofs and an expansive sky. A number of mechanical hoists provided the means by which the water was raised to these elevated terraces.

For the enslaved Children of Israel within the city of Babylon the gardens held little solace. The city area was about 200 square miles and was bounded by double defensive brick walls reinforced with powers and outside this wall was an additional wall of bricks set in bitumen. The outer portion of the twin wall extended over 17 miles.

Even had they been able to scale the walls they still had a 30 day journey over hills, desert and valley to reach home. The prophets promise from God 'Every valley shall be exalted and every mountain and hill shall be made low; and the crooked shall be made straight and the rock places plain', seemed incredible.

They waited for God for ten, twenty, thirty years. They must have wondered, 'Does God forget a promise?' Was it all just 'prophet talk'? Time passed; forty, fifty, sixty, seventy years and still the iron grip of captivity held. Waiting for God often seems like waiting for a promise long forgotten, but the important word is 'seems'. God never forgets a promise. Suddenly Persian troops were at the gates of Babylon under Cyrus. The Babylonians mocked, thinking their city impregnable, and Belshazzar and a thousand of his lords feasted, drinking out of the sacred vessels of the temple of Jerusalem. The siege outside their walls seemed irrelevant in the long term.

They were wrong, for the Persians diverted the waters of a river flowing through Babylon and marched up the bed right into the city. Belshazzar was slain and Cyrus repatriated the enslaved populations of Babylon. Suddenly the Children of Israel found they were going home. They described the experience as being 'Like those that dreamed'. The God who got the Children of Israel home is the same God today. He will get you home too. He never forgets a promise.

6

THE EVERLASTING ARMS

'His money is tainted', said someone to Mark Twain, not liking his friendship with Rockefeller. 'It is, actually, twice tainted', said the famous writer. 'It taint yours and it taint mine!' Sarcasm can be humorous.

'The Honourable Member has sat so long on the fence the iron has entered into his soul', said Lloyd George. Sarcasm can be a put-down.

Isaiah's sarcasm was certainly humorous in one sense, but, for those at the sharp end of it there can be no doubt it was a 'put-down' and it hurt. Yet, they deserved it. Imagine the incident at the fall of Babylon. Here are two Babylonish gods called Bel and Nebo being dragged off their pedestals by soldiers who have no respect for them except for the jewels with which they are studded.

July

The gods are taken by the soldiers and pitched into ox waggons. Once, when the plague swept across the city the people carried them with great pomp and ceremony through the streets. Everything has changed. The gods themselves have been carried into captivity. The situation invited the literary powers of the great Isaiah. He just could not resist it. 'Bel bows down Nebo stoops' he mocks, 'Your carriages were heavily loaded, a burden to the weary beast . . . they could not deliver the burden', (Isaiah 46:1). The bite of his sarcasm is deadly and the brunt of it undeniable.

Wisely, Isaiah issues an invitation to contrast Jehovah with all false gods. He quotes Jehovah speaking of himself; 'I have made and I will bear; even I will carry and will deliver you. To whom will you liken me and make me equal and compare me that we should be alike?' He is the great burden bearer. 'Even to your old age, I am he, and even to grey hairs I will carry you!' says God.

Some people carry a religion all their lives, others let the Lord they know carry them. Some are burdened down with ritual and observances and traditions to which they are deeply committed, others yield themselves to God and are persuaded that he will bear them and carry them as a man bears his son.

Waiting for God involves knowing that underneath and round about are the everlasting arms. Even when we are unfaithful, God is faithful. In those arms we are carried all day long. Trust them, christian, trust them.

THE TENDER TOUCH

As I came home one evening from preaching at a service in Devon, dressed in 'Sunday best', my host, who was a farmer was called to oversee a ewe who was lambing. Off came the jacket as that christian leader got down to business!

I shall never forget that delivery as long as I live. All the time the ewe kept licking him and I enquired why that was. 'Because I was with her in her time of need', replied the farmer who was also a gentle and godly leader at the local church. He could have left the ewe to her own pain and could have gone into supper which had been inviting us in the twilight as we approached the farm, but my host had a shepherd's heart and cared for his sheep. So has the heavenly shepherd.

Is is not terribly sad that we have in our day more than at any other time in human history, a generation that has been raised without a heavenly Father? Millions have worshipped the god of science and their god is hollow; it is a god with no heart and no compassion. Science cannot feel or laugh or show mercy. It can analyse and measure, disect, speculate and weigh but its world is cold, impersonal, relentless and distant. We owe a great deal to true science but those who have made a god of it will regret their action before long. How much better to repent of sin and trust in the lovely Saviour who is the good shepherd who laid down his life for his sheep, rose again, and now feeds them on food which is unsurpassed by anything that this world can offer. 'Behold the Lord God shall come with a strong arm' says Isaiah. So, is God depicted as a tyrant? No. A despot? No. A God without pity? No. He is shown as something entirely different. 'Behold' writes the prophet, 'He will feed his flock like a shepherd; he will gather the lambs with his arm and carry them in his bosom, and gently lead those who are with young'. This is our God.

8 ———————————

DOES GOD PUNISH CHRISTIANS?

She stopped me on the path as I walked with the crowds at Skegness and told me a heart wrenching story. She had had an illness over the last year and someone in her local church told her God was punishing her for her sins.

The girl was a christian and the statement really hurt her. For weeks she tossed and turned with this idea that her illness was a punishment from God and decided if she were that bad she would give up on the christian life. What was the point in going on? She decided to have one last week in a christian environment and came to the New Horizon week at Skegness. It so happened I was led by the Lord to say one morning that God does not punish christians for their sins because that punishment fell on the sacred head of the Lord Jesus at Calvary. She told me she felt like standing up and shouting with joy!

July

The sad thing is that many christians feel God is getting even with them when something goes wrong in their lives. If they sin they feel it is inevitable that God is going to 'get them' for it. If that is your thinking then meditate carefully on the words of Psalm 103:10; 'He has not dealt with us according to our sins nor punished us according to our iniquities'. God's chastening is not what satisfies his justice; the cross is the only thing that satisfies God's justice. Think long on the words: 'The Lord laid on him the iniquity of us all' (Isaiah 53:6). God's justice was satisfied at Calvary. Chastening is not God's 'getting even'. God 'got even' at the cross! So, learn it well. The punishment for your sins is over.

Chastening is inevitable, 'For whom the Lord loves he chastens'. Chastening is painful, but it is only temporal. All chastening is profitable. If a person is being greatly chastened it often indicates that God has a great work for them to do. God is not holding grudges. Chastening is a clear sign that God is not finished with us yet.

If God is chastening you, christian, remember the result could be seen long before you reach Heaven. It will make you daily more like Christ and can only be good. I leave you with this little thought in your mind today. Someone sent it to me once and it has long lingered in my mind. 'For me t'was not the truth you taught; to you so clear, to me still dim; but when you came to me, you brought a sense of Him'. Chastening makes us more like Christ but always remember it is not punishment.

July

9

THIS LITTLE LIGHT

There is not enough darkness in all the world to put out the light of one small candle.

10

BRING YOUR DADDY BACK!

My wife insisted, when she was a school teacher that it would be a good idea for me to go swimming one day with her Primary School class. I went and we had a glorious time splashing and swimming with the children. The next morning a little chap came up to her desk. 'Mrs. Bingham', he said, 'we had a lovely time yesterday at the swimming pool. Could you please bring your daddy back again next week?'

My wife diplomatically tells me that to very small children all men are Daddies. I try to comfort myself with the fact! She may not be right but I am certainly not going to argue with her on the point.

Little children are tremendous, aren't they? They have by nature a sense of wonder and live in a world governed by miracles. When they move on from the fantasy stage which is, in fact, 'artificial' wonder into the colder, practical world of scientific explanation and hard reality, the lovely sense of wonder is lost.

Have you thought, though, of the wonder of a child even in its pre-natal existence? There is no question but that the baby in the womb is a real human being. 'For you have formed my inward part;

240

you have covered me in my mother's womb', wrote David, 'I will praise you for I am fearfully and wonderfully made'. The word 'me' implied that David believed himself to be a real human being when in the womb. The physical development of the baby is one of the greatest of all wonders.

The prophet Jeremiah was called by God to do a very special task. God said to him 'See I have set you over the nations and over the kingdoms to root out and to pull down, to destroy and to throw down, to build and to plant'. The amazing thing is that God said he had set aside Jeremiah to do this work even before his pre-natal existence! 'Before I formed you in the womb I knew you; before you were born I sanctified you and I ordained you to be a prophet to the nation.' Did Jeremiah now gladly wait for God? No, his immediate response was to plead his youth. 'I cannot speak for I am a child', he said. How many of us have done that? We have all pled in our time our youth as a barrier to service for God. We feel that we are too inexperienced to be useful to the Lord.

But God reminded Jeremiah that not only had he chosen him for future service in the womb but long before it! 'Do not say I am a child', said the Lord, 'For you shall go to all to whom I send you and whatsoever I command you, you shall speak. Do not be afraid of their faces. For I am with you to deliver you'.

Tremendous truth is implied in that word of encouragement from God to Jeremiah. You and I are not called to serve God by chance and no excuse will hide us from our responsibility to get on with it. So, whether you be a daddy or but a child, if you know and love the Lord Jesus, get on with his service, now!

July

11 ——————————————

It is a fact that people will not care what you know until they know that you care. Jeremiah cared. The Book of Lamentations is comprised of five epic poems lamenting the problems that he faced in his day.

'Is it nothing to you, all you who pass by?' said Jeremiah the writer of the poems. 'Behold and see if there is any sorrow like my sorrow'. Obviously the desolation was incredible but some folk weren't too worried about it all. The indifference of many to what was happening around them cut Jeremiah to the quick. 'It is nothing to you?' he asks of the people who will not wait for God and search their hearts at the sight of the spiritual declension around them.

Is it any different today? As we see multitudes of people place their faith in our day in the tenets of spiritualism, materialism, automatic writing, clairvoyance and clairaudience we know in our heart that these are false gods. Multitudes are resorting to astrology from listening to an astrologer on breakfast television every morning, to reading horoscopes in papers and ringing the 'Starline'. As Europe moves away from the truth of Scripture the whole fear of living like the heathen did, by the stars, is returning with a vengance!

It is a mercy that God shields us from the future because if we knew what the coming week will hold we might not want to go through with it. The christian knows what the future holds and knows

242

who holds the future. That secret the christian is content to leave in God's hand and, trusting in Christ, the christian has a peace that passes all understanding. Let those who know the power of the Gospel in their lives share it with others for, as we said at the start, they will never care what we know until they know that we care. Care enough today to tell someone of the Lord Jesus. We have a great need of Christ and praise God, we have a great Christ for our need.

12

SITUATION VACANT

This little notice was seen in the window of a shop in Blackheath;

'Mature, dependable, caring Nanny wanted for professional couple. Regular employment caring for twins aged 3, spaniel, cat, tortoise, goldfish, gerbil and canary. Must have a sense of humour'.

Would you qualify?

13

DON'T FLIRT

Are you a flirt? A flirt is dangerous. Ask any girl or fellow who has been in the arms of one for soon the flirt will be in the arms of another.

If you are a husband and you came home to find another man sitting in your favourite chair taking your place in your wife's life, would the ire of

July

jealousy rise in your heart? If you were a wife and found another woman taking your place would you be jealous? If you weren't there would be something mighty wrong with your marriage. Jealousy in life which says I want what you have and I hate you for it is no virtue. Jealousy that moves to protect a marriage relationship which, in God's eyes, is sacred and exclusive is instinctive and right. God even had, in the Old Testament, a provision made for a 'jealousy offering'.

God says over and over again that he is a 'jealous God' and his jealousy is a virtue for it moves to protect his relationship with his people when they flirt with idols. No other god must be allowed to take his place in our hearts. 'For any one in the house of Israel, or of the strangers who sojourn in Israel who separates himself from me and sets up his idols in his heart and puts before him that which causes him to stumble into iniquity', wrote Ezekiel, 'I will set my face against him and make him a sign and a proverb and I will cut him off from the midst of my people. Then you shall know that I am the Lord'. It is no use waiting for God to move and bless in your life if you are all the time worshipping something else, be it the idol of public opinion, reputation, materialism, lust, pride or whatever.

'Son of man', said God to Ezekiel, 'These men have set up their idols in their hearts . . . should I let myself be enquired of at all by them?' Ponder well those words, for a double-minded person is unstable in all their ways and let not that person think that they shall receive anything of the Lord. Let us be warned that when we flirt and are seduced by idols and false gods we will be chastened by our Lord. Nothing is surer. Just stop wherever you are now and ask the Lord for a private, personal temple-cleaning session. Let us never provoke the Lord to jealousy. Remember, if he didn't get jealous when we love other things more than him, the whole relationship would be meaningless. While you wait for God, beware of flirting.

14

A CREATIVE ALTERNATIVE

'Mum', said a friend's little boy on coming home from school one day, 'I wish I was a Roman Catholic'. 'Why is that, son?', asked his mother. 'Because they have the day off school tomorrow and we haven't!', he earnestly replied.

For Daniel, the great prophet of the Old Testament the differences between him and those around him were more distinctive. At the risk of death he refused to eat the king's meat partly, perhaps, because of Jewish dietary laws laid down in Holy Scripture and also partly because of the fact that the meat had been offered first to the Babylonian idols. Imagine the confrontation that threatened when the steward pleaded that even his head would be in danger. Daniel came up with a tremendous creative alternative. 'Please test your servants for ten days and let them give us vegetables to eat and water to drink', he said. The rest is history, Daniel and his friends became not only 'better and fatter in flesh

July

than all the young men who ate the portion of the king's delicacies', but when they were examined by the monarch they were found to be in 'All matters of wisdom and understanding ten times better than all the magicians and astrologers who were in all his realm'. Daniel was a man who truly epitomises what it means to wait for God. Day after day this faithful young man obeyed the Lord, humbled himself and God exalted him.

Daniel would teach us many things but is not the lesson of what he did in providing a creative alternative to confrontation over what he could or could not eat, a lesson to us all? Let us always ask God to give us a creative alternative to confrontation. Instead of whining to your wife that you are under pressure and stress and taking it out on her, provide a creative alternative; get out and do something different — take up carpentry, ride a horse or have a swim. Go for a walk in the park. Leave confrontation behind. Instead of moaning that the work at your local church is pathetic, go and do something about it yourself. When you get up to pray in public, clear your language of well worn phrases and pray from your heart with fresh language instead of stale cliches. Instead of confronting everyone with complaints about how wrong everyone is and how bad everything is and how many problems there are, why not try to be an answer sometime? Be a creative alternative yourself.

15

KINDNESS

There is not a person on the face of the earth who does not understand the language of a kind act.

16

LET THE DEVIL TAKE TOMORROW?

Almost every day I meet it. The breakdown of marriage across the country is just epidemic. Hour upon hour is spent these days counselling individuals whose partners have walked out on them. One in three marriages are breaking down and the unfaithfulness even within marriages still standing is frightening.

There is no simplistic answer to the problem, but with all my heart I believe healing is possible. Hosea the prophet was married to Gomer who was unfaithful to him. After Gomer pursued her lovers she was to be brought back and, with patient love, re-admitted to his home, there to await in penitence and grief the time of restoration to full favour. This was a clear picture of wayward Israel in its relationship with God and showed the unending faithfulness of the Almighty. Gomer's adultery and restoration is a parable for us. God said through Hosea, in words borne out of his heartrending domestic experience, 'I will heal their backsliding, I will love them freely, for my anger has turned away from them. I will be like dew to Israel . . . those who

July

dwell under his shadow shall return; they shall be revived like grain and grow like the vine'.

Those who are unfaithful in marriage cannot be classified. They may be young or old, cultured or crude, spiritual or carnal. The conscience laden Puritan preacher is as likely a candidate as a Casanova. The people call this unfaithfulness freedom; you know the song, 'Let the devil take tomorrow for tonight I need a friend'. They see it tonight as a break from reality, from hours and years of being faithful. They see it as romantic affirmation when as yet there is no past to regret, no future as yet to dread and no present to doubt. Boredom, emotional deprivation and many other reasons are given as an excuse but adultery which seems as soft as down to begin with will become a raving, fiery flaming vulture before it is finished. If you have sinned in this area I implore of you to repent quickly. The longer you delay repentance, the dearer the price you will pay for even a short season of unfaithfulness.

I know a man who left his wife over twenty times and she loved him with incredible forgiving and against-every-odds love. She did not agree with what he did, she certainly did not condone it, but she would not give him up. Others told her to quit but she was not for quitting. She became a legend for christian hope in the midst of absolute hopelessness. That marriage is now healed and I know of no couple whom I love more dearly in Christ. Gomer came back, so did my friend and so can you.

Let the devil take tomorrow? He will take your yesterdays too, and drag you down to hell itself without a regret. Thank God that the greatest barrier to Hell is the cross of Calvary and as Betsie Ten Boom put it 'There is no pit so deep that Christ is not deeper still'. Selah.

17

RESTORATION

The Lord sent a message for Israel through the prophet Joel, once. He said; "I will restore to you the years that the locusts have eaten, the consuming locust and the chewing locust".

Do you not find it comforting that what is impossible in the natural world is possible in God's time in the spiritual life? Lost crops eaten by locusts have haunted Africa in recent years but in a spiritual sense millions look across the years of their lives and are disillusioned. I beg of you to listen to God's word through Joel for God can and will restore to you the years that the locusts have eaten. Your last days can be your very best. You need not end in disillusionment. Repent today of wasted living and return to the Lord and he will abundantly pardon. He can touch what is shrivelled up and make it live.

18

NO STANDARD CHRISTIANS

It is a very dangerous thing to standardise a christian. We must never seek to try to standardise those who love the Lord and seek to serve him.

July

Years ago I heard an old man say he had known 'Long haired saints and short-back-and-sides rascals'.

Amos is a very good example of what I am trying to say. Here was a man who had waited for God in the strictly agricultural environment in which he had grown up. His work had afforded him ample time for meditating on God's laws and their meaning for a nation in deep spiritual decline. But he did not fit the image of a prophet. He was a herdsman of sheep and goats and was engaged in dressing sycamore-fig trees. He did not seem to be a man God would choose to speak to a nation. When he went up to the king's palace to preach they didn't like it. 'Go . . . flee to the land of Judah, never again prophesy at Bethel for it is the king's sanctuary and it is the royal residence', they told him. Amos just did not fit their standards. His words hit home and they did not like it.

Amos was well aware of the fact that he seemed an unusual choice as a prophet. 'I was no prophet, nor was I the son of one', he said. 'Then the Lord took me as I followed the flock and the Lord said to me "Go prophesy to my people Israel"'. In the final analysis that was all that counted. Let us learn the lesson well today that God can use whoever he chooses, wherever he chooses, whenever he chooses and in whatever way he chooses. It could be a stammering Moses or a bigot called Saul of Tarsus — in God's transforming hand such can mould history.

I often think how the Lord was using a Dutchman who loved the poor, and as an Evangelist, was often found among them. Some christians did not like this approach to christian work and constantly discouraged him. They tried so hard to fit him in their mould. He quit and turned to painting and eventually suicide. His name? Vincent van Gogh.

The lesson is clear. Not all who wait for God and obey him may appear to do so. And, if ever you meet one who is a fig picker, treat him with respect.

19

KEEP FALLING IN LOVE

A successful marriage requires one great ingredient. It requires falling in love many times, always with the same person.

20

PUBLIC OPINION IS DANGEROUS

God thought that Jonah was very concerned about public opinion. The great test of a prophet was that his prophecies came true and Jonah had prophesied that the city of Nineveh would be destroyed. When his prophesying was over, Jonah built himself a little shelter and sat down on the east side of the city to wait for God. There was no question in his mind that he was waiting for God to destroy the city.

He waited and waited but there was no sign of any fire or brimstone. What would they say of him back at home? Jonah became very angry. He even asked

July

the Lord to take his life. He reckoned his reputation was ruined. One night God prepared a plant and made it come up over Jonah as a shade for his head to deliver him from his misery. So Jonah was very grateful for the plant but as morning dawned the next day God prepared a worm and it so damaged the plant that it withered. When the sun arose, God prepared a vehement east wind; and the sun beat on Jonah's head so that he grew faint. Then he wished death for himself, and said, 'It is better for me to die than to live'. The miserable reputation-seeking Jonah was now in for one of the most pertinent lessons any man ever received from God.

In very plain language God turned on him and in effect said, 'You care more for a plant than you do for souls. You pity a plant being destroyed and I pity Nineveh in which there are, apart from anything else, at least "120,000 children"'. The implication in all God's warnings is that if people repent they will be forgiven. Even in the words, 'Repent or in forty days Nineveh will be overthrown', the implication is there. God responds to repentance and when Nineveh repented, destruction was averted whether Jonah liked it or not.

I was up in Scotland one day preaching. Some kindly folk had me out to tea and I found myself seated beside Bert Elliot, brother of Jim Elliot the famous christian martyr to the Auca Indians. I got talking to Bert, a lifelong missionary to Peru, and we discussed public opinion and even preacher's opinions about each other. I can hear Bert, even now, as he leaned over to me at that well laden table.

'Remember that verse in Isaiah?', said Bert, 'The one which says that God gave Isaiah the tongue of the learned that he might give a word to him that is weary?' I knew it well.

'Well', he continued, 'The preachers might not have liked Isaiah's word but the weary sure did!'

Jonah could have done with a bit of the Elliot philosophy, and couldn't we all?

21

NO FISHING ALLOWED

If there is one thing I just love to do it is to water-ski in the ocean. I've skied on Lake Windermere and across a Scottish lough. I have skied by river banks and under bridges, but there is nothing to compare with the tingling exhileration of skiing across the ocean swells or hitting an ocean wave at speed and being knocked off balance and being pitched into the oceans depths! No river or lough gives such a feeling of vastness and no fresh water lake gives such a feeling of depth.

The ocean is used by God to get across his spiritual truth to us in the book of Micah. Micah writes 'Who is a God like you, pardoning iniquity and passing over the transgression of the remnant of his heritage?' He does not retain his anger forever because he delights in mercy. He will again have compassion on us, and will subdue our iniquity. He will cast 'all their sins into the depths of the sea'. Just think of the beauty of the imagery chosen to describe a person who has known God's

July

forgiveness. God has cast 'all their sins into the depths of the sea'. Someone with time on his hands once calculated there are 32 million cubic miles of sea water alone and each mile weighs 4,314,996,900 tons. Multiply those two and you have got the weight of the sea — 1,380,799,008,000,000,000 tons! The sea, miles deep at some points, is used by God to describe where he had put forgiven sins. Remember, once those sins are gone there is a little sign God has put there, reverently speaking, which reads, 'No fishing allowed!' Let's rejoice in the great truth of the little chorus 'Gone! gone! gone! gone! Yes, my sins are gone, now my soul is free and in my heart's a song. Buried in the deepest sea, yes, that's good enough for me, I shall live eternally, praise God, my sins are gone!' Praise God for Calvary.

22

ENOUGH IS AS GOOD AS A FEAST

As for a little money and a little more time, why its ten to one, if either one or the other would make you one whit happier. If you had more time, it would be sure to hang heavily. It is the working man who is the happy man. Man was made to be active, and he is never so happy as when he is so. It is the idle man who is the miserable man. What comes of holidays, and far too often of sightseeing, but evil? Half the harm that happens is on those days. And, as for money — Don't you remember the old saying, 'Enough is as good as a feast?' Money never made a man happy yet, nor will it. There is nothing in its

July

nature to produce happiness. The more a man has, the more he wants. Instead of it filling a vacuum, it makes one. If it satisfies one want, it doubles and trebles that want another way. That was a true proverb of the wise man, rely upon it; 'Better is little with the fear of the Lord, than great treasure, and trouble therewith'.

Benjamin Franklin

23

A FILM WITH A DIFFERENCE

I was in Japan and a friend of mine there told me a fascinating story of the truth of the resurrection of Christ. A Japanese man entered the cinema one day where there was a film being shown about someone called Jesus Christ. The man was totally ignorant of the facts of Christ's life and settled down to watch with interest. When it came to Christ's death he thought the film was over and decided to slip out of the cinema before the crowds milled out. To his surprise no one followed. He stood on the steps and waited. No one came out. The man was so intrigued he went back into the cinema and to his surprise the film was continuing with the story of the resurrection of the dead Christ.

A few days later the man went to the dentist and got into conversation about the strange film he had seen. 'Did you know', he said, 'The story had Christ rise from the dead. Just think of that. It seems incredible!' 'I know', replied the dentist, 'Because the Lord Jesus Christ now lives in my heart!' The

July

dentist's patient almost fell out of the chair! A few weeks later that same dentist's patient was converted to Christ through the witness of the dentist and became a christian evangelist himself! By the time I visited Japan the evangelist was in his eighties and had led a long life of faithfulness to his resurrected Lord. It may be true that you are going through a rough time today but the great truth of Christ's resurrection is your hope. Let us sing Habakkuk's great hymn of faith today as we wait for God in our lives; 'Though the fig tree may not blossom, nor fruit be on the vine; though the labour of the olive may fail, and the field yield no fruit; though the flock be cut off from the fold and there be no herd in the stalls — yet I will rejoice in the Lord, I will joy in the God of my salvation. The Lord is my strength; he will make my feet like deer's feet and he will make me to walk in my high hills'. Go to it!

24

A QUALITY OF KINDNESS

Once a certain Duke of Norfolk happened to be at the railway station when an Irish girl arrived off the train with a very heavy bag. She had come to be a maid at the castle.

The castle was about a mile from the station and the Irish girl was trying to persuade a porter to carry her heavy bag to the castle, for which she offered him a shilling, all the money that she had. The porter contemptuously refused. The Duke stepped forward, shabby as usual in appearance and offered to carry her bag to the castle. He then took her bag and walked beside her along the road to the castle talking to her. At the end of the journey, he gratefully accepted the shilling she offered him, never allowing her to know who he was; and it was only the next day, when she met her employer, that the girl knew that the Duke of Norfolk had carried her bag from the station to the castle and that she had tipped him a shilling!

In the last analysis, to the truly great man or woman, no act of service can possibly be humiliating. No task if it is going to help anyone else, can possibly be beneath their dignity.

25

PLOUGH ON WITH THE VISION

Have you ever found that if you have a vision for something and start working towards it, it seems to die before it comes to pass?

It is the corn-of-wheat-in-the-ground principle. A corn of wheat lies long in the frozen and hard earth before it ever emerges on your breakfast table in the form of bread. Anybody who has ever had a vision for something knows this death of a vision problem.

When Thomas Hardy first sent his poems to magazines they would not publish them, yet he was buried in Poet's Corner in Westminster Abbey! Handel composed the 'Messiah' under a cloud of misfortune and disappointment but whoever thinks of that as they thrill to the sound of the 'Hallelujah chorus'? The blind Milton wrote 'Paradise Lost' and

July

'David Copperfield' came from the childhood suffering of Charles Dickens. Robert Louis Stevenson showed no trace of the boredom of an invalid's life in 'Treasure Island'.

If such death and resurrection of a vision are true in the secular world, what of the spiritual? Do you think that the vision of getting to the Promised Land sank virtually out of sight when Moses saw the behaviour of the Children of Israel as they danced around the golden calf? What of Ruth gleaning corn or Esther weeping to the king on behalf of her people or Nehemiah facing the sarcasm of his enemy as he tried to rebuild the walls of Jerusalem? 'Why even a fox could knock down your wall!' sneered Nehemiah's enemy. What of Paul lashed and bleeding and left half dead or Timothy despised for his youth? All God's faithful servants have suffered immensely and found that God used their very different circumstances to show his grace was sufficient for them and his strength was made perfect in weakness. That kept vision alive in their hearts and mind.

I encourage you, weary one, to plough on with the vision God has given you. Let God's written promises of a harvest encourage your heart. The word of the prophet Habakkuk is the word for you and for me; 'Write the vision and make it plain from tablets that he may run who reads it. For the vision is yet for an appointed time. At the end it shall speak, and not lie; though it tarry wait for it; because it will surely come, it will not tarry'.

July

26

THE THINKER

"It is not what you think you are: it is what you think—you are!"

27

RUBY SHOWS THE WAY

In America he would be called 'Ivy League'. Time magazine has named him the most influential psychiatrist in the United States. A Harvard Professor, he has written more than a million words, read by millions of people. One day he made a simple but amazing personal discovery. Professor Coles discovered spiritual truth through a child.

As he was driving through the dingy, industrial district of Gentilly in New Orleans one day he noticed State Troopers had cordoned off the main roads because of a racial disturbance. Coles drove over to see what the commotion was. It was there he saw a six year old black girl called Ruby Bridges. Ruby was the first black child to attend Frantz school and all the other students were boycotting the school in protest.

Escorted by policemen, Ruby had to walk to school through a mob of white people who were screaming and yelling and waving their fists. Coles thought Ruby would make an ideal subject for

July

studying the effects of stress on young children. At first Ruby and her family were distrustful but they eventually co-operated. Coles wondered how he would have responded under similar circumstances. He would have called the police but in New Orleans the police were not on Ruby's side. He would have called his Lawyer but Ruby's family neither knew nor could have afforded one. He would have explained the mob's behaviour in the language of psychiatry, but then Ruby didn't know the language of psychiatry. Ruby was only learning to read and write.

What did Ruby do? Amazingly she did something very simple. She prayed. She prayed she would not be afraid, she asked for strength and that God would forgive her enemies. 'Jesus prayed the same thing on the cross', she told Coles, 'Forgive them for they don't know what they're doing'. In Coles book, this was not the philosophy of a six year old child from a 'culturally deprived' family. The more he studied the children of the poor the more he found courage and strength, and the more he studied the children of the rich the more he found boredom, alienation and decadence. 'Nothing', Coles had commented, 'that I have discovered about the make ups of human beings contradicts in any way what I learned from the Hebrew prophets and from Jesus and the lives of those he touched. I have known human beings who, in the face of unbelievable daily stress respond with resilience, even nobility and I have known others who live in a comfortable even luxurious environment and yet seem utterly lost. Bibical tradition belongs in our Universities and it's a privilege to call upon it as a teacher'.

Professor Coles testimony to the relevance and power of Scripture makes the words of Haggai, the prophet ring again in our generation with fresh analysis of the human dilemma. 'You have so much and bring in little; you eat, but you do not have enough; you drink but you are not filled with drink; you clothe yourselves but no one is warm; and he who earns wages, earns wages to put into a bag with holes'. Only in Christ and in Christ alone can true satisfaction be found. May we spread God's word as it is written and live it as Ruby did. Waitng for this world to satisfy us completely will be a waste of time. Waiting for God will bring satisfaction beyond compare.

28

DOUBLE TROUBLE

If a man could have half his wishes, he would double his troubles.

29

THE HIRELING

One day I walked into an Art Gallery. Musing on the paintings I was suddenly arrested by a large canvas called 'The Hireling' by Holman Hunt. In a glass case below, a letter from Holman Hunt to the

July

curator of Art at the Gallery explained what he was trying to say in his painting. The explanation was fascinating.

On a bank, in the painting, sat a young man in shepherd's garb. He was a hireling brought in for a few pennies to stay with the flock for a very short time. His heart was not in his work; he could not have cared less about the sheep. He is talking to a girl about a death head moth which he has in his hand, an object of superstition in England. While the hireling and the girl surmise what omen the moth had brought, two of the sheep are in a field eating the corn. They are as good as dead because if sheep eat corn their stomachs become bloated and they die.

This image, the artist explained, was like those who claimed to be shepherds of Christ's flock who speculate on mere superstition from their pulpits — while their flock head for perdition. The rest of the flock in the painting are all, meanwhile, standing, apart from two sheep who are sick and lying down because sheep will only normally lie down when they feel secure and safe. This flock feels neither. On the opposite side of the bank are little yellow marshmallow flowers which only grow where the ground is marshy and wet. The hireling has got his flock on the wrong feeding ground and they will develop foot rot. Holman Hunt was making a very powerful statement about the absolute necessity of caring shepherds. If there are those who are merely hirelings in positions of authority over the flock, the scattering of the flock is bound to follow. 'Woe to the worthless shepherd who leaves the flock', says the Lord through Zechariah.

Thank the Lord for the new generation of shepherds rising to feed the flock of God in many places across our land. It is heartwarming to know they care because wolves have decimated many christian churches. The best way to revive a flock is to put food, compassion, care and godly earnestness into the pulpit. When there is drivel in the pulpit there is drift in the pews. The work of God and the feeding of his people is too sacred a thing, too solemn a work to be toyed with.

It is reassuring to know that our Lord Jesus is no hireling. As we wait for him, he waits for us. His people will always be eternally secure. We will always be spiritually fed on the right food. He will never leave us nor forsake us. I love the story of the old lady in the Highlands of Scotland. Her minister called to comfort her with the words of the Lord's promise to never leave us nor forsake us. 'You understand the Hebrew meaning of that word "never" is a seven times emphasis. It reads "I will never, never, never, never, never, never, never leave you!' he said.

'Ah, your reverence', said the old lady, 'For an intelligent man like you God might have to say it seven times but for an old lady like me, once is enough!' So it is for all of us and with such a good shepherd we lack nothing.

July

30

DO IT TO IT!

What is the best form of advertisement? Do as you promise.

31

TRY THIS FOR SIZE

Imagine you are in hospital and are seriously ill. After weeks of treatment your health improves and your surgeon arrives at your bedside to have a talk with you. Let's say he begins to describe all the things he had done to you in gory detail. Would that cheer your wearied mind and lift your depressed spirits? I doubt it. Yet, if that surgeon were to sit down by your bed and with a warm smile and were simply to say, 'We are going to let you go home tomorrow', how would you react? Your heart would leap and your depression would disappear. Why? The answer is very simple; a promise is much better than an explanation!

Would you not live the life of faith by mere explanation. Faith breeds on promises. We have travelled across the Old Testament in these studies together and time and time again we have seen that the characters who have believed the promises of God and waited for him did not have explanations to lean on. They leaned on promises. Today our promise is from the last book of the Old Testament, it is from Malachi. Sometimes I wish some would take up the challenge that God makes when he says to his people through Malachi, 'Bring all the tithes into the storehouse that there may be food in my house and prove me now on this . . . see if I will not open for you the windows of heaven and pour out for you such blessings that there will not be room enough to receive it'. The explanations for all our trials and sorrows will come in a future day. God has promised if we put him first he will pour us out a blessing so large that there will not be room enough to contain it. Go on, prove him today!

AUGUST

The Ragwort, so unloved by farmers, makes a very handsome show in August and you will find all over the woodland the tall clumps of the nettle-leaved Bellflower, adorned with its numerous bell-shaped, bright purple flowers. Butterflies are all over the wood, Small Tortoiseshells, Meadow Browns and Gatekeepers by the thousand with Holly Blues and Small Coppers. Everywhere you'll find ladybirds, the seven-spot, the two-spot and the twenty two-spot variety.

Notice the Elm tree with its famous winged seeds. In many parts of the country thousands of elms have been destroyed by Dutch Elm disease. This is a minute fungus which blocks the flow of sap and kills many of the trees attacked. No strain of elm has yet been found immune to the disease.

Let us, particularly on this holiday month, be careful that we do not let anything block our way to maintaining our spiritual food supply. Prayer and Bible Study are absolutely vital and such sap will maintain our spiritual growth. Mark my words.

August

1

'VIVE LA DIFFERENCE!'

For the next month we shall concentrate on the least obeyed passage of all Scripture; the Sermon on the Mount. This is the kernel of the New Testament and its key verse is Matthew 6 : 8; 'Therefore do not be like them'. Right through the Sermon this powerful theme is taught and elaborated upon. Followers of Christ are to be different. They are to glory in the fact that they are different. In every paragraph of the Sermon on the Mount the contrast is between christian and non christian.

Are you glad, christian, that you are to be different or does it embarrass you? God forgive you if it does. We are to be different in our ethics, our devotion, our lifestyle, our ambition, and in all our relationships with others. Sham must go. We are to be the alternative to the self-centred, egotistical age around us. How do we measure up? The saddest thing that could ever be said about us is 'But you are no different from anybody else'. As you stay in that hotel on some Spanish island or on that campsite in France; as you visit your relatives in North America and wander around Disneyland or quietly stay at home and go fishing this summer may you pray in your heart; 'Lord, I am yours and because of that I'm different.' Vive la difference!

'A REAL STAR'

'And seeing the multitudes, he went up on a mountain and when he was seated his disciples came to him. Then he opened his mouth and taught them, saying . . .'

What he taught has brought more stir than any other teaching ever given by anyone. Some folks say Christ was teaching a 'Social gospel'. Communists even say that the Sermon on the Mount is really what they are about. The great Russian novelist Tolstoy claimed that because Christ said in the Sermon 'Judge not that you be not judged' he was not to recognise the courts of law and the police! Some christians teach that the Sermon on the Mount applies to the time when our Lord will return and set up his Kingdom on earth and that the Sermon on the Mount will then be truly lived: it is only meant for the kingdom age and has nothing to do with us! That explanation would mean that a christian can no longer say that they are the salt of the earth and would ignore all the Sermons gracious promises for God's people today.

The answer of course is that the Lord Jesus died in order that I might live the Sermon on the Mount. The beatitudes show me my need of the new birth and leads me to the Gospel and all it can do. The beatitudes are a highway to believing. The Sermon on the Mount is the most relevant and powerful teaching you can ever know. It states Gods demands and points to Gods supply. Don't shrink it, my reader, go for it and by God's grace live it. It will turn your world upside down.

August

3

A PORTRAIT OF YOU?

'Blessed are . . . for they shall'. The beatitudes are our Lord's portrait of the christian. Notice that they are very different to the gifts of the Spirit given to different christians in order to help them in a particular service to which they are called. These lovely christian graces known to us as the beatitudes are to mark ALL christians, everywhere.

Notice that just as the eight qualities are described so eight blessings are given. Remember the lovely word 'blessed' is not just describing what these people feel like but what God thinks of them. When God says something is 'blessed' then 'blessed' it is. This is not just God's portrait of an Amy Carmichael or a Francis Ridley Havergail. It is not God's portrait of a Hudson Taylor or a John Bunyan; this christian, is you. Be what you are!

4

THE POOR IN SPIRIT

'Blessed are the poor in spirit . . .' I'll tell you one thing the world does not believe. It does not believe that the way to success is through being poor in spirit. Check out the latest techniques taught in 'schools' of salesmanship to employees of multinationals.

Self-reliance, self-confidence and self-expression, top the list.

August

'Success, success in my hand I bring,
To my company 'product' I firmly cling,
To Yves St Laurent I come for dress,
To my company 'boss' I look for grace,
Confident, I, in Concorde fly,
Let me be a Yuppie or else I die'

The words, 'Blessed are the poor in spirit', does not mean that christians are weaklings or lacking in common sense, it simply means that they do not look to education, position, or money to transform them. The poor in spirit do not look to themselves but to God. It is a lovely quality.

5

NO PERMANENT GRIN

'Blessed are those who mourn'. Does this mean 'Happy are the unhappy?' No. This means the sorrow of repentance. Is the christian life not all joy? I believe every christian joy is tinged with sorrow, the sorrow that even as we glory in the cross we are aware that it was our sins that put Christ there. Do you think God was filled with joy as Christ died on the cross? There was sorrow in Heaven that day. Remember the Bible does not say there will be no tears in Heaven, the Bible says that God shall wipe away all tears. Nowhere in Scripture am I told that the christian has to go around with a permanent grin. Twice our lovely Lord wept in public. Once over

August

the grave of Lazarus and once over a city called Jerusalem. If we were filled with the Spirit more we might weep more for the condition of our land. The christian has a deep doctrine of sin and a high doctrine of joy. Let's get it in balance.

6

WHICH WORLD?

'Blessed are the meek'. This is the quality of humility and gentleness. It is as having nothing and yet possessing everything. You can afford to be magnimonious, christian. Why? Because the meek shall inherit the earth. 'But if you go to Ireland and preach you will never get on in this world!', said someone to a friend of mine. 'Which world are you talking about?' he answered. One day christians will live and reign with Christ and there will be a new heaven and a new earth for them to inherit. Be meek and you'll win, eternally, if not immediately.

7

GIVE THE OLD MAN SIX MONTHS

'Blessed are those who hunger and thirst after righteousness for they shall be filled'. It is a mark of a true christian that they are hungry and thirsty for righteousness. If you are a believer you stand legally righteous before God; you have a right relationship with God. But there is a moral righteousness that we should look for, an inner righteousness of motive.

We should hunger and thirst for sincerity of heart in our everyday living. There is no excuse for claiming a righteousness that does not reach your home or public life.

The story is told of the chap who was up before the Judge for an offence. He was a christian and pleaded that it was his 'old man' that had committed the offence. This is a phrase used by the apostle Paul to describe the old nature of a christian that wars against the new nature he receives on conversion 'Well, then', said the Judge, 'we will just give the "old man" six months!'

8

MERCY AND GRACE, UNITE

'Blessed are the merciful for they shall obtain mercy'. There is no more beautiful quality in the life of a christian than the quality of showing mercy. To show mercy and to receive mercy are indissolubly linked together. Mercy is compassion for people in need. There is a very clear distinction between mercy and grace. Grace deals with the sin and guilt itself. Mercy deals with what we see of pain, misery and distress. Mercy extends relief, grace extends pardon. Mercy brings healing and help. Grace cleanses and reinstates.

August

9

THE SINGLE MOTIVE

'Blessed are the pure in heart, for they shall see God'. There is nothing worse than having your heart divided against itself. It is, in fact, a tyranny. All around you are people with ulterior motives, manipulators who live for themselves and their own ends. Outwardly they smile, inwardly they smolder. They are always making moves. You feel a real Plain Jane because you are not shrewd and manipulative. Fear not. Live in your every action with a single motive; the glory of God. Even as you go out today, perhaps, on your holiday, do all to the glory of God. Is it possible? Of course it is. Didn't Eric Liddell say 'When I run I feel his pleasure'? If ever there was a man who lived for God's glory and who didn't manipulate it was Eric Liddell. Such lives, count. They become real Chariots of Fire. They also see God.

10

WHAT PRICE PEACE?

'Blessed are the peacemakers, for they shall be called the Sons of God'. Who are the best peacemakers? The pure in heart, I reckon.

The story is told of the parents who had parted because their love for each other had died. Their little child took very ill and the doctors in the hospital in which she lay asked her mother to find her father.

August

The father eventually arrived in the hospital and sat down at the side of the bed, his wife sitting opposite to him. They would not look at each other. All they could do was look at their desperately ill child. Suddenly the child reached out and took her mothers hand and then reached out and took her fathers hand. Drawing both parents hands together across her little chest she held them close. In the process of doing this she died. Tell me, do you think that those parents fought with each other any more?

On the cross of Calvary the Son of God reached out and took his fathers hand and at the same time reaches out for your hand. Only he can bring you together. And he died in the process. Are you still continuing to fight God? Have you rejected the reconciliation offered by the greatest peacemaker of all?

11

No need to be surprised

'Blessed are you when they revile and persecute you, and say all kinds of evil against you falsely for my sake. Rejoice and be exceedinly glad, for great is your reward in Heaven, for so they persecuted the prophets who were before you'. Are you being despised and rejected, slandered and persecuted for the Lord's sake? Notice that this last beatitude is actually a double beatitude. Jesus stated it in the third person like all the other seven and then he repeated it in the direct speech of the second person. To be persecuted for your Lord's sake is as

August

much a normal mark of being a christian as being a peacemaker, meek, poor in spirit, or any of the other qualities which the Saviour spoke of. We are constantly surprised when we are persecuted for being a christian. Let's quit being surprised and start realising that it is normal.

12 ——————————————

I went to school in the town of Downpatrick in Co. Down. I look back on my schooldays with great pleasure and Down High School was, for me, one of the happiest periods of my life. On lots of days I used to call in to a little shop on my way to catch the school bus home. I had one great purpose in mind and that was to buy a packet of Smiths crisps because they had inside every packet a little blue bag of salt. It was lovely to be able to salt ones own crisps! I love salt to this very day.

The Lord Jesus described the christian as being 'the salt of the earth'. This was saying a lot about the society around the christian for salt was used to prevent things from putrifaction. Jesus was saying that the society was rotten and that christians are put into it as an anti-putrifaction agents.

It may seem to you that since there is so much rottenness and evil in the world what effect can the few christians there are in it have upon it? The answer is to be found in the metaphor Christ uses of salt. It only takes very little salt in anything before you are aware that it is present. If someone dropped a few grains of salt into your tea you would soon realise what had happened. Christians may be few but their presence can make a tremendous difference anywhere and at any time. So, christian be good salt today and make life tasty for others.

13

SAVOURLESS IS USELESS

Salt in itself is pure but if it is mixed with other chemicals it is absolutely useless. In the Middle East contaminated salt is used to make roads.

So it is that if a christian mixes up his or her life with impurity the effectiveness of their testimony is wrecked and people walk all over it. Are there things in your life today that are threatening to contaminate your witness for Christ? With all my heart I say be done with them. Savourless salt is simply good for nothing. As the Saviour put it 'If the salt looses its taste, how shall it be seasoned?' It is then good for nothing but to be thrown out and trampled under foot by men. We have been warned.

14

'LIGHTHOUSES DON'T BLOW TRUMPETS'

It was an incredible statement of the Lord Jesus when he called christians 'the light of the world'. You will notice that he did not mention Aristotle or Plato or Socrates. He looked at Peter, and Thomas and Andrew and Matthew and the rest of his

August

disciples and referred to them as being the light of the world. That implied of course that the world around them was in darkness. It implied that it was not education or culture or money or prestige or social standing that gives christians spiritual influence. It is because they are partakers of the Divine nature since coming to know Christ as their Saviour that gives so few such an influence among so many. Wherever you are today, christian, you are, according to Christ, the light of the world. Lighthouses, you know, do not blow trumpets or fire guns, they just shine. Even a city, Christ taught, 'That is set on a hill cannot be hidden. Nor do they light a lamp and put it under a basket, but on a lampstand, and it gives light to all who are in the house. Let your light so shine before men, that they may see your good works and glorify your Father in Heaven'. So, for the Lord's sake, christian, get out there today and shine!

15 _____

'ALLEYS LEAD TO THE METROPOLIS'

You know how it is that you can wander along a little lane in the country or up an alley in a village. Just remember that every single lane in the country and every single alley eventually joins up with a road that leads to the metropolis. That applies to any country in the world. If you follow even the smallest track it will eventually lead you to the very heart of the capital city of the country.

August

The older I grow the more I have come to see that every lane and alley of Scripture leads to the great metropolis which is Christ. Everything in Scripture culminates in Christ. He said 'Do not think that I came to destroy the law or the prophets. I did not come to destroy but to fulfil'. When you think about it it is the most stupendous claim that he ever made. He was saying that everything in the law and the prophets eventually leads you to him. He was backing the authority of the Old Testament. If you say you are a christian and do not believe the story of creation, or the story of Jonah, or look upon the law as a very clever bit of Jewish legislation produced by man with good ideas for public health and hygiene, you are contradicting everything our Lord and Saviour said about himself. Everything has meaning. 'For assuredly, I say unto you', said Christ 'Till heaven and earth pass away, one jot or one tittle will by no means pass from the law until all is fulfilled'. You realise that a jot is the smallest letter in the Hebrew alphabet and almost identical with our apostrophe sign. A tittle is a small, horn shaped mark to indicate accent in Hebrew. So the Lord Jesus was teaching that everything in Scripture will be carried out down to the smallest detail imaginable. His word cannot be broken. He fulfils every detail predicted of him and everything that the law demanded. Such a majestic Saviour is yours today, christian.

I find the older I grow in a christian life the more I am turning to the Old Testament to look for Christ in it. I am finding he is everywhere. Look for him in the lanes and allies of Scripture today and you will soon be in the metropolis. None of the Bible is wasted.

August

16 ———————————

'A NUMSKULL?'

'But I say unto you that whoever is angry with his brother without a cause shall be in danger of the judgement. And whoever says to his brother, "Raca!" shall be in danger of the council. But whoever says, "You fool!" shall be in danger of hell fire'. What on earth did our Lord mean by this statement?

First he meant that we are not to be angry without a cause. Secondly he was warning us about using the word raca regarding our brother. The English equivalent for the word raca is to literally call someone a numskull, blockhead or nitwit. It means to have contempt for a person's head. It is to call him stupid. Thirdly he was warning that to call someone a fool is to have contempt for their heart and character. These three thoughts may never lead to murder but Christ was teaching clearly that they are tantamont to murder in God's sight. 'You have heard that it was said of those of old, "You shall not murder", said Christ "And whoever murders will be in danger of the judgement" . . . but I say unto you'. The warning is very powerful and goes very deep and the message is that wherever you go today and whatever country you find yourself in, be very, very careful what you call other folk even in casual conversation.

'HEART CONTROL'

'You have heard that it was said to those of old', said Christ, "You shall not commit adultery." But I say unto you that whoever looks at a woman to lust for her has already committed adultery with her in his heart'.

Control of the heart is due, by and large, to control of the eyes. Have you ever noticed, men, what Job said about the problem of lust. Job said, 'I have made a convenant with my eyes; why then should I look upon a young woman?' That's pretty straight talking. It was quite obvious that Job had a problem with lust and he overcame it by making a promise to keep his look wholesome. I always remember reading that when the godly Jim Elliot, martyr of Ecuador, was tempted to look to lust, particularly when travelling alone, he used to think about the cross and the two could not live together in his mind. His advice has helped me and it may help you.

Let me balance this very sensitive subject by saying that it would be very wrong of me to legislate for fashion. Ladies you know it is one thing to make yourself attractive and it is another to make yourself deliberately seductive. You ladies know the difference — so do we men. Selah.

August

18 ————————————

'If your right eye causes you to sin, pluck it out and cast it from you: for it is more profitable for you that one of your members perish, than for your whole body to be cast into hell', warned Christ. 'And if your right hand causes you to sin, cut if off and cast it from you; for it is more profitable for you that one of your members perish, than for your whole body to be cast into hell'.

What exactly is the Lord Jesus driving at in this powerful statement? He is warning that we must have discipline in guarding the approaches of sin. We must use military tactics and post sentries in our lives. It would be very foolish if we allowed the enemy to overwhelm us simply because we did not post sentries to warn us of the enemies approach. I certainly do not believe this passage is saying that Christ's disciples should blind or maim themselves but I certainly do think that the command will require the elimination from our lives of certain things which could easily become our downfall.

We shall have to decline to see certain films and to read certain books and to visit certain exhibitions. As John Stott, the Queen's chaplain put it we shall have to become culturally 'maimed' in order to preserve our purity of mind. It will be better to forego some experiences this life offers in order to enter the life which is life indeed. It is far better to accept some 'cultural amputation' and to ask for the soft drink and be considered 'soft'; it is better to turn away from the attraction of lust knowing full well the deadly sting in its tail; it is better to resist the temptation to gossip and be considered 'very-quiet-tonight' and 'unsociable'; it is better to say 'no' to many things than to say 'yes' and be popular.

We have to decide quite simply whether to live for this world or the next; whether we are going to follow the popular crowd or the Lord Jesus. Have you made up your mind?

19

'WOULD CHRIST DIVORCE HIS CHURCH'

We now come to our Lord's statement regarding the question of divorce 'Furthermore it has been said, "whoever divorces his wife, let him give her a certificate of divorce". But I say unto you that whoever divorces his wife for any reason except sexual immorality causes her to commit adultery; and whoever marries a woman who is divorced commits adultery'. A lot could be said about this statement but all I wish to do is to ask you, christian, a simple question. Do you think it would ever enter the Lord's head to divorce you as a member of his church? Do you think the Lord would ever divorce his bride, the church? The very thought is unthinkable. Nowhere in Scripture are we commanded to divorce our partner and since God hates divorce (see Malachi 2:16) and I promised to love my partner until death parted us; I must keep my promise. Husbands are to love their wives as

August

Christ loved the church. How did Christ love the church? He loved her unto death. The duty of a christian husband is plain. For me, christian marriage is for keeps.

20 ――――――――――

'I DARE YOU'

Honesty in speech is an absolutely vital quality of the christian. 'Do not swear at all; neither by heaven, for it is God's throne; nor by earth, for it is his footstool; nor by Jerusalem, for it is the city of the great King. Nor shall you swear by your head, because you cannot make one hair white or black. But let your "yes" be "yes" and your "no" be "no". For whatever is more than these is from the evil one,' said our Lord.

The mosaic law prohibited false swearing. It was prohibited that any person should make a vow and then break it. Their whole world had become chaotic because people could not rely upon one another's word or statement. So the law was to check and control this lying. What Jesus was saying for the christian is that we must keep our promises and be people of our word. If we do this then vows become unnecessary. Both vow taking and divorce were permitted by the law but neither was commanded. The plain fact is that neither should be necessary. I do not know any more powerful words in the English language than the two little words 'yes' and 'no'. Try using them without embellishment for a while and see what happens. I dare you.

'PERSONAL REVENGE PROHIBITED'

There are few Scriptures that have been twisted as much as the little statement 'An eye for an eye and a tooth for a tooth'. The Lord Jesus commented 'You have heard that it was said, "An eye for an eye and a tooth for a tooth". But I tell you not to resist an evil person. But whoever slaps you on your right cheek, turn the other to him also.' The context of the statement about an eye for an eye and a tooth for a tooth is taken straight from the law of Moses. This instruction was given to the judges of Israel. It expressed the principle of exact retribution. It had the double effect of defining justice and restraining revenge. No one was allowed to take the law into their own hands and exact ghastly vengeance with a family feud, for example. You see, if someone hurts me on the arm, in vengeance I am inclined to want to take his head off!

It is almost certain that by the time of Jesus literal retaliation for damage had been replaced in Jewish legal practice by money penalties or 'damages'. Exodus 21 : 22-29 gives us evidence of this, much earlier. The problem with the Scribes and Pharisees was they wanted to extend this principle of just retribution from the law courts where it belongs to personal relationships where it doesn't. They tried to use it to justify personal revenge, although the law explicitly forbade it. The Lord Jesus is teaching here that an individual christian is given a God given function not to repay evil for evil. 'Whoever slaps you on your right cheek, turn the other to him also', taught Christ. So when a person becomes a

August

christian in their personal relationships they no
longer demand the exact retribution the law
demands. They should react to those who hurt them
in love.

22 _____

'THE CASE OF THE SUNBATHER'

In 1928 a very interesting case came before the
courts in the State of Massachusetts. It concerned a
man who had been walking on a boat dock when
suddenly he tripped over a rope and fell into the
cold, deep water of an ocean bay. He came up
spluttering and yelling for help and then sank again,
obviously in trouble. His friends were too far away
to get to him but only a few yards away, on another
dock, a young man sprawled on a deck chair,
sunbathing. 'Help! I can't swim!' came the
desperate shout. The young man, an excellent
swimmer only turned his head to watch as the man
floundered in the water, sank, came up spluttering
in total panic and then disappeared forever.

The family of the drowned man were so upset by
that display of callous indifference that they sued
the sunbather. They LOST! The court reluctantly
ruled that the man on the dock had no legal
responsibility whatever to try and save the other
man's life.

The Lord Jesus would teach that the christian's
attitude is to be very different to that of the American
sunbather. 'Whoever compels you to go one mile,
go with him two', taught the Lord Jesus. Are you a
second miler?

23

WILL WHITEFIELD BE IN HEAVEN?

When I think of the Sermon on the Mount it reminds me of a story concerning two very famous christian leaders whom a man tried, once, to divide. It was a sick and subtle way the man, with sugar coated piety, tried to get John Wesley to criticise the great open air preacher George Whitefield. 'Shall we see Mr. Whitefield in Heaven, sir?', he asked. 'No!', replied John Wesley, 'Because Whitefield will be so near the throne and we shall be so far back we shall scarce get a sight of him'. That's the spirit!

24

VANITY AND COWARDICE CONDEMNED

'Take heed that you do not your charitable deeds before men to be seen by them', warned Christ, 'Otherwise you will have no reward from your father in Heaven'. Does this contradict Christ's earlier command to 'Let your light shine before men, that they may see your good works and glorify your father which is in Heaven'? No. The first statement is warning against human vanity which would want us to practise our piety before men. The second is warning against human cowardice which would prevent us from letting our light shine before men. What is Christ saying then? He is saying 'Show when tempted to hide and hide when tempted to show'.

August

25

WHEN IS A GOOD ACT, BAD?

'When you do a charitable deed, do not let your left hand know what your right hand is doing, that your charitable deed may be in secret; and your Father who sees in secret will reward you openly'. This statement of Christ's on christian giving is clearly saying that we are not to stand with a penny in one hand and a trumpet in the other in the posture of hypocrisy. Do not let your left hand know what your right hand is doing when you do a charitable deed is to take deliberate steps to make sure that you do not gloat even in your own heart with self-congratulation. Even a good act can be turned into a bad act with wrong motivation.

26

THE TREASURE HOUSE

They tell me that in a Greek restaurant the name over the cashier's desk is exactly the same word as is used by Christ when he said 'When you pray, go into your room'. In Greek the word means 'The storeroom where treasures might be kept'. The implication is that there are treasures waiting for us when we pray. Christ is not talking here about public prayer, that comes later in the Sermon on the Mount. Here he is talking about private prayer. 'But you, when you pray', says Christ, 'When you have shut your door, pray to your Father who is in and your Father who sees in secret will reward you openly'. Have you been in the treasure house today?

27

WHICH SPECTATOR MATTERS?

The sad countenance of the hypocrite drawing attention to his fasting was 'roasted' by Christ. If I may paraphrase his teaching; 'Fasting?', he implies, 'Have a wash and a brush up so that no one but God will know'. Our Heavenly Father is always looking for opportunities to bless us but he won't find one if our fasting or praying or giving is done to draw attention to ourselves. Which spectator matters most? Earthly or heavenly?

28

TEMPORAL VERSUS THE ETERNAL

The recent crash on the Stock Exchange has certainly shown us the vulnerability of earthly treasure. Treasure that is laid up in Heaven is very different. 'Neither moth nor rust destroys' and 'Thieves do not break in and steal', as far as heavenly treasure is concerned. But what is it? It seems to me that it is temporal activities that have eternal consequences. If an act, even as humble as washing a dish is done for the glory of God then you will meet it again. If an act has not the glory of God in mind then the act itself is all. Think about it for where your treasure is there will your heart be also.

August

29

WORRY IS WASTE

Divided loyalty will bring about instability in your life. You cannot serve both God and wealth. It seems inconceivable but some people try. 'Which of you by worrying can add one cubit to his stature?', said the Lord. I knew a man once who said that he had done just that. He told me that he had literally married a girl called Cubit!! I smiled but in fact the statement of Christ still stands. Worrying will not make you grow nor will it make anything better. Worry is incompatable with the christian faith. Christ commanded us to consider the little birds of the air. Do they worry? I'll tell you one thing, they certainly work. There are a pair of bluetits who have raised a family in the eaves of my house this year and I can tell you they were a very busy pair. Little birds store food for the winter and many of them migrate thousands of miles to warmer countries. But they don't spend their lives worrying. If God takes care of the little birds of the air will he not take care of you? Do birds die? Of course they do. Are the flowers of the field cut down? Yes. Will we face problems in our lives? Of course we will. God is not promising us freedom from trouble but he is promising us freedom from worry. Worry is a waste. Cut it out.

August

30

MAKE THEIR CHILDHOOD GLAD

'If you then, being evil, know how to give good gifts to your children, how much more will your Father who is in Heaven give good things to those who ask him!' Apart from teaching your children spiritual truth what do you think is the greatest gift you could give to them? I am no great father, I wish I was, but in my reckoning giving our children our time is, next to spiritual things, the most important gift we can give them. I wrote a little poem about it once. It may help you.

It is not hard to make a child's heart glad,
Often a little thing will please, will ease,
A tear-filled afternoon,
A walk, a ride across the park,
A story read, a small surprise,
A 'Let's pretend',
Will make their childhood glad.

Father, busy in your office, plush,
Rushing around so much, you cannot touch,
Your children's heart that way,
Oh! It may buy them food or toys,
But you must give them time,
Your time, if you would ever say,
'I've made their childhood glad'.

Mother, who daily makes the mould,
In those first years, edged by fears,
Fears of how they'll fare,
Make yours the encouraging word,

291

August

And hold their love, even when they rebel,
Always care, always care,
And you'll make their childhood glad.

Then, when they've left your patient care,
Leaving the nest, and the rest,
To make their own,
When you are old and their childhood's gone,
Far from your grasp and reach,
They'll say of you to children of their own,
'They made my childhood glad'.

31

WITNESS TO HIM

'And so it was, when Jesus had ended these sayings, that the people were astonished at his teaching, for he taught them as one having authority, and not as the Scribes'.

What was it, after all, that made the Lord Jesus different to any other kind of teacher? Many things could be said but amongst them we would have to point to the fact that Christ assumed the right to teach absolute truth. The Scribes and the Pharisees claimed no authority of their own. They conceived their duty in terms of faithfulness to the tradition they had received. The Old Testament prophets did not claim any authority of their own. They said 'Thus says the Lord'. Jesus was different. He claimed to be Lord. 'You call me master and Lord; and you say well; so I am'. Those of us who seek to live for him are not just guarding and handing on the tradition of his teaching; we are 'witnesses to him'.

August

So, as we leave August days behind let us remember that as all seasons will one day pass away, and everything we know around us will pass away, Jesus Christ will still be Lord. Let us then take his Sermon on the Mount with deadly seriousness. May its values ever pervade our lives. It is what our Lord calls us to and when we obey it the world will notice the difference.

SEPTEMBER

There are mushrooms on the floor of the forest and Speedwell and False Fox Sedge and Shaggy Ink Caps. Trooping Crumble Cap is swarming over the roots of trees. In the balmy September afternoons the forest is full of the drowsy hum of bees and when the sunset comes the crickets still chirp on, far into the night.

The Walnut tree has long since produced walnuts and the green husk is withering away and the delicious kernel is about to be fully exposed. The juice will stain your fingers and some people use it as suntan lotion! Solid walnut furniture is very costly and rare. It is a very stable wood. We too shall know stability in this changing world as we seek to follow the one who is the same, yesterday, today and forever.

September

1 ⸻⸻⸻⸻⸻

THE DEVIL NEVER SIGNS HIS NAME TO ANYTHING

If the Sermon on the Mount is the essence of our Lord's teaching, then Romans is the essence of Paul's teaching as given to him by the Lord. For the next two months let's have a fresh look at some of that great teaching. Written about thirty years after the resurrection of Christ there are no letters that have ever been written anywhere to hold a candle to the impact that Romans has had upon human history. It raises momentous questions for just about everything. It is, if I may coin a phrase, a mind-bender. It opens up a way through the woods of 'woolly thinking' and if you understand it you have a sure road to the whole of Scripture.

Notice how it opens. 'Paul', it says. What, a name right at the beginning? Is it not a bit pompous? Certainly not. Paul was not ashamed to identify his name with what he wrote. Are you? The devil never signs his name to anything.

2 ⸻⸻⸻⸻⸻

'A SERVANT OF JESUS CHRIST'

We all have labels. You know how it is when you are introduced in a crowd. 'This is Mary from . . .', 'This is Tom from . . .' or 'This is Valerie who is Mrs.

so-in-sos neice'. I once sat in a crowd at Wheaton, Ilinois and watched a ceremony where Mrs. Ruth Graham, the famous Evangelist's wife received a Doctorate. In her speech she said she was looking forward to now being introduced as 'Dr. Graham' for a change!

It is always intriguing to see how Paul introduces himself at the beginning of his letters. In Romans he calls himself 'a servant of Jesus Christ'. He reckoned his time, strength and plans belonged altogether to another. He meant that he was entirely at the Lord's disposal. Are you?

3

IT TAKES TWO

A golden wedding is when a couple have gone fifty-fifty.

4

THE EMPIRE BUILDERS

The Roman Empire was something else. The Romans crushed any nation standing in their path. They could build roads like no one else. They made laws which were truly great laws. Their Imperial city teemed with aqueducts, bridges, quays, temples and monuments of civic pride. Ceaser Augustus said he had found the city of Rome built of brick and left it built of marble. The welfare was truly amazing.

September

Yet, the Romans with all their powers couldn't eliminate violence, corruption and evil in the hearts of their citizens. They thought their Emperors were the big cheese and hardly a line in their literature of million of words is devoted to those referred to by Paul as 'To all who are in Rome, beloved of God, called to be saints'. Yet, the gospel those few believed outlived the empire as it will all empires. Don't be ashamed of it. The Roman Empire is now Mediterranean rubble but the Gospel is as relevant as today's news. Even more so!

5 _____

OUT OF MEDIOCRITY

What was it the christians at Rome were famous for? The size of the congregations? The size of the buildings they operated? The kind of church suppers they laid on? The chariots they drove? The horses they owned? The houses they lived in? No! It was their faith. 'I thank my God', wrote Paul, 'Through Jesus Christ for you all that your faith is spoken of throughout the whole world'. Isn't that a beautiful thing? Do they speak of your faith in the world you live in?

Faith lifts you out of mediocrity. Faith is possible in anyone, it can flourish in any heart. Faith can master impossible difficulties. Without faith it is impossible to please God. Faith helps you to go on. True faith is not wishful thinking or imagination but it feeds on the promises of God, they are its native food. So, feed on them today and watch your faith grow. And, by the way you will find the promises of God are even better than ready money any day. The Romans had plenty of the latter and where are they now?

--- **6**

Luckin' for han's to use

'For I long to see you that I may impart to you some spiritual gift'. Did Paul mean by this statement that he carried spiritual gifts around and dealt them out? No. Only God can give spiritual gifts. What Paul wants to do is to share the gifts God has given him with the christians at Rome. I know what you are thinking. You are thinking 'But what gift do I have?' Well, at the risk of sounding simplistic, you've got hands haven't you? Start with them.

Let me quote the heroine of Ulster's famine in the last century, Anna Irvine from the book 'My Lady of the Chimney's Corner'. The conversation is in the broad dialect of the Antrim town at the turn of the last century but it is none the worse for that. I am all for the retention of dialect. Without dialect, colour would be taken from our language. This piece of conversation was taken from the words spoken in comfort to a lady called Eliza Lecky whose son Henry had died suddenly. Henry had been famous for bringing home trout and for giving them to the famished children of Antrim's entries. Anna was trying to comfort his mother on his death. Speaking of God Anna said 'He takes the han' of a docther t' relieve pain, th' han' of a mother t' guide her chile,

September

an' sometimes he takes th' han' of an aul' craither like me t' give a bit of comfort to a neighbour. But they're all han's touch't be His Spirit, an' His Spirit is everywhere luckin' fur han's to use'.

Eliza looked at her open-mouthed for a moment. 'Tell me, Anna', she said, as she put her hands on her shoulders. 'Was th' han' that bro't home trouts fur the th' childther God's han' too?'

'Ay, 'deed it was'.

'O, glory be t' God — thin I'm at pace — isn't it gran' t' think on — isn't it now?'

7 ────────────────

No time

A lazy man, have you noticed, never has time.

8 ────────────────

Two kinds of debt

Was Paul a debtor? He says he was, 'To Greeks and non Greeks, both to wise and unwise'.

There are two ways of getting into debt to somebody. One is to borrow money from him or to be given money for him, by somebody else. Paul was the latter kind of debtor. His Lord had entrusted him with the gospel for the whole gentile world, as Philipps puts it 'From cultured Greek to ignorant savage'. And he says he was not ashamed of the gospel. He must have been tempted to be so. Yet he overcame the temptation when he thought on what the gospel is. Think of it! As to its source; 'The gospel of Christ'. As to its nature; 'The power of God'. As to its purpose; 'Unto salvation'. As to its scope; 'To everyone'. As to its reception; 'Everyone who believes'. As to its quality; 'In it is the righteousness of God revealed'. As to its outcome; 'The just shall live by faith'. So, christian, if this is what you have believed, what are you worried about?

9

DON'T PRESUME

There is a notion abroad that wrath is unworthy of God. People think that God's wrath is like ours, and that he gets mad and irritable and even cruel like we do. Such is simply not true; God's wrath is right and necessary. It is a reaction against evil. It is righteous anger. It is never cruel. God's wrath is something people choose. If you refuse God's offer of love in Christ then you must face his righteous anger. 'For the wrath of God is revealed from heaven against all ungodliness and unrighteousness of men, who surpressed the truth in unrighteousness'.

Notice God's wrath is mentioned in the present tense. It is revealed in our conscience. It is revealed in the physical consequences of sin, it is even seen in the thorns and thistles in your garden. We have said much in this book of God's love but let me remind you there are more references to the wrath of God than there are to his love in the Bible. Too often we presume. Don't. A man Uzzah presumed.

September

Men were told to keep 1,000 yards distance from the Ark of the Covenant. He presumed to touch it when it swayed while being carried and he was a dead man. Look up the story in second Samuel chapter 6 and read it. When God says something he means it.

10

GODLESSNESS — WHAT IS IT?

What is godlessness? Is it atheism? Not necessarily. Godlessness can be acting as though God didn't exist.

11

EARTH IS CRAMMED WITH HEAVEN

Did you know that truth from God is breaking out all around? It's blowing in the wind. 'It is', writes Paul 'Understood from what has been made'. It is, 'Since the creation of the world . . . clearly seen'. Earth is crammed with Heaven. 'If you seek his monument, look around you', said the great architect Sir Christopher Wren. 'It is', said my good friend Dr. Harold Love, 'Far harder not to believe in God than it is to believe in him'.

Of course, adds Paul, men 'surpress the truth'. They call God 'Fate' or 'Destiny' or 'Mother Nature'. Isn't it amazing, though, you never hear people say 'By nature, I'm going to do this' or 'By nature if you don't stop that I'll hit you!' Strange.

12

THE TRAGIC EXCHANGE

One of the devices people use to surpress the truth is to exchange God's immortal glory for images, 'Made like corruptible man ... birds, animals and reptiles.'

Have you noticed the names we use for our cars? 'Jaguar', 'Mustang', 'Pony' etc. Our society is no different to the world Paul lived in, only now people worship rock stars, athletes, movie stars, television shows and images. Everywhere there are images. Huge advertising agencies are paid millions to produce images for companies. The logo is the image. The medium is the message. People worship beauty, and it fades, youth and it passes, adventure and it disappoints, leisure and it even bores. Some nations even worship military power in the form of tanks, planes and guns. Others measure power in the form of computers, technology, etc. These are gods to them. Materialistic secularism is all around us.

Imagine exchanging the glory of the undying, majestic and great God for an image? Imagine swopping the Creator for an image of one of his creatures! Don't do it.

13

FUEL EFFICIENCY

Did you realise that if you cut your own wood it will warm you twice?

September

14

HOPE IN THE DARKNESS

One of the disastrous results of idolatry in any nation is widespread sexual immorality. Paul writes in Romans 1 that because of idolatry God gives people 'Up to uncleanness, in the lusts of their hearts, to dishonour their bodies among themselves, who exchanged the truth of God for the lie, and worshipped and served the creature rather than the Creator . . . for this reason God gave them up to vile passions. For even their women exchanged the natural use for what is against nature. Likewise also the men, leaving the natural use of the woman, burned in their lust for one another, men with men committing what is shameful, and receiving in themselves the penalty of their error which was due'.

Does this mean that God washes his hands of these people? No, but he allows men and women to experience the full effects of their sin and to discover that they don't have the answer.

I have no doubt in my mind that one of the signs of a Godless society is homosexuality. It was common in Paul's day because fourteen out of the first fifteen Emperors were homosexuals. The sad thing about it in our day is that homosexuals widely believe the lie that their condition is biological and can't be helped. As long as they believe that there is no help for them. But if they see it as a sin, it can be forgiven and they can be delivered and freed from its power. There is tremendous hope in the midst of their darkness. That hope is in Jesus Christ.

 Avoid a colourless marriage

In a time when AIDS is rampant, because of sexual immorality, it seems to me a glorious opportunity for christian morality to shine. Single, celibate christians can be a joyful witness to the advantages that Christ gives when they obey his word.

Christian marriage has now a glorious opportunity to witness as never before. Instead of boring, arguing, sarcastic, introverted, colourless couples whose only phrases seem to be 'Wash the car', 'Empty the bin', 'Wash the dishes', 'Is my meal ready?', 'Why did you spend that much?', 'Keep quiet', 'Leave me alone'. We could have homes and lives filled with phrases like 'Forgive me', 'Please', 'I'm sorry', 'Thank you', 'I love you', 'What a delicious meal' etc.

Try and look at your partner today and smile. Call her during the day and tell her something pleasant. When you leave this morning blow her a kiss. The neighbours might die of shock, never to speak of your wife! Oh, I know that you may look like a cross eyed discus thrower. Cross eyed discus throwers are not very good discus throwers but I'll tell you one thing, they sure keep the crowd awake! Go for it!

September

'THEY MAY NEVER LOOK AS HIGH AGAIN'

It was Mark Twain who said that to do good is noble but to teach others to do good is nobler — and no trouble!

In Romans chapter 2 Paul has a devastating passage against the person who claims to teach others and who does not teach himself. 'You, therefore, who teach another, do you not teach yourself? You who preach that a man should not steal, do you steal? You who say do not commit adultery, do you commit adultery? You who abhor idols, do you rob temples?'

The passage is full of solemn searching and startling lessons for all who profess God's name. Inconsistency dishonours God and leads people to reject and even blaspheme the christian gospel. Let us by God's grace make sure that no person is ever turned away from God because of us.

I know of no worse accusation than the chilling words 'People have been turned away from God because of you'. Just remember that someone may never look as high again if you have been hypocritical. Selah.

17

THE HOLE IN THE WALL!'

There was an old black mother once who had a lot of confidence in God. Someone, impressed with her confidence said to her 'Why, you have so much faith in the Lord that if the Lord told you to jump through a stone wall you would start jumping'.

The old lady quickly replied with a twinkle in her eye that 'If de Lawd tole me to jump through a stone wall it would be mah business to jump and His business to make a hole in de wall!'

There are no dilemma with God. Remember that.

18

RECONCILIATION

In the Book of Proverbs the question is asked 'Can a man take fire in his bosom and his clothes not be burned?' In the Book of Romans it seems to me another question is being asked which is saying 'Can God take you and I who have sinned and make us his friends and not be soiled as a result?' The answer is 'Yes'. Through the cross of Christ, God can be 'Just and the justifier of the one who has faith in Jesus'.

I love the illustration of the little girl whose parents were separated. The little child took dangerously ill and the doctors asked her mother to find her father. He came to the hospital ward and sat at one side of the bed with his wife at the other side but neither parent would look at each other, they would only look at the little girl. Quietly the little girl slipped out one hand and took her mother's hand and then slipped out her other hand and took her father's hand and brought them both together across her little chest, and died. Tell me, do you think that the mother and father fought and argued any more? They were, in fact, reconciled through the death of their daughter.

So it is that the Lord can put out his hand and take his Father's hand and put out his other hand and take your hand and mine and bring us to God. If we accept his death as enough to atone for our sins and receive him as Saviour we can literally be reconciled to God through the death of his son. God is therefore both just and the justifier of the one who has faith in Jesus. Have you put your hand in his yet?

19 ————————————

'THE BAVARIAN WOODCARVER'

You know how people argue that James and Paul contradict one another. Paul says 'We conclude that a man is justified by faith apart from the deeds of the law' and James says 'Faith without works is dead'. It is a contradiction? I do not believe that it is. James is not contradicting salvation by faith he is illustrating it. Let me tell you a story.

There was once a Bavarian woodcarver. He saw a piece of wood in the mouth of a sack of grain. The wood was the precise colour of the grain. The man took the wood and began to carve imitation grains of wheat. Finally he had a small handful of them and mixing them with real grain defied his friends to tell them apart! In the end, in fact, he couldn't tell the difference himself. Ultimately the only way to tell the two apart was to put them in water for a day or two. The grains that were from nature, sprouted, and the others remained exactly what they were — dead imitations.

September

So it is that there is no personal salvation apart from real faith in Christ but a professed faith in Christ that is not followed by good works is a dead imitation. Which do you and I have?

20

WHERE IS YOUR FAITH PLACED?

So, you think God only chooses good people to be his great people? If you read Romans chapter 4 you will learn how Paul destroys that myth. The Rabbis were always teaching that Abraham was chosen as the father of Israel because he earned the position by his good works. Paul sets out to prove this to be untrue. Make no mistake about it what Paul says about this matter is the very heart of christian theology.

If Abraham couldn't be justified before God by works, nobody could. 'Abraham', wrote Paul, 'Believed God and it was accounted to him for righteousness'. So, if you climb all the mountains in the world out of penance, pray all the prayers possible, go to all the religious services possible, never swear, never hurt anyone, be kind and decent; all of it couldn't save you. Abraham believed God long before there was a law of Moses. He was justified by faith alone.

Remember that it is not the bank note that has the value, it is the promise the bank makes on the note. So faith is not the valuable thing but the one in whom the faith is placed. Where, oh where, with

September

everything within me, I ask you, is your faith placed? Be sure, mighty sure, it is in Christ alone for salvation. If it isn't make sure this very moment that it is.

21

THE STRANGER

I wonder have you ever heard the story of the famous organ in the cathedral in Freiburg, Germany. The man who played it for many years had become quite old. One day a stranger came in and asked if he could play the organ. The man said, 'No, I'm the only one allowed to play this organ'. The stranger persisted and finally the old man gave in. The stranger began to play music more beautiful than the old organist had ever heard, and his eyes began to fill with tears.

When the stranger had finished playing he asked him, 'What is your name?' The answer came back, 'My name is Felix Mendelssohn'. The old man used to tell the story over and over again and he would always end by shaking his head and saying, 'And to think I almost did not allow the world's greatest master to play on this organ!'

Jesus Christ has spoken to you and you could be on the verge of missing God's great call to your life. Answer him yes and like the old organist of Freiburg you will not be sorry you let the Master have access.

HARRY VAUGHAN'S POSSESSIONS

My friend, Harry Vaughan was a policeman; I loved Harry for he loved the Lord and he loved to sing. He would come to our Bible Class and with hundreds of others would lift up his heart and sing with such enthusiasm. His favourite hymn was Andrae Crouch's lovely hymn 'Soon and very soon we are going to see the King'. The day came when I had to conduct Harry's funeral service and standing by his graveside there was but one text I felt I could preach upon. It was from Romans; 'Therefore, having been justified by faith, we have peace with God through our Lord Jesus Christ, through whom also we have access by faith into this grace in which we stand, and rejoice in hope of the glory of God'.

I remember pointing out that the text says that there are three things the christian has that the non christian hasn't. The first is 'Peace with God'. That means his past is dealt with and he is no longer at war with God. The second thing he has is 'Access by faith into this grace in which we stand'. That means he has something to go on with. Thirdly he has 'Hope of the glory of God'. That means his future is secure. The past? 'Dealt with' The present? 'Helped with'. The future? 'Secure with'. I miss Harry to this very day but one thing makes me very glad; Harry is now looking upon the face of the one who gave him those three possessions when he trusted him as Saviour. One day, so can you.

September

23

ALL YOU NEED IS . . .

'What more of us need most, is in fact, to need less'.

24

THE BEST MEDICINE FOR PRIDE

Brer Rabbit was born in the brier patch and was used to it, but I'm not. I hate the place and when I fall into life's brier patch I find I thrash about to try and get away from those thorns. The problem is, the more I thrash about the greater are my scratches. How about you? The best thing to do when we get into such a place is to 'sit still' and be quiet and let the Lord extricate us. He'll only be too glad to do so. As Ray Stedman put it 'The route to the main highway from the thorn patch is usually back to where you left the road'. I find I usually have left the road because I have not been prepared to wait for God in the first place. Some tribulation, you know, is corrective. 'Glory in tribulations also', writes Paul. Corrective tribulation is the best medicine for pride I know. I've had to drink it often and although it doesn't taste nice I have learned to thank God for it.

25

AUGUSTINE'S ANSWER

Augustine, who had led a very immoral life, was converted to Christ. A girl from his past life ran after him one day after spotting him on the street. 'Augustine!', she said. 'Augustine, it is I!' He turned to her and replied 'It is not I but Christ that liveth in me'.

Augustine was learning that as a christian he did not have to obey sin. He now had Christ's power to overcome it. 'We should', say Scripture, 'No longer be slaves of sin . . . do not let sin reign in your mortal body'. Now just as a christian was once a slave to sin and the end of all that was death so now a christian is a slave to righteousness and the result of that is eternal life; eternal life is the capacity to know God! Whose slave are you?

26

WHERE WILL YOU SOW TO-DAY?

How, on earth can we explain the little verse which says that christians 'Do not walk according to the flesh but according to the Spirit' (Romans 8:4) You may say that as a christian you seem to find that your old nature is still very much with you. What does this statement mean?

Let me give you an illustration. It may seem a far fetched illustration but it serves the point. Here is a

September

gardener who goes out into a desert with rich soil and plenty of supplies of water. He plants a tree in this new soil and irrigates it every day. Now answer me a question. What is the tree in? Is it in the desert? In a sense the answer is 'Yes' and in a sense the answer is 'No'. The desert is all around it but the tree is actually planted in different soil to the desert's.

You are now 'In Christ Jesus', christian, and are planted in him and one day when you go to be with the Lord you'll get a body like his glorious body (Please see Philippians 3 : 21 and 1st Corinthians 15 : 40-44). You shall be changed. The unbelievers won't be changed; they will rise with their rebellious nature, exactly as they died. When the Lord comes for you, either through the article of death or in the air you will leave the old flesh behind forever. At the moment the flesh is still 'in' you although you are not 'in' the flesh. The real roots of your personality are in God's Spirit. So you owe the flesh nothing. If you sow to the flesh even as a christian you will reap corruption even in this life; if you indulge yourself you will reap the consequences. But, if you sow to the Spirit, you will reap spiritual blessing both now and in eternity. Where will you sow today?

27 ——————————————

OPPORTUNITY KNOCKS?

One reason why so few recognise opportunity is because it is disguised as hard work. True?

ALL THE GOOD GOD CAN THINK OF

Are you troubled by past sin? Are you being made to feel an outsider because of your faith? Have you gone down with a terminal disease? Have you just been bereaved of a much loved relative? Maybe you are a relative of a murdered victim or someone badly hurt in an accident? Maybe you are looking for guidance in your life and you are finding it difficult? Are you going through the mid-life crisis? Are you going through 'the change'? Do you feel depressed? Are you lonely? Have you lost your job and can't find another?

Listen to Paul; 'What shall we say to these things? If God be for us who can be against us?' He is saying that no opposition or problem can finally crush you. No good thing will be withheld from you. If God spared not his own Son for you how shall he not with him also freely give us 'all things'.

The 'all things' means all the good God can think of, not all the good that you and I can think of. Does 'all things' mean that we shall be cured of all our diseases in this life? It certainly does not. 'Tell me', said my good friend David Gooding one day, 'Did the weeds stop growing in my garden the night I got converted?' Neither did disease and illness stop the night I got converted, either. God heals according to his mercy but it is not guaranteed. What is guaranteed is that nothing, no nothing, can finally wreck or crush your soul and all that God has for you in Christ. Keep asking yourself today, that little question, 'If God be for me who can be against me?' It will make mountains, molehills.

September

29 ⎯⎯⎯⎯⎯⎯⎯⎯⎯⎯

GOD'S VERDICT

'Who shall bring a charge against God's elect? It is God who justifies. Who is he who condemns?' asks Paul.

If someone were to rise in your local church service and say, publicly, that they were going to accuse you of things you had done in the past; what would you do? How would you react?

George Whitfield, the great evangelist, said that he would tell them that when they had finished he could tell them worse things about himself than anything they knew! We all know our own hearts and what goes on in them. Too well we do. It is so comforting to know that no one can ever disinherit us by any accusation they can make. It is God who justifies and nobody can challenge his verdict. Nobody.

30 ⎯⎯⎯⎯⎯⎯⎯⎯⎯⎯

MORE THAN CONQUERORS

There are in the local church to which I belong a couple who lost two of their boys within eighteen months. Their deaths were heartbreaking. Recently when our young people were reaching out to other young people in a tough area of Belfast some prayer meetings were held to pray for them. There, I spotted the parents who had lost their lads with bowed heads praying for other young people that they might find Christ. I thought, there go a couple whom Paul's letter to the Romans would call 'More than conquerors'.

To be a conqueror is to win. To be more than a conqueror is to actually lose and still retain your faith in God. To be a conqueror is good but to be more than a conqueror is better. May coming autumn days see you become more than a conqueror.

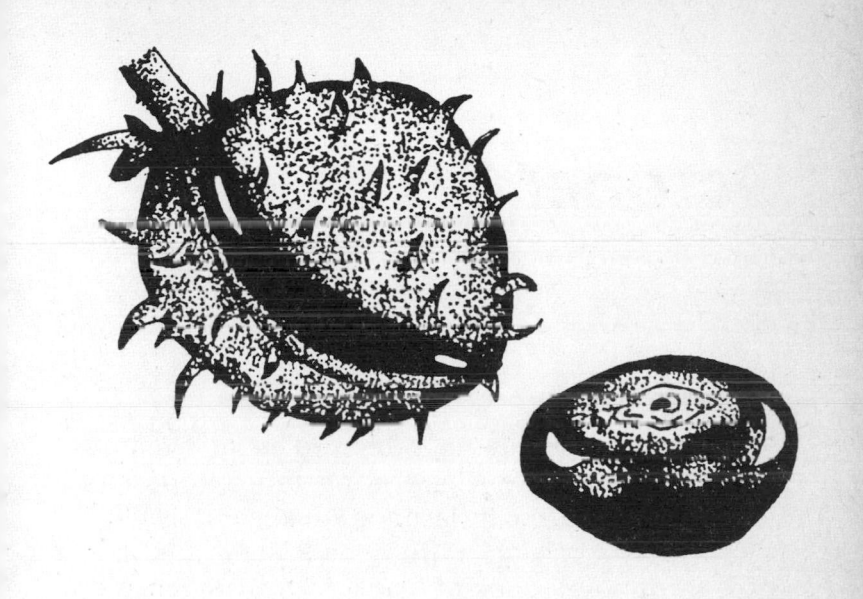

OCTOBER

Its seed used to be fed to broken winded horses and so it was called the horse chesnut. Most animals, except the deer, don't like its bitter seeds.

Animals apart, there are tens of thousands of young eyes that watch the hard dark brown horse chesnut seed mature with relish. Into the branches of the horse chesnut tree sticks are thrown to even encourage the seeds to fall because the boys who throw them prize the nuts for a game of conkers, known originally as "Conquerors". Each player bashes his nut against that of his opponent till one cracks and the harder nut wins.

In the life of the Spirit may you find that it is not the harder that wins but one thing, and one thing alone, and that is love. Stoop, this autumn, to conquer.

October

1

THE DIVIDING LINE

We want to continue our studies in Romans through this month. There is no more important book in the Bible and its lessons are absolutely vital.

Paul is now talking in Romans 9 about Pharaoh who, through plagues of frogs, flies, pestilence of animals, hail and locusts had known God's power and mercy. But Pharaoh kept saying 'No' and then he said 'No' once too many times and God hardened his heart. He found it impossible to change. He stands as a beacon of light. Why did God do it?

We cannot for ever trifle with God. If a man puts thousands in slave labour camps and persistently refused to obey God, would you have God say 'It doesn't matter, Pharaoh, do as you like?' Would you want God to say sin doesn't matter? You can blast somebody's brains with drugs, destroy somebody's home with immorality and it doesn't matter? You wouldn't respect a God like that. And he isn't like that. God endured the treatment he got from Pharaoh to show us his tolerance, mercy and longsuffering (Romans 9 : 22) But enough is enough. There is a dividing line and Pharaoh crossed it. I hope you never do.

October

2

A VESSEL OF MERCY

Just as Pharaoh was what the Bible calls a 'Vessel of wrath' so there are 'Vessels of mercy' (Romans 9 : 23); people who become an exhibition of the great mercy of God. Paul says he is one of them, 'Upon me Jesus Christ had mercy that in me first who am the very chief of sinners Jesus Christ might show forth all his longsuffering as an example to the rest'.

When God takes a man or a woman or a child and makes them a 'Vessel of mercy' it isn't that he takes them and uses them and confines the rest to Hell. He chooses them that they might be advertisements of his mercy to all the rest of the world. It is so that people might look at them and say 'Did you ever know such a God? If God would have mercy on Saul of Tarsus, for example, he would have mercy on me!' You see, 'The same Lord, over all, is rich to all that call upon him, for, whosoever shall call upon the name of the Lord shall be saved'. Tell me, my friend, what sort of an exhibition are you?

3

'A TRULY VALUABLE EXHIBITION'

If salvation is by good works and you are held up as an exhibition of good works to me it is of absolutely no value to me, for, I am a sinner. But, if

October

you are a sinner saved by the mercy of God and are held up by God's Spirit as an exhibition of that mercy, my, there is hope for me, indeed. See the difference? There's Heaven or Hell in it.

4

'A THERMOMETER IS NOT MEDICINE'

A well known preacher delivered a message before his congregation in which his wife was present. 'How did I do?', he asked her afterwards. 'Fine', she replied, 'Only you missed several opportunities to sit down!'

It might interest you to know that preachers also discuss their congregations and in Romans chapter 10 Paul discusses his. He says that he sees Israel going about 'seeking to establish their own righteousness . . . for Christ is the end of the law for righteousness to everyone who believes'. What does that mean?

Imagine you have a temperature and you are given a thermometer which says that your temperature is sitting at 105 degrees. O.K.? Imagine what your friends would say if you declared that you didn't believe the doctors and that you believed if you sucked the thermometer you would get the temperature down to where it should be! That would be crazy, wouldn't it? The thermometer surely is given to you to drive you to the doctor so that the doctor can make you better.

So it is with God's law. It is given to us to show us that we are spiritually sick and no matter how hard we try to keep the law we can't. The law is given to us to drive us to the Saviour who can make us right with God. It's time millions put their thermometers down and got to the great physician, don't you think?

5

READ THE WORD MORE

There is a school of thought who will tell you that God gives you faith, then, you hear God's word and believe. They say that some aren't given that faith.

But notice Paul does not say that. He declares that 'Faith comes by hearing and hearing by the word of God'. Mark that well. It is the reading, preaching and communication of the Word of God that brings faith. So, if you want to increase your faith — read the Word more.

6

GOING PLACES?

It's no use galloping if you are going in the wrong direction, is it?

October

7

A FOUR THOUSAND YEAR DAY?

Is God patient? In Romans 10 : 21 we read a quotation of God saying a remarkable thing. He says 'All day long I have stretched out my hands to a disobedient and contrary people'. Four thousand years ago Abraham set out for Canaan. Four thousand years later God is still holding out his hands to Israel and longing to draw Israel to himself. But not only Israel, surely. You and I have known this stance of God extending his hands to us even when we have resisted his will, haven't we?

Try, sometime today, to stretch out your arms and hands for five minutes. You'll know pain and in ten minutes excruciating pain. If you try it all day long you'll be calling for an ambulance. What about a four thousand year old day? Our God is patient. But don't whatever you do presume on his patience.

8

GOD IS NO KILLJOY

'Let their table become a snare and a trap', King David is quoted by Paul as saying in Romans 11 : 9. What does he mean? He means that there is such a thing as the table of the saved and the table of the lost.

The word table in the Bible is a metaphor. It speaks of the infinite delights which Christ has obtained for the believer; innumerable blessings include forgiveness, justification, reconciliation and redemption. It speaks of all God's plans yet to be revealed in Heaven. The Saviour described it all as a banquet. Salvation is like a banquet! God is no killjoy!

And the table of the lost? There are certainly pleasures there but such pleasures become a trap. King Saul was an example of that. Look at him who had once known a palace now sitting in a house of a Spirit medium doing his best to enjoy himself and tomorrow brings disaster and he knows it. The table of the lost dishes up blackness of darkness forever.

Tell me, tell me, at what table do you feed?

9

'THE ROOT'

If there is one thing I detest it is the view held by some people that the killing of millions of Jewish people by the Nazis was God punishing them for those Jews who had said at the time of Christ's death, 'His blood be on us and on our children'. This view, in my opinion, has been the root of anti-Semitism in Western Europe. Hitler fed that root.

Why do I not believe it? Listen to Paul; 'And if some of the branches were broken off, and you, being a wild olive tree were grafted in among them and with them became a partaker of the root and fatness of the olive tree, do not boast against the branches. But if you boast remember that you do not support the root but the root supports you', (Romans 11 : 17/18)

October

What is Paul saying? He is saying 'Don't get uppish in the christian church against Jews. Don't boast, for the Jewish nation was the root from which you have come. Israel was the tree that bore a testimony for God when your western fore-fathers were running about painted blue, but, she fell into unbelief. The branches were cut off and non Jews (Gentiles) were grafted in.'

We cannot go around calling the Jews 'Christ murderers' when we ourselves are invovled. I would never accuse the Jews of crucifying my Lord other than the way I crucified him for it was my sins that put him on the cross, too. It is at the cross that the Jew and Gentile meet. Christians must not boast except in the cross. I oppose anti-Semitism with all my heart.

10 ——————————

He has the answers

Paul now comes to one of his great high points in the letter to the Romans; 'Oh, the depth of the riches both of the wisdom and knowledge of God! How unsearchable are his judgements and his ways past finding out! For who has known the mind of the Lord?'

It is a good question, isn't it? Have you ever been able to anticipate what God is going to do? Have you ever been able to figure out how God is going to handle the situations you get into?

'Whose picture is on this coin?', asked Christ. 'Caesar's, they said. They wanted to know if they should pay taxes to Ceasar. If he said 'No' the Romans would be angry, if he said 'Yes' the Jews would be angry!

'All right', Christ is saying, 'If a coin is what Ceasar puts his image on then give it to Ceasar but God has put his image on you and that is what you owe God — yourselves!'

You see there is no situation to which your Lord does not know the answer. Our thoughts are not his thoughts. So let's stop arguing with him for it is foolish to argue with the very power that makes it possible to argue at all. If you really knew the Lord's mind you would quit worrying. So, wait for him, he will make his mind known to you. Be sure of that.

11

THE BATTLE FOR YOUR MIND

The problem with television's script writing is that it often attempts to harmonise two contradictory values; hedonism and decency. People get dazzled by a programme's entertaining qualities and don't realise its downright wicked message. The message often is; 'Don't take life too seriously; enjoy it. All moral codes are restrictive. Seek pleasure as long as you balance self-indulgence with moderation and good taste. A modern sense of decency requires that you only accept the possibility of a God; it neither accepts nor requires true holiness'.

Paul says the very opposite. 'Be not conformed to this world but be ye transformed by the renewing of your mind that you may prove what is that good and

October

acceptable and perfect will of God'. (Romans 12 : 2) You will find that what the world counts reasonable God does not count reasonable. The mind is where the battle is. If I soak my mind with the world's standards then I must not be surprised if my standard become the world's standards. Be careful what you soak your mind with today, especially through your eyes.

12

BIG SPENDERS

It's always easy to be liberal when you are spending someone else's money. Agreed?

13

'THE REBELS'

When the firstborn were redeemed out of Egypt the Lord claimed them as his (Exodus 13 : 1). As they moved out across the wilderness 22,273 Levities were substituted for them. That left a shortfall of 273. Were they to be 'Let go' easily? No, those 273 were to be redeemed at ten times the price a man would have to pay at 30 years of age when his name was first entered on Israel's census sheet!

The Levites, then, were very special. Their service was to be a living sacrifice. One day a Levite called Korah rebelled against this idea that they were special and God opened the groud and swallowed him and his rebels, alive. Their censers were nailed to the altar of sacrifice to perpetually remind Israelites that when God said something was his, he meant it.

Is it any wonder that Paul said 'I beseech you therefore, brethren by the mercies of God, that you present your bodies a living sacrifice, holy, acceptable to God, which is your reasonable service' (Romans 12 : 1). Paul is beseeching because he had Korah in mind. Selah.

14

THE COMING DAY

Let us not think for one moment that whatever we sow, we reap applies to this life alone. If such a thing is true then what do the words of Revelation 3 : 11 mean when they say: 'I am coming soon, hold fast what you have that no one may take your crown?' We judge things by 'Man's day' but in the light of that coming day I'll wish I had given him more.

15

'SINK YOUR PRIDE'

Fangio was a hero of mine as a boy. The great racing driver knew how to leave his challengers behind. Imagine Fangio sitting at the traffic lights in your town or city as you go to work this morning. Here are some local lads in a car who spot him and with great joy they rev their engines and pass Fangio as he pulls away from the lights, leaving him

October

behind. Does he chase them? No, for he sacrifices his pride for the sake of his example.

'Therefore', says Romans 14 : 16 'Do not let your good be spoken of as evil'. There are many things christians could do but they abstain from them lest they be a bad example to others. Such action brings their Lord great delight and His pleasure in them is earth's highest joy.

16

'NO. 1 IS SOMEONE ELSE'

Is there any more challenging question in all of Scripture than the question asked in Romans 15 : 3; 'For even Christ did not please himself?' Where would we be if he had? If you set out today bent on pleasing yourself alone I warn you now that your day will ultimately be utterly wasted. Utterly.

17

CHRISTIAN HOPE IS NOT "HOPE SO"

'Whatever things were written before were written for our learning that we through the patience and comfort of the Scriptures might have hope', says Paul encouragingly. Please notice that christian hope is not 'Hope so'. There is absolutely no trace of uncertainy in it. Christian hope is ultimate, final and absolute. 'Which hope we have as an anchor of the soul both sure and stedfast which entereth into that within the veil', says the letter to the Hebrews.

October

They tell me when ships were entering harbour long ago they would put their anchor in a small boat which would carry it into the harbour and the sailors would sink it in the sand. The ship was out on the ocean but the anchor was in the harbour. That's the kind of hope you have, today, christian. It enters into Heaven itself ahead of you. Enjoy it.

18

'DON'T TRY TO EXPLAIN'

I'm not so sure about the phrase, sometimes spoken to people in distress; 'God only let this happen to you because he knows that you are strong enough to bear it'. A minister said that to a lady once and she replied 'If only I was a weaker person my son would still be alive'.

When folk have been bereaved keep away from any temptation you may have to explain why their bereavement has come. I know of deep, deep hurt which has been brought to hearts already broken by such well meaning naivety. Don't try to explain, just get along side and help. O.K.?

19

'KOSSOF IN ULSTER'

I sometimes speak of hearing the great storyteller David Kossof when he visited Northern Ireland once. We clapped and clapped for more when he had finished, but he only came back onto the platform once.

October

'My father was a poor Russian tailor in London', he told us, 'And he once said to me, "David you will be with people of an evening or wherever and the chemistry will be good between you but my advice to you is — don't stay too long!" With that the most famous Bible story teller of my day walked away from his audience and I have never cast eyes on him, in the flesh, since.

You see, there comes a time to move on and the great apostle Paul knew it. 'Now', he wrote, to the christians at Rome, 'No longer having a place in these parts . . . I shall come to you'. Think of those little words; 'No longer having a place in these parts' (Romans 12 : 23). He knew his time was up, that the Lord was moving him on. The place God had given him had passed it usefulness; it was someone elses turn now. God had work for him elsewhere and it was time to go. Paul had the wisdom to know it when the time had come. Have you?

20 _____

'PHEBE'

Do you often wish you could get a glimpse of first century church life? The last chapter of Paul's letter to the Romans will give you that. Let me draw your attention, over the last few days of October to a few of the people Paul mentions. The church is people and here are a few first century ones. Let's start with Phebe.

'I commend to you Phebe', says Paul, 'Our sister, who is a servant of the church in Cenchrea, that you

October

may receive her in the Lord in a manner worthy of the saints, and assist her in whatever business she has need of you; for indeed she has been a helper of many and of myself also'. (Romans 16 : 1-2) Phebe is generally reckoned to be the one who carried Paul's letter to the Romans and if she did she carried more than she knew. The Reformation was in her luggage, John Bunyan read the letter and got so caught up with its truths he wrote Pilgrim's Progress, and the list of people who have been influenced by the letter is countless.

Wouldn't you like to follow in Phebe's steps and be a helper? You might say it's not much. Is it not? What if Phebe had lost the letter? You are vital as a helper in whatever you do for the Lord and don't forget it.

> 'For want of a nail the shoe was lost,
> For want of a shoe the horse was lost,
> For want of a horse the message was lost,
> For want of a message the battle was lost,
> For failure in battle the war was lost'.

21

'NEVER FORGET A FRIEND'

It is very easy to forget a friend, especially a friend of early days in your life. Events come to separate you, circumstances distance you and it is not long before you get out of touch. Paul shows he cared deeply about past friends and it is moving to see him keep up contact.

October

'Greet my beloved Epaenetus, who is the first fruits of Achaia to Christ', he writes. Obviously Epaenetus was the first person to believe the gospel when Paul went to the Province of Asia. Paul saw a great spiritual awakening in Pro-Consular Asia especially at Ephesus. The awakening spread to Smyrna, Pergamos, Thyatira, Sardis, Philadelphia, Laodicea, Colossae, Heirapolis but Paul never forgot the first convert. He considered him a 'first-fruit'. Paul saw himself as a branch and a vine from which converts, by God's power were borne. They tell me at Hampton Court near London a 1768 vine still bears several hundred pounds of grapes every year!

You see, christian work is often thrilling particularly in the way it bears spiritual fruit even for long years after the first seed has been planted. Yet, as you see the spiritual fruit grow from work you have done for the Lord in your life, don't forget the first folk who trusted Christ through your witness. Why not write a letter or phone some of them today? A young chap looked me up recently after a service I had taken and I discovered I had taught him in Sunday School nearly thirty years ago. I was deeply touched that he looked me up. So, go on, touch the heart of someone you knew long ago by getting in touch today.

22 ——————————

SENOIRITY IS NOT SUPERIORITY

Respect is a fast receding quality in many peoples lives. Youth is a time of great vitality and it brims with ideas, fresh initiative and 'zip'. The young

October

people in church life are vital, they are its future but it is also vital that they remember in their first years of joyful christian experience that there are folk around who knew the Lord long before they did. Paul says 'Great Andronicus and Junia, my kinsmen and my fellow prisoners who are of note among the apostles who also were in Christ before me'. Let's keep respect for those who are older-in-the-faith; Paul did. At the same time let the older-in-the-faith remember that although there is seniority in a christian church there should be no such thing as superiority. Paul was a great apostle, the greatest christian writer in history and the best Bible teacher the church has ever known but he didn't forget those who knew Christ before he did.

23

THE OPEN-ENDED COMMITMENT

Is someone reading today's entry and you are working hard for the Lord? My heart goes out to you because christian work is an open ended commitment; it does not begin at 9.00 a.m. and finish at 5.00 p.m. There is no earthly end to it, is there? Anybody who has ever been in any way involved in christian work knows this to be true. 'Great Tryphena and Tryphosa who have laboured in the Lord. Great the beloved Persis, who laboured much in the Lord', asks Paul. Obviously these were hard working christian women and Paul is commending them for their hard work.

October

There is nothing wrong with hard work for the Lord but in the midst of it let's remember the word of a man caught up in the midst of the recent scandal ridden problems of American T.V. evangelism; 'I was working so hard in God's work, I forgot about God'. Selah.

24

LINES OF COMMUNICATION

The one who says they have no Call have probably left the receiver off.

25

KEEP IT UP, MOTHER

Can I add a personal note in today's reading? In my experience in the christian life I have found what I call 'Mothers-in-Israel' to be a power of strength to me in the christian ministry; I mean godly christian women who have helped me and 'mothered' me in the faith. I thank Paul for such people and so did the great apostle Paul. 'Greet Rufus', he wrote, 'Chosen in the Lord and his mother and mine'. Rufus's mother treated Paul like a son and he appreciated it. I reckon the christian church would be much the poorer without our spiritual mothers. Paul certainly thought that. Am I being read by one today? Keep up the good work, mother!

26

TIME TELLS

Paul is now drawing his great letter to the Romans to a close. He lifts his pen for the last warning and challenge to the people of God. He warns that there will come into their christian lives and churches people who do not serve Christ but who 'serve their own appetites'. Just let that warning sink into your heart today. These people, warns Paul 'By smooth words and flattering speech deceive the hearts of the simple'.

There is a very real difference between those who serve Christ and those who serve their own appetites, but the difference is not always easy to discern. Time tells, though, doesn't it? Time tells. And if not time, certainly eternity. Let's not 'duck' the issue; is my christian service to Christ or is it serving my own ego? Am I doing what I'm doing in christian work out of love to Christ? You and I might answer 'I assume so!' Don't assume; make sure.

27

BE SIMPLE CONCERNING EVIL

'Be wise in what is good and simple concerning evil', says Paul.

The story is told of a couple in a group one night where an off-colour joke was told. Some laughed and the wife turned to her husband and said; 'I don't get it. What are they laughing at? I don't see the point'.

October

'Thank God. You can't', replied her husband, 'It's dirty'. Let's be unsophisticated concerning evil.

Sow a thought, reap an action,
Sow an action, reap a habit,
Sow a habit, reap a character,
Sow a character, reap a destiny.

28

SATAN CAN BE BRUISED UNDER YOUR FEET

Man first heard the gospel in the Garden of Eden. 'I will put enmity between you and the woman, and between your seed and her seed; he shall bruise your head and you shall bruise his heel'. It was good news then and it still is.

Now, because of the victory the christian has in Christ, Satan can be bruised under our feet. 'And the God of peace will crush Satan under your feet, shortly', says Paul to the hard pressed Roman church. Isn't that a lovely promise? Whatever you face today, in Christ's strength, Satan can get a bruising and a crushing instead of you. Resist him and he will flee from you.

29

YOU MATTER TO GOD

Paul adds a little Post Script to his letter. In it he brings greetings from his frineds and notice that 'Tertius' and 'Quartus' are mentioned. Tertius means 'third' and Quartus means 'fourth'.

October

According to Dr. Donald Grey Barnhouse black mothers during the slave trade did not want their boys to be called 'One', 'Two' or 'Three' etc. They poured over boys names and instead of Tertius and Quartus they choose 'Rastus' because of Romans 16 : 23.

Yes, my friend, you matter, you are not a number. Don't get overwhelmed by other people's views of you. You do really matter. Even the very hairs of your head are numbered by God. Walk in the conscious knowledge that you are beloved of the Lord. Our cat caught a baby blue tit recently and landed It with a cat grin at our front door. My heartbroken wife took the wee thing, still alive, to the vetinary surgeon! Now if a human heart would do that for a baby bird what would God not do for those who trust Him? Keep going', 'Rastus', God cares!

30

ACTIONS SPEAK LOUDER

The person who does big things is too busy to talk about them.

31

DON'T KEEP THE SECRET

According to the best authorities Paul wrote the letter to the Romans over a three month period, December 56AD to February 57AD. In those three months he communicated truth which is worth

October

spreading. He implies in his last word in the letter that the Gospel he has been expounding was once a secret but that it should be no longer so. 'Now to him who is able to establish you according to my gospel and the preaching of Jesus Christ, according to the revelation of the mystery which was kept secret since the world began but now has been made manifest and by the prophetic Scriptures has been made known to all nations, according to the commandment of the everlasting God, for obedience to the faith — to God, alone wise, be glory through Jesus Christ forever. Amen'. Paul certainly did not let the great truths that God had taught him lie dormant in his life. He poured his life into communicating them to others. So must we.

I was deeply moved recently to read that when the great Dr. Barnhouse preached on the Epistle to the Romans on his radio programme he received 2 million letters in the mail. Recently I preached a weekly series of messages on the letter to the Romans for a 33 week period and although I cannot claim 2 million letters in the mail I did receive one of the most moving letters I have ever known. It came from a young man who had come to those services and because of what he had learned had led his mother to faith in Christ just a few weeks before she died. When the Lord returns and that precious body is raised by His power I know in my heart that I shall not be sorry I spent those months in the pulpit expounding the truths of Paul's great letter. Wherever you go today, as God gives you opportunity, don't keep the Gospel a secret.

NOVEMBER

Beech-wood fires are bright and clear
If logs are kept a year,
Oaken logs burn steadily
If the wood is old and dry.
Chesnuts only good, they say,
If for long it's laid away.
But ash new or old
Is fit for a Queen with a crown of gold.

Birch and fir-logs burn too fast
Blaze up bright but do not last.
It is by the Irish said
Hawthorn bakes the sweetest bread.
But ash green or ash brown
Is fit for a Queen with a golden crown.

Elm-wood burns like churchyard mould —
E'en the very flames are cold.
Poplar gives a bitter smoke
Fills your eyes and makes you choke.
Apple-wood will scent your room
With an incense-like perfume.
But ash wet or ash dry
For a Queen to warm her slippers by.

Author unknown

November

1

'A WORD TO ALL EXILES'

Now, as winter seeps and then freezes into the woods, I want to draw your attention to the writing of a child of much sorrow. Tempered by age, mellowed by suffering, his words had once burned with rashness and self-centred boasting. All that has gone; Peter the fisherman is now Peter the comforter. He sets himself to encourage the christian church of his day, a church that was going through the fires of trial. Lied upon, hated and despised for their faith in the Lord Jesus these christians found sustenance for troubled times in Peter's inspired writing. So can you.

These words were not written to combat doctrinal heresy, they were written to strengthen people. Here are winsome, affectionate, loving, humble, warm words which appeal to the human heart.

'To the pilgrims of the Dispersion', he wrote. It was a technical term for Jews scattered in exile in all countries outside Israel, but it is now applied by Peter to the christian church scattered abroad. We are, you see, the exiles of eternity; we are in this world but not of it. A christian sees everything in the light of eternity and decides what importance anything in life has in relation to eternity. A christian doesn't envy the godless any more than envy the passengers on the Titanic.

343

November

2

'CHECK YOUR MAP'

Sometimes christians forget the tremendous spiritual inheritance that is theirs. It is like a child born into an aristocratic family who is not aware, nor can be fully aware, of all that birth has given him. 'The Lord is our portion', says the Bible. This is our inheritance and one day we shall enter more fully into all that it implies. The full joy of knowing God awaits us in Heaven.

What kind of qualities does this inheritance have? It is 'Incorruptible'; time, people, shifts in opinion or human values cannot touch it. It is 'Undefiled'; no flaw, crack, or freckle, taints it. Pollution cannot even touch the edges of it nor creep to the heart of it. 'It does not fade away', it never palls, it never bores, it will never weary us. 'It is reserved in heaven for you'; just think of that, as the swirl of events of the coming day sweep around you, christian. No one will be able to contest your inheritance no matter how bad your day gets. You are the heir, the Bible is your map to the lands you will inherit. Explore it and it will cheer your heart. Have a good day!

3

'KEPT'

Not much good having an inheritance if you will never be able to enjoy it. It is just thrilling to read Peter's word to inheritors; he comments, 'Who are kept by the power of God through faith for salvation

344

ready to be revealed in the last time' (Chapter 1 : 5). Kept. Kept. Get a hold of that little word. When God says he will keep something, he means it. If I may be so bold as to write — God's credibility is at stake if he doesn't keep his inheritors for their inheritance. David spoke of the Lord as leading his sheep in the paths of righteousness 'For his names sake'. His name behind it, guarantees it. If he has the power to lead, he has the power to keep.

Are you worried about a loved one, a son or a daughter, a relative or a friend who has gone away to college or work or a new life? Don't be. He who can keep them for an inheritance yet to be fully enjoyed can keep them on the way there.

'BURNING OFF THE SCUM'

Trial is compared by Peter to fire. That 'The genuineness of your faith', he writes, 'though it be tested by fire may be found to praise, honour and glory at the revelation of Jesus Christ'. Fire can't endure impurity and goes for it. Fire is a refiner and God uses his refining fires to cause the 'outward man' to perish and the 'inward man' to be renewed day after day. God's trials are only 'for a little while' (Chapter 1 : 6) and you can be sure as he turns up the heat in your life that he is after some scum that needs to be burned off in order that you may reflect his glory.

November

The trial you are passing through is not aimless. It is not a punishment. It proves you are very valuable to the Lord. It shows there is some higher service coming up. You will eventually be compensated at the sight of what the trial has accomplished. You will be able to lay it as a crown at the Lord's feet.

5 ───────────────────

'SOMETIMES WE NEED PRESSURE'

I remember reading that the athlete Steve Cram once ran a 2,000 metre race in Budapest in 4 minutes 51.39 seconds. A very interesting fact emerged from that race. Steve Cram was leading the race but at the halfway stage his pacemaker dropped out and he had no first class challengers. 'It was very, very tough', he said. 'I'm not going to do anything like that again for a long time'. Even world class athletes need pressure to make them do better.

'Now they do it', says the Bible, 'To receive a corruptible crown, but we an incorruptible' (1 Corinthians 9 : 25). Let us remember then as Peter's first epistle has been teaching us that we must accept trial as from the hand of God. If our faith would grow stronger by the use of exercise and strain we must not be surprised if God exposes us to discipline. If an athlete needs pressure so do we in order that we might be able to gain that incorruptible crown. Don't fear that tension that is gnawing at the edge of your faith today. Plunge into the day with enthusiasm and he will use the pressure to make you run an even better race for him.

346

'DO YOU WISH YOU COULD SEE CHRIST?'

I often wish I could have the Lord physically before me every day so that I could ask him, as he sat in my house, 'Where to now, Lord?' 'What should I say in this situation?' 'What do you want me to do today, Lord?'.

Why do you think great film makers attempt to make films of the life of Christ which are then watched by millions? Why do you think great painters have attempted to produce masterpieces depicting the face of Christ? It is the desire in millions of peoples hearts to have a Christ who is present, physically.

Yet, the Scripture is very clear on the matter that those who have not seen Christ are at an advantage over those who, in the past, have seen him on earth. How? Those who saw him would have been well aware that domestic or other duties would have taken them away from him. It would have been a much interrupted view they would have had of Christ. Crowds flocked around him and eventually the cross came and the ascension.

'Whom having not seen, you love', wrote Peter. 'Though now you do not see him, yet believing, you rejoice with joy inexpressible and full of glory'. The fact is that those who have not seen Christ have to exercise faith in a way those who saw him never had to. It is a deeper, more arduous faith that is absolutely independent of every circumstance that happens. An unseen Christ is no hindrance to sheer downright christian joy. You have the edge, for, 'Blessed are they that have not seen yet believe'.

November

7

'NOT THE CHRIST WHO "WAS"

Isn't it fascinating that no apostle ever remembered Christ in the sense that they spoke of him in the past tense? They always spoke of him in the present tense. They did not say 'My, you should have heard him, you should have watched him as we did. Then you would really live for him!' No, they spoke of our Lord in the present continuous tense. You see, Jesus Christ is the same, yesterday, today and forever. No wonder George Muller had a little text framed in his room which read, 'And today'.

I shall never forget going to the garden tomb in Jerusalem. At the tomb there was a little door and on it were these words 'He is not here, he is risen'. Praise God our Lord Jesus is not a Lord just of the past but of the present, too. Come on, cheer up, you and I change and so do our moods and our day but nothing changes him. Time is foiled in Jesus. Come to him in a billion years time and how will you find him? Just the same. Hallelujah!

8

SILENT WORSHIP

Peter calls it a 'Joy unspeakable!'. Aren't there times in your christian life when you have experiences of Christ which are just inexpressible? Words seem empty. Don't try to analyse such times with words. The nameless woman who stood at

Christ's feet behind him weeping and then washed his feet with her tears and wiped them with the hairs of her head and anointed them with fragrant oil, worshipped without a word. It was one of the most significant acts of worship in history and not a word passed her lips. Silence, you know, is sometimes a great aid to conversation.

9

THE ANGELS DESIRE

I had just finished preaching at a service in North Wales one evening when I was approached by an old lady. She was very ill, if not dying and being Irish by birth and having seen my name on a board outside the church building she had come in to listen. For a long time she had been a reader of one of my columns and having never met me she was determined to shake my hand before the evening was through. I found the situation very moving as she sat down beside me and encouraged me in the things of God. She said she felt the Lord was urging her to encourage me to keep preaching about the cross and then she let slip a little statement which has stayed with me for months. 'Paul', she said 'put his learning on the shelf and preached the cross'. It was an Irish way of putting it but how true her statement was. Peter would have agreed with her.

Peter says the Spirit of God spoke through the prophets witnessing 'Beforehand of the sufferings of Christ' (Chapter 1 : 11). The sufferings of Christ were the burden of the prophets. He also says that

November

the sufferings of Christ was the centre of the apostles preaching. 'To them it was revealed that not to themselves but to us they were ministering the things which now have been reported to you' (Chapter 1 : 12). He even adds that the cross of Christ was the theme of angels for these are things, he says, 'Which angels desire to look into'. In fact even though angels cannot penetrate all the mysterious depths of the cross they declare what they know for in Heaven they cry 'Worthy is the lamb that was slain'.

Now if angels find opportunity of knowledge in the cross of Christ, where do we who have enjoyed its blessing stand? I love what one of the Queen's chaplains, John Stott says in his classic book 'The Cross of Christ'. 'I could never myself believe in God, if it were not for the cross. The only God I believe in is the one Nietzsche ridiculed as 'God on the cross'. In the real world of pain, how could one worship a God who was immune to it? I've entered many Buddhist temples in different Asian countries and stood respectfully before the statue of the Buddha, his legs cross, arms folded, eyes closed, the ghost of a smile playing around his mouth, a remote look on his face, detached from the agonies of the world. But each time, after a while I have had to turn away. And in imagination I have turned instead to that lonely, twisted, tortured figure on the cross, nails through hands and feet, back lacerated, limbs wrenched, brow bleeding from thorn-pricks, mouth dry and intolerably thirsty, plunged in God-forsaken darkness. That is the God for me! He laid aside his immunity to pain. He entered our world of flesh and blood, tears and death. He suffered for us. Our sufferings become more manageable in the light of his. There is still a question mark against human suffering, but over it we boldly stamp another mark, the cross, which symbolises divine suffering. The cross of Christ . . . is Gods only self-justification in such a world as ours'.

10

RUMOUR

There is one thing that will grow like wildfire in any kind of soil, in any climate, anywhere on earth and that is idle rumour.

11

'NO MORE POSTAL ORDERS'

'As he who called you is holy, you also be holy in all your conduct', challenges Peter (Chapter 1 : 13-15) What is holiness? Well, I like the story of F. B. Meyer preaching at the Keswick Convention on the subject of Scriptural holiness. The next morning the local Post Office ran out of postal orders because christians who had heard Mr. Meyer's message from the word of God were so challenged by it they decided they would pay their debts immediately. That's holiness in action.

November

12 ——————————————

We talk about the Russian bear or the British lion, and the Americans have their eagle symbol and other countries choose animals fleet of foot or wing to symbolise what their country stands for. Nowhere in the world do I know of any country that has a lamb as its symbol. Innocence and tenderness are not qualities which nations want to be associated with their place in the world.

The christian church thinks very differently. Their Lord is constantly depicted as the Lamb of God. Peter says 'We are not redeemed with corruptible things, like silver or gold .. but with the precious blood of Christ, as of a lamb without blemish and without spot'. The lamb is a beautiful analogy for our lovely Lord Jesus Christ.

The city of the book of Revelation is a city where its light is the face of Christ, its music is the name of Christ, its harmony is the praise of Christ, its theme is the love of Christ, its joy is the presence of Christ, its employment is the service of Christ, its strength is the omnipotence of Christ, its duration is the eternity of Christ, and its super glory is Christ himself. Let theological fashions come and go. Let gimmicks be what they may. Let men deride and let the demons fume. The only message which saves people is the gospel of the lamb. Behold the Lamb of God.

13

HAVE YOU BEEN RECENTLY BEREAVED?

Isn't it a great thing that we are not redeemed with corruptible things such as silver and gold? The soul that trusts in money will never be ransomed but the soul that trusts in Christ will never be lost. Tell me, have you been recently bereaved of a loved one who has gone to be with Christ? How can you say you have lost a loved one if you know where they are? Isn't that a comforting thought?

14

WHITE AS LIGHT

We are, according to Peter, to have 'unfeigned' love for fellow christians. That means 'sincere'. You could easily kiss those you would betray. Gossip, you know, is what you say behind folks backs that you would never say to their face. Flattery is what you say to their face that you would never say behind their backs. Often our politeness, even, is but skin deep. Peter says we are to 'love' one another fervently with a pure heart. Let your motivation today be as white as light.

November

15 ————————————

THE BURNING HEARTS

It is vital that christians love one another but it must always be remembered that the mere meeting of christian with christian does not bring a burning heart. Peter speaks of having sincere love one for another but he also adds 'Having been born again not of corruptible seed but incorruptible through the word of God which lives and abides forever'. If you set two mirrors one over against the other they won't reflect much light. Yet, set a candle or an electric light between them and see what happens.

So it is when christians have the knowledge and obedience to 'the truth of God' (The Bible) between them; burning hearts result. What did the two on the way to Emmaus say when the Saviour opened up the Scriptures to them? Their burning hearts came as a result of the Scriptures being set between them. The same experience can be yours with fellow christians when the Scriptures are between you. That's why I count it the privilege of my life to set the word of God between believers and teach it. Burning hearts result. Try it.

16

'THE THREE GIFTS'

The story is told of the old minister who at the end of his ministry was given, on a special evening, three gifts; some money, a clock, and a copy of a new Bible. When asked by someone a few years later as to how he was, he replied 'The money has gone, the clock is still going but the word of the Lord endures forever!' It was a very good way to put it for Peter says 'All flesh is as grass and all the glory of man as the flower of the grass. The grass withers, and the flower falls away, but the word of the Lord endures forever'. Do you really believe it?

17

'DISALLOWED?'

There was a division among the builders. A specially prepared and cut stone lay ready to their hand. Some admired it and some even praised it but most criticised it and derided it. After some discussion they rejected it. 'Disallowed' was the word they used. They began to build their building without the specially prepared stone and it became a monument to their folly.

This is the metaphor that Peter uses to describe what people do with the Lord Jesus. They reject or disallow him a place in their lives and plans and the end result is a disaster. I warn you today that if you are building your life on any other foundation no

November

matter what you become or what you have it will be wrecked when the storm hits it. It was Samuel Rutherford who pointed out that as it is no shame for a drowning man to throw himself upon a rock so it is no shame for a sinner to throw himself or herself upon Christ. He or she is a fool who rejects the Rock of Ages.

18

'ALL BELIEVERS ARE PRIESTS'

The metaphor that Peter uses to describe Christ as a stone is now taken a stage further. 'Coming to him as to a living stone, rejected indeed by men, but chosen by God and precious, you also, as living stones are being built up as a spiritual house, a holy priesthood, to offer up spiritual sacrifices acceptable to God through Jesus Christ'. Notice that the stone lives and draws to itself other stones which are lying all around and one after another as they slowly approach it, they also begin to live. Stones as if gathered by unseen hands begin to build up, not a material, but a spiritual house. The metaphor suddenly changes. These stones are now referred to as a holy priesthood. Just as the priests in the old Testament temple did not serve God with empty hands so the priests in this new building offer spiritual sacrifices, acceptable to God by Jesus Christ.

Let me emphasise once again that every believer is a priest in the sight of God and can offer, at any time of day or night, a spiritual sacrifice which will bring pleasure to the heart of God. You will notice that when Bartimaeus got his eyesight back he no longer returned to his begging. He no longer said 'give me' anymore at the side of any road. He followed Jesus in the way of service. So, today, why not give the Lord something instead of always asking him to give you something?

19

CHECK THEM FOR IT

The stone that the builders rejected is the stone which we consider a chief corner stone, elect, precious! 'And he who believes on him shall not be confounded' As far as a christian is concerned the one in whom they believe 'Is precious'. Because Christ is precious that is why we cannot stand people taking his name in vain around us every day. The tragic thing at the moment in Great Britain is that the two chief swear words are 'God' and 'Christ'. As you go through your day I am quite sure that you will come across someone somewhere taking your Lord's name in vain. Why not gently check them for doing so and your witness may result in bringing them to revere and worship his name? They too, like you, may come to consider him precious. Think about it.

November

20

AT LEAST WE CAN PRAISE HIM

The metaphors now begin to really pile up in Peter's writing. 'You are a chosen generation, a royal priesthood, a holy nation, his own special people, that you may proclaim the praises of him who called you out of darkness into his marvellous light'. Are you, christian, proclaiming his praises today? A young lady told me recently of sitting at a breaking of bread service in a little hall in the heart of the Ulster countryside. The girl told me how that that morning there was a long silence as the christians sat at the Lord's table, no one taking part. Suddenly an older man rose to his feet and looking around those christians he said with great passion in his voice, 'At least we can praise Him' and proceeded to announce a christian hymn. I often think of what he said for he spoke, in his frustration with the barrenness of that morning's worship a truth which applies to any of us on any day. Whatever kind of a day you have had or are going to have today, at least you can praise Him. Don't forget to do it.

21

THERE IS A WAR ON

Quietly and earnestly Peter begins to move from the more purely doctrinal part of his writing to the more practical. 'I beg you', he writes 'as sojourners and pilgrims, abstain from fleshly lusts which war against the soul'. Notice that little word 'war'. It means there is an army marching against you. In practical terms it means that if you go in for self indulgence this army will attack and conquer your inner life. They will sully it, pollute it, lower its tone and sap your moral and spiritual strength. Eventually it will cripple your endeavours for your Lord and lead you to failure and defeat. The much talented and sensitive David gave in to it and became a murderer. His son, the wisest man in all the earth did the same thing only on a far greater scale and became an effeminate fool. Samson, despite his great gift gave in to self indulgence and wasted so much of his precious life. Demas, Paul's companion gave in to self indulgence and fled the cost of being a disciple and became a deserter in the spiritual battle.

Indulge the flesh and you will be weak. Curb it by God's strength and power and you will be strong. May you know a great victory over self indulgence today. Walk in the Spirit and you will not fulfil the lusts of the flesh. The fulness of the Spirit of God within your life makes it easy to abstain from fleshly lusts. The person filled with the Spirit finds that they lose a taste for the very things in which they formerly delighted. Satisfied with the provision of their Father's house they turn with disgust from the husks of the swine trough. May you be filled with the spirit of God today.

November
22

WHO IS THE BEST PREACHER?

The great Latimer rose to preach at St. Paul's cathedral on the 18th January 1548. He had just been released from the Tower of London and what he said in those moments still rings down through years. I leave it with you today.

'And now I would ask you a strange question. Who is the most diligent Bishop and prelate in all England that passes all the rest in doing his office? I can tell for I know who it is, I know him well. But now I think I see you listening and harkening that I should name him. There is one who passes all the others and is the most diligent prelate and preacher in all England and well you know who it is? It is the Devil. He is the most diligent preacher of all others. He is never out of his diocese. You shall never find him unoccupied. He is ever in his parish. You shall never find him out of the way. Call for him when you will, he is ever at home. He is the most diligent preacher in all the realm. He is ever at his plough. No lording or loitering can hinder him. He is ever applying his business. You shall never find him idle, I warrant you. Where the devil is resident and has his plough going there away with books and up with candles. Away with Bibles and up with beads. Away with the light of the gospel and up with the light of candles. Yeah at noonday, up with mans traditions and his laws and down with God's traditions and his most holy word. O that our prelates would be as diligent to sow the corn of good doctrine as Satan is to sow cockel and darnel. There was never such a preacher in England as he is'.

ARE THEY BEING UNREASONABLE?

So you wish to live according to the will of God only? Good. You will soon discover that God's will works through the appointments of men who are often foolish and even ignorant. There is hardly a biography in the Bible of any of its great heroes who did not discover the will of God in their lives through the appointments of ungodly people above them. Think long on the life of Joseph. Think long on the life of Esther. Even Peter knew what it was to be cast into prison by an evil man and God to overrule in his circumstances. That is why Peter writes 'Submit yourselves to every ordinance of man for the Lord's sake whether to the king as supreme, or to govenors, as to those who were sent by him for the punishment of evildoers and for the praise of those who do good. For this is the will of God that by doing good you may put to silence the ignorance of foolish men'. Has your boss made a foolish decision regarding your life today? Are you fretting under what some shop steward has done to you? Has the ward sister been unreasonable as you have tried to nurse in the hospital? Just remember, christian, God's permissions are ultimately his appointments.

November

24

————————————————

THE BALANCED LIFE

'Honour all people. Love the brotherhood. Fear God. Honour the king'. Here are four things that every christian should do. The first is saying that we must value and esteem people. People are not things. Every person has a precious soul. If you were to be able to put the most degraded soul in the world on one scale and the weight of a world of gold in the other the world would kick the beam. It has been well said that the only equivalent to the value of a soul is the precious blood of Christ. That's how much God thinks of a persons value. We must not think any less. The second thing is to show a family spirit within the christian church. The third thing is to fear God and that means to fear causing him any pain. It is to always hold him in awe and reverence. The fourth thing is to respect human institutions and governments. If a christian does all four things then that christian will have an all round application of the christian faith in the nitty-gritty of every day life. They will be thoroughly balanced.

25

NOT WORTH IT

It is a wise saying that 'There is nothing in this world worth doing a mean action for'.

362

26

HOW TO "HIT" AN ENEMY

Peter gently points out that when our Lord Jesus was reviled he did not revile in return; 'When he suffered, he did not threaten, but committed himself to him who judges righteously'. Why not follow our Lord's example today? The best way to get an enemy is to hit them with an act of loving kindness. As you do it commit yourself to your Lord and ask him to vindicate you. He will certainly do that. Just because our Lord Jesus did not threaten when he suffered does not mean that a time of divine retribution is coming. This is a very unpopular truth in many circles today. People try to teach that God will never bring retribution. The fact is simply not true. If people refuse his offer of mercy presented in Christ and His Calvary work they will one day go down under the wrath of God. You do not need to revile nor threaten your enemy. 'Vengenance is mine', said God, 'I will repay'.

27

CALVARY BROKE HIS HEART

Is there any more moving statement in all of Scripture than Peter's statement 'Who himself bore our sins in his own body on the tree'? This lovely statement about the Lord Jesus reminds us that he will never have to bare our sins again. His wonderful Calvary work was accepted by his Father and to all who accept him as Saviour true salvation is given.

November

I once wrote an article on my good friend Dr. Victor Glasgow of Newtownards. He had been fifty years in Christ and gently prodding him about his life as a student and then as a Doctor with the RAF during the war and his subsequent life as an elder in a local church in Newtownards I began to gather some fascinating information about what he had been through. I can see him yet standing by his own fireside in the presence of his wife. With tears running down his face he looked at me and said 'Bingham, when you write this article let the people know that when I was a little boy of nine a man called Mr. Storey came to preach at a Sunday School prize-giving service. He broke my heart with the story of Calvary. That's fifty years ago and Calvary still breaks my heart'. Could you say that? God pity you if you can't.

28

THE PATH OF SUFFERING

'Christ also suffered for us'. Peter lays great stress on the sufferings of Christ as vital for our relationship to God. Notice that he says that Christ suffered 'for us'. Is there a more important preposition in all of the Bible? This preposition is showing that Christ took upon himself the consequence and curse of our sin. The sins of untold myriads of people were made to meet upon him. To all who trust him as Saviour those sins are put away for evermore through what the Saviour accomplished.

November

But notice what Peter says after pointing out that Christ suffered for us. 'Christ also suffered for us, leaving us an example that you should follow his steps'. Following the Lord Jesus will inevitably involve suffering for you. Do not think that you will escape suffering because your Lord did not escape it. Those footprints of his went through many days of deep suffering and if we will follow in his steps we must know them too. Let us never be ashamed to associate ourselves with the fellowship of his suffering. Let me remind you of the forgotten beatitude 'Blessed is he who is not offended in me'. Are you offended because you must suffer for Christ's sake. Then you are missing a very real blessing. If you are led by the Spirit of God you will come inevitably into the same collision with the spirit of society around you.

29

WATCH YOUR TONGUE

I like the little warning which says 'Watch your tongue. Remember it is in a wet place and likely to slip'.

30

RETURNED

We have now come to the end of November and soon the trees of the forest will be plumed with snow and their tops will be filled with a swirling pepper of snowflakes. I leave you with the lovely

November

words of Peter 'For you were like sheep going astray, but have now returned to the Shepherd and Overseer of your souls'. Once you were stray sheep. Once you were enticed by the sweet grass and strayed until at last you wandered alone and fell into pits you do not even want to think about. You became the easy prey of the one who goes about as a roaring lion. You were certain to perish unless you were rescued by the good Shepherd. He found you and now you have returned to his fold. Put up with the sarcasm and the roughness of people around you who persecute you because you belong to his fold. What will their censure look like when you are gathered as part of the whole flock on the hills of eternity? If we suffer, we are told, we shall also reign with him. Surely the greatest blessing in all of life is to be identified with Christ. Be glad of it.

DECEMBER

In millions upon millions of homes it will be covered with love. Everybody knows the Norway Spruce as the Christmas tree.

In my childhood home our Norway Spruce was brought every year by a friend who was a forester as a gift and off I would go as a lad to the nearby seashore to get sand to fill the base in which it stood. To this day its very smell evokes a vision of that crackling fire reflected in the red and blue baubles we hung from its branches and the childhood delight in those mysterious parcels piled lovingly around its base.

May this month be a very precious time for you and your family. Enjoy it, for, this too shall pass.

December

1

I want to devote our readings for this final month of the year to the subject of Mary of Nazareth. If ever anyone in history waited for God, Mary was that one. Jesus was called 'Jesus of Nazareth' chiefly because his mother was Mary of Nazareth. People did not call our Saviour Jesus the Bethlehemite but Jesus of Nazareth. It was to the town of Nazareth that the angel Gabriel was sent by God to speak to Mary about the coming Saviour.

I remember walking for the first time in the streets of Nazareth and thinking to myself that if I wanted to influence the world on any matter probably the last place on earth I would have chosen would have been Nazareth. Even when I went to preach to some of the christians in Nazareth I walked by an open sewer which ran down the middle of the street of the old city. It reminded me of the great Bible teacher Dr. Harry Ironside and his wife when they visited Nazareth. Mrs. Ironside was moved to tears as she walked through the streets of Nazareth. 'To think, Harry', she said 'that my Lord lived here in this place'. The great Dr. Ironside opened his coat and pointing said 'I'll show you a worse place than Nazareth where Christ lives now', he said 'He lives in my heart'. Does He live in yours? No place is too lowly or sinful for the Christ of God to enter and transform.

APOLOGISE TO AMERICA?

In city after city the Lord Jesus did mighty works during his lifetime. Yet, those very cities were denounced by him; Chorazin, Bethsaida, Capernaum no longer exist. They were small, ordinary sized towns and their peoples were privileged to hear the gospel from day to day but they sorely neglected Christ's great salvation and where are they now?

Nazareth is not mentioned in Christ's judgement of the cities in which he had been because he had not done any great and mighty work there. You see witnessing the power of the Lord is a very great privilege but it brings a very special responsibility with It. Do you not find that familiarity with the things of the Lord often tempts people to despise them? I trust that no one is reading this little book who has been brought up with all the privileges of a christian home and background and who has lived in a town where the gospel has been preached powerfully all through their lifetime and where they have witnessed the transforming power of God in lives all around them and yet they have despised the very gospel they know so well. Sometimes those cities and countries which are most privileged are the most wicked. I often think of what Dr. Billy Graham's wife, Ruth once said; 'If God does not judge America he will have to apologise to Sodom and Gemorrah'. I say to you today 'How shall you escape if you neglect so great a salvation'? If you have been highly privileged in knowing of spiritual truth and you despise it, greater will be your judgement, Selah.

December

3 ⎯⎯⎯⎯⎯⎯⎯⎯⎯

What a fantastic thing it must have been when the great angel Gabriel appeared to the virgin, Mary, to tell her that she would conceive in her womb and bring forth a son, saying, 'He will be great, and will be called the Son of the Highest, and the Lord God will give him the throne of his father David. And he will reign over the house of Jacob forever and of his kingdom there will be no end'. Mary had been chosen for an unprecedented, unrepeatable and gigantic task. Suddenly, out of the blue, she learns that she is to give birth to the Son of God. Can we ever begin to imagine what must have dawned upon her mind. How would she ever be able to stand the psychological and spiritual strain of waiting for the Son of God for nine long months? Her first reaction was to question the angel because of the moral difficulty. She could not see how an unmarried girl was going to become a mother. The angel explained 'The Holy Spirit will come upon you, the power of the Highest will overshadow you; therefore, also, that Holy One who is to be born will be called the Son of God'.

There is absolutely no doubt that such a staggering annunciation needed great faith to believe and that faith needed to be mightily confirmed. The angel was not slow to give Mary that confirmation for he told her of her cousin Elizabeth's miraculous pregnancy and was virtually suggesting that Mary should go and visit Elizabeth to have her faith confirmed and strengthened. When she

December

eventually got there Mary discovered that Elizabeth knew by prophetic inspiration without Mary having to tell her that Mary was going to be the mother of the Son of God. Her faith was immediately confirmed.

What do we learn from this? We learn that no matter how difficult a task God may call us, to or no matter what he may ask us to believe in His name he will not leave us without confirmation. Are you, like Mary, troubled about something the Lord has asked you to do or go through for Him and you want your faith confirmed? You will not have to wait long.

'AN UNBORN PROPHET PRAISING AN UNBORN KING'

It must be over twenty years ago now when I heard the gentle Bible teacher Mr. Albert Leckie say something very precious about Mary's visit to Elizabeth who was expecting her baby, John the Baptist, in her home in the hill country of Judah. You will remember that when Elizabeth heard Mary's greeting her baby leaped in her womb for joy and Elizabeth said, filled with the Holy Spirit, 'Blessed are you among women, and blessed is the fruit of your womb! But why is this granted to me, that the mother of my Lord should come to me? For indeed as soon as the voice of your greeting sounded in my ears the babe leaped in my womb for joy. Blessed is she who believed, for there will be a fulfillment of those things which were told her from the Lord'. Mr. Leckie said of the movement of Mary's baby in her womb 'That was an unborn prophet praising an unborn king'. What a lovely thought.

December

5 ———————————

'MARY'S HUMILITY'

We know absolutely nothing about the childhood and early years of Mary but in Mary's song of praise and prophesy she exposes her heart and mind. She bursts into song with the words 'My soul magnifies the Lord, and my spirit has rejoiced in God my Saviour. For he has regarded the lowly estate of his maid-servant; for behold, henceforth all generations will call me blessed. For he who is mighty has done great things for me'.

Is it not fascinating to notice that nowhere in her song does Mary mention the fact that she is going to be the mother of the Son of God? Her joy arises from the fact that God is acting as her Saviour. Fully aware that she is going to be transformed from obscurity into world wide fame and realising that 'all generations shall call me blessed' Mary nowhere says that it is because she was going to be the mother of Christ. The thing that stands out to her is not what she is but what God has done. Her remarkable humility is touching to read. Her eye is not upon herself but upon the Lord. The greatest honour ever placed upon any human brings the moving response 'For He who is mighty has done great things for me'. Let us, particularly when God choses us to do something special for Him maintain Mary's humility. Remember her humility was not mere poverty for the fact remains that many poor people live and die among the proud. Selah.

December

6

Suddenly Mary breaks into a string of verbs in her beautiful song. Speaking of God she says 'He has shown strength with his arms; he has scattered the proud in the imagination of their hearts. He has put down the mighty from their throne, and exalted the lowly. He has filled the hungry with good things, and the rich he has sent away empty'. It is very important to notice that in these verbs Mary is not just speaking of God in the past but God in the present and God in the future. What he has done in the past he will continue to do in the present and will do in the future. In her humility and spirituality Mary is pointing out in her song that what God has done for her in salvation in lifting her and using her is the kind of thing he always does. A friend of mine recently went to a church which was extremely wealthy. A man who belonged to the church lived a mile away from the church building and only attended once a year. He did that by helicopter! What did my colleague preach on amongst that wealthy congregation? He preached on the text 'He has filled the hungry with good things, and the rich he has sent away empty'. He was a brave man but he certainly had caught the spirit of Mary!

December

7

MOTHER, BE ENCOURAGED

If Mary's song proves anything it proves that she knew and loved the Old Testament. It does not contain any actual verbal quotations from the prophets but everything she says is founded on the Lord's promises as contained in Holy Writ. The Scriptures that she knew so well were to be fulfilled exactly in everything he said and did from childhood to death. She who was to know his light had to eventually watch him go into darkness and suffer the penalty for her sins and ours. She who was to be made whole had to eventually watch him be rent and torn. Mary must have known the prophesy of Isaiah which said He was to be wounded for our transgressions and bruised for our iniquities. She saw the word fulfilled before her very eyes.

The lesson is very powerful. No mother who knows the word of God and passes it on to her children will find that the Word returns empty. I encourage every mother reading these lines today to keep on feeding your children on the sacred truths of Scripture. It seems to me that Mary's quiet life and love for the word of God played no small part in the fact that God chose her for such a sacred task. God still chooses to use those women who know his word to influence their children and hence the history of the world. Mother, be encouraged.

December

8

MARY WAS NOT FOUND UNPREPARED

It must always be remembered that while Mary's choosing was unexpected it certainly did not find her unprepared. Notice what she said in her song of God. 'He has helped his servant Israel in remembrance of his mercy, as he spoke to our Fathers, to Abraham and to his seed forever'. There is no reference in the angels message to Abraham. Gabriel certainly told Mary that her son was to be the expected Messiah and the promised King of Israel but it was Mary's own mind that traced the promise right to its source in the life of Abraham. Mary remembered the allusion in God's original promise to Abraham when God said 'In your seed shall all the nations of the earth be blessed'. (Genesis 22 : 18) The ancient promise had long been a cherished promise in Mary's heart. The lesson is very clear; may we look for the second coming of our Lord Jesus Christ as Mary had waited and looked for the coming of the Messiah. As his first coming did not find Mary unprepared, may his second coming find us working, watching and waiting.

9

'MARY'S GODLY FEAR'

There is another beautiful feature of Mary's character which is a very powerful lesson to us in our day. Notice that Mary said of God that 'His mercy is on them who fear him'. Mary claimed

December

God's mercy because of her fear of him. She had a sacred awe and reverence for God. How many others have cast off their fear of God, Adam included and did not tremble at God's word, Mary took God's word very seriously? The Bible distinctly says that 'The secret of the Lord is with them that fear him and he will show them his covenant'. It may be that you will be surrounded at work today or in the environment in which you will find yourself by people who do not fear to take God's name in vain. Yet, you fear the Lord despite what others do. Correct? Is it worth it? It certainly is. 'Godly fear', taught Bunyan, 'is the key to the keeping of the town of Mansoul'. We are told that the angel of the Lord encamps around about those that fear him. Don't, wherever you go today, or, whatever you do, lose a fear of God. It is the beginning of wisdom.

10 ────────────────

MARY'S FAITH

We now come to one of the most sacred subjects in all of Scripture; the incarnation of Christ. Incarnation is from the Latin meaning 'becoming flesh', i.e. 'becoming human'. The doctrine of the incarnation is saying that the God who took a motherless woman out of the side of a man took a humanly fatherless man out of the body of a woman. The doctrine is teaching that Christ was not like any Greek mythological hero. He was not a half man and a half God. He was fully God but at the same time he became genuinely a man. With all my heart I believe this great doctrine that the Almighty appeared on earth as a helpless little human baby, as someone has put it 'unable to do more than lie and stare and wriggle and make noises, needing to be fed and taught to talk like any other child'. The more you think about it the more staggering it gets, our God contracted to a span, incomprehensibly made man.

Let us never forget that the end of Mary's faith was exactly the same as her Father Abraham's. As Abraham trusted God when he said he would give him children as the stars of the heavens in whom all the nations of the earth would be blessed so Mary trusted in God for the incarnation of the Messiah. Let us never forget that Mary had a great trial of faith. The trial of Mary's faith was unprecedented in human history. The virgin birth that she was faced with was and still is to this day foolish to human reason, and sight. Could we just stop for a moment and try to put ourselves in Mary's shoes? Imagine trying to explain a pregnancy by claiming that an angel had told her that she was going to become pregnant by divinely induced conception and that the child would prove to be the Messiah, the Son of the living God. Can we begin to imagine how conservative believing Jews would react to her story? If Joseph reacted the way he did when he first heard it, imagine how others reacted. Yet Mary believed and, as was said about her Father Abraham when he was faced with God's promise, she staggered not at the promises of God. Despite all a woman's instinct at such incredible news, Mary's simple and unquestioning faith helps our faith too.

December

Do not, christian, stagger at the promises of God for you today no matter how incomprehensible they are to others around you. That is what matters most.

11

Do people around the world believe in the incarnation of Christ as Mary did? Let me tell you that at least 540 million people disagree with her, to start with. Moslems believe that Mohammed at the age of forty went to a mountain called Hira to meditate and think quietly. They believe the archangel Gabriel summoned him to go and preach that there was only one God and that he was his prophet. He fought battles, attacked Mecca and smashed down its idols turning it into a shine of Islam. The baby born at Mecca 570 years after Christ certainly didn't believe that the baby born in Bethlehem was God. So, you can see that it is very important what you believe about the incarnation for it deeply affects your view of Christ. Touch my blest Saviour first, take Him from Gods esteem . . . then tell me I'm unclean.

12

'THE INCARNATION IS NOT OPTIONAL'

If you think that 540 million Moslems disagreeing with the christian doctrine of the incarnation is a lot of people let me tell you about another entirely different 530 million people on earth today. They are

378

the Hindus who believe that God is present in everything and shows himself in many different ways and through other lesser gods to whom they sacrifice animals in their temples. They have their caste system where you take your caste from your parents and If you behave better you will be born into a higher caste. You can imagine how they would treat the one who said 'I am the way, the truth and the life no man cometh unto the Father but by me'.

Then of course there are the Buddhists who follow Buddha who was originally a wealthy Hindu but was disillusioned with it all and founded Buddhism which believes that all men can attain a state of perfect peace of their own efforts. You can imagine their attitude to the one of whom it is said 'For there is no other name under heaven given amongst men whereby we must be saved' or 'Look unto me and be ye saved all the ends of the earth for I am God and there is none else'. There are millions upon millions of Buddhists in the world today.

Of course, not only do Hindus and Buddhists oppose the doctrine of the incarnation but some modern theologians do not want to make any distinction between the purely mythological nature of Hinduism or the basic teachings of Buddhism and the Lord Jesus. The claim has been made that the church has deified the Lord Jesus just like Buddhists have deified Buddha who made no claim to be divine. The attempt has been made, it has been said to demythologize the incarnation. It has been said that to speak of Jesus as different in kind from all other men is to threaten, if not destroy his total

December

solidarity with all other men. These modernistic theologians want to make a belief in the incarnation optional. They merely want us to recognise that the Lord Jesus was a man approved by God for a special role and that the conception of him as God incarnate is a poetic way of expressing his significance for us.

Let me categorically state that the Scriptures won't let us have this nonsense for they constantly ascribe to him a status which can only be described as divine. We are faced with a choice either the church declares itself a mere interesting chapter in the history of religion or else it faces the inescapable truth of the incarnation and of the resurrection. Any teaching which concentrates on Christ being Emmanuel, God with us at the expense of teaching that Christ is God the Saviour is abhorrent. Let us thrill once more to those marvellous words of John 'In the beginning was the Word, and the Word was with God, and the Word was God. The same was in the beginning with God. All things were made by Him and without Him nothing was made that was made. In Him was life, and the life was the light of men .. He was in the world, and the world was made by Him, and the world knew him not. He came to His own, and His own did not receive Him. But as many as received Him, to them He gave the right to become children of God, even to those who believe in His name'.

13

'THE BABY WHO WAS GOD'

Since childhood I have loved the little carol 'Away in a Manger'; its tender words have brought across the truth of God incarnate to millions. Yet we must be careful with the line of the carol which says 'The little Lord Jesus no crying he makes'. Let us never forget that 'tears and smile like us he knew'. It is also worth remembering that the birth of the Lord Jesus was a natural birth it was his conception that was super-natural. What a mystery! The baby who was God.

14

'MARY NEVER APPEALED FOR PITY'

I have been pondering those sacred words of Matthew chapter 1 : 18 where we are told that Mary 'Was found with child of the Holy Spirit'. I wonder what lies behind those words? One thing is absolutely certain that Mary was now exposed to reproach for the Lord's name. She certainly had the favour of God but a darker cloud never rested upon any believer on earth purely for the sake of Christ than the cloud that now covered Mary. Joseph is not himself persuaded of her innocence, he has no assurance of it, in the natural course of events Mary will within a few days be divorced as an adulteress, privately. One day the highest angel in heaven had saluted her as being highly favoured of the Lord and

December

is she now to become the song of the drunkard? Is she now to be branded as a hypocrite? Is she to be thought of as someone who covered a life of immorality with a cloak of superior sanctity? The amazing thing is she appears to have said absolutely nothing and done absolutely nothing to vindicate herself. Nowhere do we read that she complained to anyone of wrong or appealed to anyone for pity. But she quietly waited for God, literally. What no human person could do for Mary and what Mary could not do for herself the Lord did for her in a direct and miraculous intervention. As Joseph thinks of privately divorcing her the angel of the Lord appeared to him in a dream by night, explaining everything.

Just remember that God always knows the things that you need before you ask. If you interfere to try to deliver yourself you will only bring yourself into deeper waters. Leave your cause with Him, wait for Him and as Mary found, you will not wait in vain.

15 ────────────────

ARE YOU A PONDERER?

Eventually the Saviour of the world enters the world and is laid in a manger. Could ever a group of shepherds take a journey with such anticipation as those men who came from the hillsides of Judea to Jerusalem? No wonder the Scripture comments 'They came with haste'. They were not disappointed for they 'Found Mary and Joseph, and the babe lying in a manger'. The shepherds made it widely

December

known what had been told them concerning this child. The people who heard it marvelled at all those things that were told them by the shepherds. There must have been some talk in that district at that time. Yet, we do not read of any comment that Mary made despite all the talk around her. We are simply told that 'Mary kept all these things and pondered them in her heart'. (Luke 2 : 19). The shepherds may marvel and the people may talk but Mary thoughtfully ponders. It is a beautiful quality in her life.

Are you a ponderer? 'Ponder the path of your feet and let your ways be established' (Proverbs 4 : 26). It is a very healthy breakfast. In the world around us very few people ponder, much. They take most things for granted but we should be different. We are aware of the awful wrath to come and that we have been delivered from it. We are aware that sin is great and that Christ has given us victory again and again over its power. We are aware of what Satan is doing across the world and are looking for signs of our Lord's return. No christian should treat anything in their life as common because nothing happens to us by chance. Do you not think that one of the reasons why Mary was chosen was because she had been raised by the Lord with a heart that pondered the paths of her feet? I challenge you to ponder well today the place and the circumstances where God has placed you. Try and trace today in your mind how God has led you through these past few months and through the trees of the wood of life to where you are now. You will soon see that it is your own blindness that has made you think your life is little instead of great, dull instead of full of interest. If you and I would only wise up and observe the Lord's

December

goodness and kindness to us we would as Paul said to Timothy 'Stir up the gift within us' and be glad that we have it and that we are placed where we are. Mark well my words that if you ponder the path of your feet, your movements will be established by the Lord.

16

THE POWER OF OBSERVATION

'To those who are given to observation, things happen that are worth observing'.

17

YOU CAN WELCOME DEATH

Mary and Joseph now go the Jerusalem to offer a sacrifice of a pair of turtle doves and two young pigeons. As they bring the child Jesus into the temple they are suddenly confronted by one of the most wonderful characters in Scripture. His name was Simeon. Simeon was a very devout man who had for many a long day waited for God. He too believed God's promises and had been patient in waiting for them to be fulfilled. Can you imagine his joy when the little child is brought into the temple? Immediately Simeon takes the Saviour up in his arms. Imagine holding God. Notice that the Scripture says Simeon had come 'By the Spirit into the temple'. Those who wait for God are always assured of being led by the Spirit of God. Notice also

December

how that those who wait for God are content with whatever the Lord wants. Simeon had been promised that he should not see death till he had seen God's Christ and now he says 'Lord, now let your servant depart in peace, according to your word; for my eyes have seen your salvation'. Simeon is quite content to die. He departs in peace, peace with God, peace with his own conscience, and at peace with death. He was able to face death because his eyes had seen God's salvation.

Could it be that some dear one reads these lines today and you are facing death? This lovely Saviour, even when he was in the form of a little boy in the arms of Simeon took the terror of death away from the old man's heart and made it into gain. If you have welcomed Christ you can welcome death.

18

SPEAK OF HIM

Simeon was not the only one who was waiting for Christ. We read that there was an 84 year old woman Anna who served God with fastings and prayers night and day. She came into the temple at the very same time as Simeon was holding Christ in his arms and immediately 'She gave thanks to the Lord, and spoke of him to all those who looked for redemption in Jerusalem'. I believe that light is given to every person who comes into the world and if they follow that light when they are presented with Christ they will see that he is that light. The chief priests and the Scribes and the Pharisees refused the light but thank

December

God that Anna and her friends recognised it for what it was and worshipped. Notice that it says that Anna 'Spoke of him to all those who looked for redemption in Jerusalem'. It is a sad business whenever christians meet for dinner, or socially that sometimes the lovely Lord Jesus is never spoken of. Why not when you are in the presence of other christians today 'Speak of him to them all'? It sure beats gossip.

19

NEVER LOSE SIGHT OF JESUS

We now move into a very remarkable set of circumstances in the life of Mary. Mary had been a believer even before Christ's birth. Now her relationship as a mother begins to fade and her relationship as a believer starts to be paramount. She now becomes in a very real way the disciple and follower of Christ. He now starts to guide, teach and rule her. The outstanding circumstance in the discipleship of Mary now becomes reproof. You and I know that every child of God has to suffer chastisement and Mary had to have her share. It happened on three outstanding occasions. Let us look at the first. It has to do with her losing sight of Jesus.

When the Lord was twelve years old he was taken up to Jerusalem for the Feast of Passover and when his parents returned home 'The boy Jesus lingered behind in Jerusalem. And Joseph and his mother did not know it; but supposing him to have been in

December

the company, they went a days journey, and sought him among their relatives and acquaintances'. When they could not find him after three days searching they eventually went into the temple and found him 'Sitting in the midst of the teachers, both listening to them and answering them questions'. Mary complained. 'Son, why have you done this to us? Look, your father and I have sought you anxiously'. The answer he gave must have burned into her very soul. 'Why is it that you sought me? Did not you know that I must be about my Father's business?'

Mary's losing sight of the Lord Jesus was certainly chastened by her long and difficult search but now Jesus marks that chastening with a truth which she ought to have known well; his Father in Heaven has claims upon him far above Mary and Joseph's claims. How very easy it is to forget who the Lord is, what he is about and what his eternal objectives are! Abraham lost sight of his Lord and went down into Egypt and experienced a real disaster in his life. Peter when he was walking on the water lost sight of his Lord and started to sink. Again, at the home of the High Priest, Peter lost sight of his Lord and denied him with oaths and curses. What Mary did was a very reasonable act for any mother to do and yet in the midst of it she lost sight of who the Master really was and was chastened. The lesson is clear; never lose sight of Jesus.

December

20 ——————————

The scene now changes from the temple at Jerusalem with Christ as a little boy to the scene at a wedding at Cana of Galilee, eighteen years later. Now both Jesus and his disciples were invited to the wedding. And when they ran out of wine, the mother of Jesus said to him, 'They have no wine'. Jesus said to her 'Woman, what does your concern have to do with me? My hour has not yet come'. His mother said to the servants, 'Whatever he says to you, do it'.

There can be no doubt that Christ's words to his mother is the plain language of reproof. He did not show his mother disrespect by calling her 'woman' for the term was applied to women of any rank. The words were reminding Mary that it did not belong to her to prescribe to him what he was to do. There seems to be a clear reproof for her in presuming to hurry him along. By the fact that she immediately told them to do whatever he asked them to do proves that Christ had given her a real cause to hope. He had not done any miracle before but she knew that he was perfectly capable of performing miracles. The lesson was that she must leave both the time and the manner of his work to himself alone.

Don't we all need such reprove as Mary got that day? Aren't we all tempted to dictate the time and manner of God's work and aid? Surely patience is the crowning grace. Let patience have her perfect work that you may be mature and entire, wanting nothing. Your Lord will be a very present help in time of need. But notice that it is in time of need. If you need it he'll give it to you.

21

DON'T INTERRUPT YOUR LORD

The third reproof of Mary came when one day Christ had entered into a house for rest and food but the multitude pressed so hard upon him to hear the word that he couldn't so much as eat bread. They seated themselves around the house and from the inside he continued to speak to them.

Then his brothers and his mother came, and standing outside they sent to him, calling him. And a multitude was sitting around him; and they said to him 'Look, your mother and your brothers are outside seeking you'. But he answered them saying, 'Who is my mother or my brothers?' And he looked around in a circle at those who sat about him, and said. 'Here are my mother and my brothers! For whoever does the will of God is my brother and my sister and mother'.

It would seem a very severe reproof of his mother and yet when you think about it it was no such thing. Mary it seems had not yet learned her lesson that she was not allowed to interfere with the work of the Lord. The Master stood in the midst of that huge crowd and proclaimed to them and to all of us as well that as the Saviour of the world all who trust him as Saviour are equal, and without the

December

least distinction, his children. There are no favourites. Not even his own earthly mother. Would that millions would not try to go to God through her. All they need to do is to go through him.

22 ————————————————

TELL THE MEANING OF HIS BIRTH

Preparation is vital. God is constantly moving us on to greater things. We want to linger with what we've got, to cling to it. God has far wider horizons and greater things to give us than we have yet imagined or dreamed of. We must bow to God's method of preparing us for them. He will use, perhaps one method with me and another method with you. Be assured the result whatever method he uses will be thrilling.

The Son of God had come to redeem Mary and she must now be prepared for the cross. Notice that between the incident of Mary's interrupting Christ at his work and the cross of Christ there is not a line of scripture about Mary. There is no news of her until the moving statement 'Now there stood by the cross of Jesus his mother' (John 19 : 25)

There can be no doubt that Mary had been prepared by God for she did not have the same spirit at the foot of the cross as she had when she had interrupted Christ in his preaching and teaching ministry. Mary had learned not to interrupt but to wait. Her silence in waiting is a lesson to you and to me today. Mary had learned the meaning of his coming.

December

In the hectic bustle of Christmas week as celebrated in the western world, let's get near to the meaning of his birth; namely, that he was born to die. Let's get near to the cross and remember that the woman who had stood by a manger later stood by a cross. As the office parties start to swing this week and millions across the nation get drunk, you will, christian be naturally standing off from such behaviour. Yet, as it swirls all around you be positive. This week will give you a great opportunity to tell others of the true meaning of it all. As the opportunity arises this week tell those around you that the manger led to the cross and the cross leads to God.

23

REVEALED TO BABIES

How must Mary have felt when the little children in the temple cried to her son 'Hosanna to the Son of David'? The chief Priests, Scribes and Pharisees and the leaders of the people hated him and dragged him before Pilot and Herod. They had him scourged, crowned with thorns and condemned to die. Yet, the little children cried Hosanna to him which was a prayer concerned with Messianic salvation for the children regarded Mary's Son as the Messiah.

Christs comment was that God had hidden these things from the wise and intellectually clever but revealed them to babies. May the little children in your house be given an opportunity this week to cry

December

Hosanna once more. Don't let them be like the lady I happened to be standing beside one day in the Christmas rush. As we watched the 'Santaclaustaphobia' around us I said to her 'It's far from the original story, isn't it?'. 'And what was that?', she smiled.

24 _____

THE UNSPEAKABLE GIFT

'Behold', old Simeon had said, to Mary, 'This child is destined for the fall and rising of many in Israel . . . yes, a sword will pierce through your own soul, also, that the thoughts of many hearts may be revealed'.

The sword had come. The little baby of Bethelem was taken at 33 years of age at midnight, blindfolded, spit upon, beaten and led eventually to a cross. Is this the one of whom Gabriel said 'He shall be called the Son of the Highest and the Lord God shall give to him the throne of his Father David and he shall reign over the House of Jacob forever and of his Kingdom there shall be no end'? This is the very same Lord Jesus.

Mary had to have her heart torn in order that she might be made whole. As millions think on this Christmas Eve of the manger and the incredible gift God gave us, let us also think of what that gift cost God. Let us meditate on the lovely words of the great young Scottish preacher Robert Murray McCheyne.

'When this passing world is done,
When has sunk yon glaring sun,
When we stand with Christ in glory,
Looking o'er life's finished story,
Then, Lord, shall I fully know
Not till then, how much I owe.

When I stand before the throne,
Dressed in beauty not my own,
When I see Thee as Thou art,
Love Thee with unsinning heart,
Then, Lord, shall I fully know,
Not till then, how much I owe.

Thanks be unto God for His unspeakable gift.

25

'OH! SO FAIR'

I love the tune to the song we know in Ireland as 'Scarlet Ribbons'. Once, musing upon the Christmas story these words came to me. I leave them with you. Why not gather your family around you today and sing these words to 'Scarlet Ribbons?'

'In a country far away
In a manger lying there
Was a baby, precious baby,
Was a baby, oh! so fair.

Chorus
Yet throughout eternity
We shall ever thankful be,
That this baby, precious baby,
Came to die for you and me.

December

From a Country far away,
Came those men so very wise,
Looking for the princely Saviour,
Looking always to the skies.

On a skull hill far away,
Three and thirty years now gone,
Stood a cross upon that hilltop,
Nailed upon it God's own Son.

In a Country far away,
Lies a city built four square,
Trusting Jesus you can enter,
Through those pearly gates so fair.

26 ————————————

YOUR WORST DAY MAY TURN OUT TO BE YOUR BEST

"Now there stood by the cross of Jesus his mother, and his mother's sister, Mary the wife of Cleophas, and Mary Magdalene. When Jesus therefore saw His mother, and the disciple whom He loved standing by, He said to His mother, 'Woman behold your son! Then He said to the disciple, 'Behold your mother!' and from that hour that disciple took her to his own home".

Do you think it was easy for Mary to hear those gracious words from her son on the cross? She could easily have said that John was not her son and that she was not John's mother. She could have railed upon Christ and said you are my son and you healed the sick and cleansed the lepers and cast out devils and walked on raging seas and fed starving thousands and raised people from the dead and you could come down from that cross and save yourself and me. And Mary said no such things. She submitted to the will of God and went home with John.

Is it not good for us to accept the death and burial of our most cherished hopes? Mary had waited for God before and she would wait for God again. It could be that at this time in your life you have just watched the death and burial of one of your most cherished hopes. Do not panic, my friend. What Mary may well have thought the worst day of her whole life was in fact the door to the greatest adventure any human soul could ever know. Not one thing had failed of all the good things which the Lord her God had spoken concerning her. Not one thing will fail of all the good things the Lord your God has spoken of concerning you. Bow to the will of God today, and receive the sentence of death in yourself, that you may not trust in yourself but in God who raises the dead and calls the things that are not as though they were. Selah.

27

BECAUSE HE LIVES WE CAN FACE TOMORROW

At last the dark night of sorrow for Mary has passed. All her fears have gone. Not from the darkness of Mary's womb now, but, from the tomb of death Christ comes, never to die again. Our friends may bring us to the grave and leave us there

December

but God will not. Because Christ lives we shall live also. As the man said, 'We are more sure to arise out of our graves than out of our beds!' Mary rejoices and once more waits for God; this time for God the Holy Spirit.

Mary is the only one of the women to be actually mentioned by name as waiting for the Spirit. She was not disappointed for she got a blessing greater than she had looked for at the end of a long, holy, tested and tried, but truly amazing life. Scripture leaves us with Mary continuing in 'Prayer and supplication'. (Acts 1 : 14). Waiting for God became Mary's hallmark and after this year's journey together may it be ours. Many christians pray less as they grow older but not Mary. She waited for God in Nazareth and she waited for Him in Jerusalem and she now shines as a beacon to us all of faithful, patient, quiet endurance. When I ask of you in thirty years, if we are spared, will you still be found faithful to your Lord? Will I? May it be so.

28 ───────────────

TRUE BEAUTY

Mary's was marked by what the Scripture calls a "Meek and quiet spirit which is in the sight of God of great price". I do not wish in any way to be hurtful, for we men could do with a lot of improvement, me especially, but, ladies, don't you think true beauty is a very handy thing to have at any time, especially for a woman who isn't handsome?

29

A GLIMPSE OF HIM

Not merely in the words you say,
Not only in your deeds confessed,
But in the most unconscious way,
Is Christ confessed.

Is it a beautific smile?
A holy light upon your brow?
Oh, no, I felt his presence
When you laughed just now.

For me, 'twas not the truth you told,
To you so clear, to me still dim,
But when you came to me, you brought
A glimpse of him.

And from your eyes he beckons me,
And from your lips his love is shed,
Till I lose sight of you, and see,
The Christ instead.

30

'FASTER THAN A MAN CAN RUN'

Eve used words badly and Adam fell. At Babel
they said a lot and look what happened. The children
of Israel used grumbling words and provoked God
to anger. Sweet talking women turned the brilliant
Solomon into an effeminate fool. Job's friends
talked pious but broke his heart. The wise David was

December

deceived by a clever talking widow and lost his throne. Peter said 'I know not the man:' how different it all would have been had he said 'I'm glad to say that I know him well, he is my Saviour.'

Words. Words. Words. They go faster than a man can run. Are you ready to let rip against an individual? Don't. Are you ready to say 'I'm sick to death of my local church?' Don't. Are you ready to defend yourself against people who have twisted your words for their own evil ends? Let them go. Remember that a tongue three inches long can kill a person six feet tall. When you have a word on the tip of your tongue sometimes it is better to leave it there. The only part of the human body that never gets tired, eventually, is the tongue. Just keep in mind, even in December days that in the world of using words you are skating on thin ice and can get into hot water.

31

'He remains faifthful'

And so we come to our last day together. I pray that the distinction between the woods and the trees is a little clearer. I trust that you are able to get 'the big picture' as well as the more local scene a little more clearly into focus. I have found, in writing this book for you that God has met me at every turn. Through the daily round of preaching and teaching God's Word, of travelling across the country, of counselling broken hearts and in the midst of it seeking to raise a little family, God's promises and help have not failed at any time.

In my neck of the woods over the last ten years, 30,825 people have been injured and 2,654 have been killed through terrorism and civil strife. I have found, with thousands of other believers that one promise is true; as christians we have, none of us, been what we should have been but the promise still stands. It is found in 2 Timothy 2 : 13. These words are in the very last letter Paul wrote. They were written to a young man starting out on the journey of the life of faith. Mark them well, for though you and I may never meet again this side of Heaven, the promise still stands. What is it? 'If we are faithless, He remains faithful; He cannot deny Himself'. Waiting for God? It is a hard task. If you have done it, I'm glad but as I leave you always try to remember that even though we may fail to wait for Him He will remain faithful. That should really encourage you to wait for Him, next time around.